# 100
# GREAT GAA
## CONTROVERSIES

# 100
# GREAT GAA
## CONTROVERSIES

## JOHN SCALLY

BLACK & WHITE PUBLISHING

First published in the UK in 2022 by
Black & White Publishing Ltd
Nautical House, 104 Commercial Street, Edinburgh EH6 6NF

A division of Bonnier Books UK
4th Floor, Victoria House, Bloomsbury Square, London, WC1B 4DA
Owned by Bonnier Books
Sveavägen 56, Stockholm, Sweden

Front cover design by Richard Budd.
Cover images © INPHO / Ken Sutton (Hannah Tyrell) & © SPORTSFILE /
Brendan Moran (Ger Loughnane & Lee Keegan), Ray McManus (Pat Spillane),
Piaras Ó Mídheach (Jackie Tyrell)

This book is a work of non-fiction, based on the recollections of the author
and interviews conducted by the author. The author has stated to the publishers
that the contents of this book are true to the best of their knowledge.

A CIP catalogue record for this book is available from the British Library.

ISBN: 978 1 78530 415 6

1 3 5 7 9 10 8 6 4 2

Typeset by Data Connection
Printed and bound in Great Britain by Clays Ltd, Elcograf S.p.A.

MIX
Paper from
responsible sources
FSC
www.fsc.org    FSC® C018072

www.blackandwhitepublishing.com

*'Taitneamh a bhaint as'*
Joe Connolly

*To the humbling heroism of the Ukrainian people*

*And the Irish people who remember that while charity begins at home, it does not stay there.*

*Both have been inspirational.*

# CONTENTS

## PART II: CONTROVERSIES FOR ALL SEASONS

## PART III: POWER TO ALL OUR FRIENDS

## PART IV: THE HAND OF HISTORY

## PART V: THE PUNDIT'S CORNER

# FOREWORD

*by Charlie Redmond*

Nothing excites GAA fans like a big controversy.

Trust me, I know!

I think it is fair to say that it will be a long time before Dubs' fans forget that I was once sent off twice in an All-Ireland final!

Now anyone who has forgotten will be reminded in this book!

Since I have retired from the inter-county scene, I see the world of GAA controversies in a new light and am ever more aware of their power to get the nation talking.

Over the last 130 years in its rich history, the GAA has generated many great controversies and this book celebrates them.

While it features the obvious ones like: Newbridge or Nowhere; the Cork Hurlers Strikes, the Ban, Bloody Sunday, the Battle of Omagh, Mayo and Meath's fisticuffs, and, of course, the gripping events of the never-to-be-forgotten hurling summer of 1998, I am pleased to see a few less obvious ones covered in these pages.

Gaelic football, women's football, camogie and hurling are featured. As the GAA is a thirty-two-county movement it is good to see that this is reflected between the covers of this publication.

Those of us with an interest in history will particularly understand why the stories of some of the controversies in the world of Gaelic games need to be situated in the wider context of society as a whole.

Of course, it features the 'greatest hits' of the most controversial personalities in the Association's history like Joe Brolly, Ger Loughnane, Pat Spillane and Babs Keating.

I hope you will enjoy it.

# INTRODUCTION

*'The ultimate measure of a man is not where he stands in moments of comfort and convenience, but where he stands at times of challenge and controversy.'*

MARTIN LUTHER KING

Heartbreak, betrayal, misery, ruptured relationships, pain, truth and sin are the staples of country music. They are also common ingredients in the canon of GAA controversies.

If love did not hurt and scar, there would be no country songs. If our love for Gaelic games did not cut so deep, we would not feel our controversies so keenly. Fans love the spectacle of great games; the thrill of watching great players who leave us watching in awe like David Clifford or Cian Lynch or Tony Kelly. However, nothing causes the pulses of GAA fans to get agitated like the conspiracies of circumstances that become great controversies.

When we are emotionally engaged, like when our county is involved, the stakes rise still further. I learned that lesson at first hand when I played for Saint Brigid's at under-12 level. I sucked in the noise of the stadium beginning to fill like a distant ocean rising and crashing. When I was beaten for a challenge,

1

I heard low whispers at first, faraway, then closer and closer, clearer. My breath came shallow and fast. Something like a stone moved in my stomach. Then, self-conscious and embarrassed, I heard someone say in a familiar voice: 'He's too lazy to scratch himself.' It was the local priest. My veils of delusion about my abilities as a footballer lifted immediately.

Forgive and forget is a noble aspiration but one we find remarkably difficult to achieve because it is human nature to take things personally. Some years ago, a lawyer in America, who stole his clients' money and faked his own death, watched his own funeral while sitting in a tree. He was caught but he never forgave his friends who had not attended his funeral and burial. Fans of Gaelic games take a slight on our teams as a slight on ourselves leaving shadows on our souls. The agitation is sharpened in our years of grief like a soldier's blade on the eve of battle.

It is the big controversies that turn our national games into our national soap opera. They are the topics that get fans and enemies of the GAA, leaden down with moral indignation, to ring Joe Duffy on *Liveline*. In this world, history is often altered by imagination.

They are like bad loves we cannot quit.

I was spoilt for choice and reluctantly leave out many notable controversies because of the constraints of space. No two fans would pick the exact same 100 Great GAA Controversies so this selection invariably is a personal one. In selecting controversies from over the last forty years, my sole criteria was to include the ones I could remember most clearly.

### GET A GRIP

One of the biggest talking points of the 2022 Championship was the furore over the frosty handshake between Brian Cody and Henry Shefflin when Galway beat Kilkenny in Salthill. There were acres of press coverage about 'Handshakegate'. A few weeks later when both sides met again in the Leinster final the build-up was dominated by how 'Handshake the Sequel' would unfold. After Kilkenny won Cody strolled onto the pitch to congratulate his players, while King Henry stayed rooted in the same spot on the sideline. After what seemed like an eternity Shefflin finally made a move towards Cody in the centre of the field and there was a perfunctory handshake and just a few words. Afterwards King Henry shook his head in apparent frustration. Again there was more extensive analysis of the handshake than of a less than stellar match.

## A TOWN CALLED MALICE

More seriously the 2022 campaign saw the reoccurrence of an ongoing issue for the GAA. After Andy McEntee stepped down as Meath the scale of the personal abuse he had been subjected to emerged. His daughter Aisling tweeted: 'I really hope the next manager doesn't have a family with access to social media. I also hope I never raise anyone to be as pathetic as to abuse people from behind a keyboard. Would they put in an ounce of the effort and dedication he did? . . . doubtful.'

Meanwhile Joe Brolly was at the centre of yet another storm. In an article published in the *Sunday Independent* in the aftermath of the Ulster final, Brolly wrote of a young boy charging for parking outside his house, squeezing multiple cars into the front lawn with 'no gaps between them' and no lane for exiting after the match. 'Welcome to Calcutta, Ireland,' Brolly opined. The piece prompted Monaghan County Council to pass a motion calling on Brolly and the *Sunday Independent* to apologise for the 'critical and disrespectful' comparison. True to form Joe did issue an apology – but to the people of Kolkata claiming: 'In no way did I intend to demean them by comparing them to Clones.'

Pat Spillane was agitated by the All-Ireland SFC quarter-final between Armagh and Galway. The match went to extra-time after a 1–17 to 2–14 draw. Then a brawl broke out between members of the panel from both teams as they made their way towards the dressing rooms in which Galway forward Damien Comer suffered an eye-gouge.

Unlike some of the players that day Spillane pulled no punches: 'We should be here praising a great game but we're looking at disgraceful scenes. Shame on all the players involved. There was a gouging incident. There's a million rules and regulations and you send two teams running into the same spot straight after full-time. It's crazy and you have fellas who are not subs involved. The possible eye-gouging was done by a fella who's not on the official panel. That was disgraceful, scandalous and shame on all involved.'

*The Sun*'s front page headline the next morning was 'The Sunday Shame'. Meanwhile revulsion at the eye-gouging incident prompted *The Mirror*'s front page headline 'Eye Sore'. Given the frequency of violent incidents in the GAA down the years and the failure to meaningfully address it, there was a competition on social media to see which pundit would be the first to say: 'The first rule of GAA fight club is that nobody talks about GAA fight club.' Another fan described it as 'Armagh-geddon.'

The game spawned another controversy. Galway manager Pádraic Joyce hit out at the decision by the GAA in having spot kicks to decide a championship match. As the teams were still level after extra time, Galway won 4-1 on penalties. Joyce stated: 'It's a horrible way to lose it and that's not the fault of the Armagh players, it's the fault of the GAA and the condensed season. It beggars belief as to why we couldn't have had a replay next weekend. To decide the outcome on a penalty shootout . . . we're not soccer, we're GAA. To me it's disgraceful it had to happen.'

In the accidental truths of the heart, controversy is the sweaty syntax of the language of Gaelic games.

Bittersweet memories are made of this.

# PART I

# If You Want an Audience Start a Fight

I grew up in a household of seven, including grandparents and an aunt. One Christmas we were gifted with the most beautiful cake I had ever seen. It had been divided into eight sections. We each took a slice and savoured every mouthful for the culinary delight it was. After we had finished, my little sister surged forward and licked the remaining slice of cake to claim it for her own. She beamed in satisfaction at her ingenuity. We all recoiled in horror apart from my grandfather. He reached forward and licked the other side of the slice of cake. His point was to highlight that it was not fair for somebody to get an extra slice when nobody else could get one. It was an early insight for me that fairness can come in unusual forms. Watching the GAA's disciplinary system in action in recent decades has caused me to stretch my definition of fairness in ways I could never have imagined.

Controversies have always been part of the GAA. In 1925 Sligo took no less than six games to decide the first round of the Connacht Championship against Roscommon. The epic featured three draws and two objections. Sligo won the sixth and final game.

Kevin McStay claims that the 'culture of machismo is the greatest stain on the GAA'. He went on to say that it is deemed better for a Gaelic footballer to be an 'assassin or a thug than soft or windy'.

The greatest controversies generally fall under the umbrella of 'discipline'. 'Tough' players have always been part of the GAA landscape. Former Limerick great, Shane Dowling, gives a lovely snapshot from his career about playing a club game marking a player of mature years. 'All I knew about him was his age, and that his best days were behind him. I thought I'd go in and swan about this ould lad now. Five minutes into the game he hit me an awful slap, fair and honest, turned around to me and said, "Hey kid, I'm a butcher back home, and for the rest of the game I'm going to go at you like I mince all my meat."'

Our deeds are our greatest monuments.

But in the world of GAA controversies it is our misdeeds that generate our greatest talking points.

This section chronicles some of the most high-profile controversies in the broad area of discipline.

# 1

## TOP CATS

*Kilkenny Playing on the Edge*

The playwright Eugene O'Neill argues that our tragedy is that we are haunted not just by the masks others wear but by the masks we wear ourselves. We are acting all the time because life makes us unnecessary deceivers – apart from sometimes when we are all alone. This man, though, is a study in authenticity.

He believes that attitude is the little thing that makes the big difference. He has the voice that, when he needs it to, cuts through the air like a reaper's scythe.

Just ask Marty Morrissey.

He has a steely stare that could send the meek and the mild hiding under their beds.

We fell asleep in one world and woke up in another. In spite of the posturings of various media figures, the reality is that we did not see this coming, even though a handful of enlightened prophets did issue some unheeded warnings. Chief among them was Ger Loughnane's observation, 'We're all in trouble now.'

Loughnane always has had the capacity for sharp observation. I once asked him how I could best learn the secrets of GAA politics. His answer was short: 'Watch *The Godfather*.'

When Brian Cody was appointed Kilkenny hurling manager he began the most successful managerial career hurling has ever known. The glow from his fire would light up the hurling world though he would guard his secrets as if they were the most sacred of Masonic mysteries. He knew how to unravel the threads of probability and possibility and held the past, present and future of the black-and-amber jersey surely in his hands, cupping them in a chalice of self-belief. His team became the sun around which all the others were moving orbits.

The team was powered by some of the greatest defenders in the history of the game: Tommy Walsh; Jackie Tyrell; Noel Hickey; Brian Hogan and J.J. Delaney. Cody said Delaney was the greatest defender he had ever seen. That is some endorsement. All those defenders had the talent and the hard work. Some, like Brian Hogan and Noel Hickey, were surprisingly fast. To be hit by Brian Hogan was like being hit by a JCB.

In 2007, Ger Loughnane, at a time when he was managing Galway, created a tidal wave of controversy when he suggested that some of the Kilkenny backs 'played on the edge' and possessed a mastery of 'the dark arts'. He drew attention to their tendency to 'push the rules to the limits' which was code in the GAA vernacular for saying they went way beyond that. In particular, he expressed a concern for the fingertips of his players if they tried to catch the ball in the vicinity of Tommy Walsh. While conceding that this was only a relatively minor part of their play, he claimed that it was a dangerous one.

The great and the good of Kilkenny hurling led by Eddie Keher were quick out of the blocks to accuse him of hurling heresy. A few months later, after they comprehensively beat Limerick in the All-Ireland hurling final, the controversy continued and was a major talking point on *The Sunday Game* that evening as if Loughnane was a sinister apparition in a dark fairy tale.

I texted Loughnane during the programme. His reaction was a mixture of amusement and bemusement. 'Can you believe it? They have just won back-to-back All-Irelands. They should be celebrating it but instead they are still giving out about me!'

## SAVAGE

The publication of Jackie Tyrell's autobiography years later confirmed that for all the importance of skill on Cody's team Kilkenny did not play like altar boys. Tommy Walsh encapsulated that robust approach: 'If you can't see the ball, you pull where you think it is.' For his part, Cody's mantra is very simple: 'Savage intensity'.

In 2019 journalist Dermot Crowe revealed two stories about Cody which offer suggestive snapshots into his personality. In the first he was examining portraits of the Black and Tans and the Kilkenny hurlers of the 1920s at an art exhibition. When someone commented on the similarity of the images, Cody observed, 'Both killing machines.' When he was asked if he wanted a player who would die for the Kilkenny jersey, Cody replied, 'No, I want a lad who would kill for it.'

In 2022, after twenty-four years patrolling the sideline, Cody stepped down as Kilkenny manager.

Ní fheicfimid a leithéid arís.

# 2

# THE LYNCH MOB

*Christy Ring Gets Suspended*

'The key to immortality is first living a life worth remembering.'
BRUCE LEE

When Gareth O'Callaghan interviewed the philosopher John O'Donohue he asked him where do we go when we die. John answered: 'Nowhere. We remain here.' Jack Lynch remains a lingering presence in the GAA.

For a few hours I entered the land of hopes and dreams. I felt like the children who climbed into the wardrobe and emerged in Narnia.

One of the most memorable evenings of my life came when a mutual friend arranged for me to meet Jack Lynch some years after he had retired from the political stage. Outside through the glass window a silvered swirl of stars settled in. He was so serene that I imagined that if a bomb exploded under his bed he would turn over and go back to sleep. To get some context for his career as one of the GAA's most decorated stars I began by asking him about his early life. Words seeped slowly from the edges of his memory:

'My father's family came from a small farm in the townland of Baurgorm, south of Bantry. The farm was later amalgamated with another and this, in turn, was again amalgamated. The fact that the holding is still a very small one gives some idea of the size of the original holding. My father came to Cork City at the turn of the century and became an apprentice to a tailor, first at Daniel's, a merchant tailor on Grand Parade, and later on at Cash's, one of the main drapery stores in Cork.

'He got married in 1908 to Nora O'Donoghue, whose family originally came from a farm near Glounthaune, but they had moved into the city by the time my father came in contact with them. She was a seamstress and continued to work part-time after they got married – a much needed supplement to my father's income. Although we were not well off, we were always well dressed, even if our clothes were usually hand-me-downs. My mother's training as a seamstress made her fussy about our clothes and appearances. I suppose I learned a certain fastidiousness in that regard from her.

'My father was a tall, dignified-looking man, quiet and modest in all his doings. He liked a drink occasionally and was interested in sports. In his day he played football, first in west Cork and then for a Cork City team, Nil Desperandum, now defunct, whose members were associated with the drapery trade in Cork. He was interested in all sports, attending soccer and rugby matches as well as Gaelic football and hurling. His main recreation, when I was young, was walking and occasionally throwing a bowl along the road, which, of course, is still a favourite pastime in west Cork and the environs of the city.

'My memory of him is as a strict but fair father. I was regarded as the wild boy of the family and, therefore, came into conflict with him more often than did my brothers, but we had a good father/son relationship. He took particular interest in my sporting career and was often quietly critical of my performances, but always in a helpful way. I remember once after a match I had played for Glen Rovers, him commenting: "You were rather lackadaisical today", which was quite true on the occasion and, coming from him, a stern rebuke.'

It was during his schooldays that Jack Lynch the GAA star was born:

'My first school was St. Vincent's convent in Peacock Lane. I was there for two years until 1925, when I went to the primary section in the North Mon and was in "the Mon" for eleven years in all. One can't remain in a school for such a length of time without it having a profound effect and, I suppose, the North Mon has left its mark on me. How, it's difficult for me to say. It's a very competitive school, however, and maybe some of that rubbed off. They used to publish examination results in the papers and pushed scholarship classes very hard as a result. They also concentrated strongly on sport and it was in this sphere, I'm afraid, that I made most impact in school. My older brothers were all involved in sports, so it was natural for me at an early age to play both hurling and football. At quite an early age, I remember feeling that I had an ability, especially as a hurler. This may sound rather cocky, but I think it was just a self-confidence which is really an indispensable ingredient in any successful sportsman, or maybe even politician!'

He nodded sagely in agreement with himself and there was a suppressed amusement in his expression.

'Early on I played in local parish leagues and, of course, I started to play with North Mon in the Cork Colleges and Munster Colleges competitions – there were no All-Ireland Colleges Championships at the time except at interprovincial level on the lines of the Railway Cups. I think it was recognised fairly early on that I had an ability as a hurler and, frankly, I took advantage of this for missing an occasional class, as I used to have allowances made for me by teachers who were convinced I was otherwise preoccupied, which may not have been always the case.

'My older brothers – Theo, Charlie and Finbarr – had joined Glen Rovers at an early age and I did likewise. There I came in contact with one of the great father figures of the Glen, Paddy O'Connell, who took a special interest in my progress, which suggested to me that he thought I had some potential. He used to take me to some of the big Munster Championship matches and point out facets of play to me and the techniques of various players. For instance, I remember him getting me to watch Mickey Cross, the Limerick left half-back in the early thirties. He was one of Paddy's own favourites. I noted how he moved towards a ball, how he sized up to it, how occasionally he would let it pass him in order to create better space for himself. I learned quite a lot about tactics and I suppose about how to think about the game during these outings. I won a scholarship to get from primary to secondary school – I remember coming first in English in the scholarship exam, but not doing as well in other subjects.'

### RINGSIDE VIEW

Lynch went on to become a barrister and T.D. while playing hurling for Glen Rovers and football for St Nicholas', the sister club of Glen Rovers. On both sides he would line out with Christy Ring and literally became a witness to one of the most controversial episodes in Ring's career.

Ring was sent off when St Nicks' played Macroom in the 1949 county football semi-final. The referee in his report said Ring had obstructed him in the course of his duty by making a remark. The club vigorously pleaded Ring's innocence and Jack

Lynch, who also played in the match, left the Dáil to travel to Cork to attend the board meeting as a witness on Ring's behalf. The referee's report, however, stood, and Ring received a one-month suspension.

Lynch was angry at the time about the way Ring had been treated. However, years later when I asked him about it he took me by surprise when he quoted from Shakespeare's Sonnet 60:

> Like as the waves make towards the pebbl'd shore,
> So do our minutes hasten to their end;
> Each changing place with that which goes before,
> In sequent toil all forwards do contend
> [. . .]
> Time doth transfix the flourish set on youth
> And delves the parallels in beauty's brow,
> Feeds on the rarities of nature's truth,
> And nothing stands but for his scythe to mow:
> And yet to times in hope my verse shall stand,
> Praising thy worth, despite his cruel hand.

# 3

## ANOTHER ONE BITES THE DUST

*Paddy McBrearty Is Bitten During a Match*

*'There is a code of omertà in the Dublin camp and a player risks having his tongue cut out if he leaks any information.'*
COLM O'ROURKE

The aggression was rising like waves.

It was one of the most infamous episodes in sporting history.

In June 28, 1997, Iron Mike Tyson bit Evander Holyfield's ear in the third round of their heavyweight rematch. The attack led to his disqualification from the bout and suspension from boxing, and was the strangest chapter yet in the champion's roller-coaster career that included marrying and divorcing actress Robin Givens (after being accused by her of domestic violence), firing and suing his manager, breaking his hand in an early-morning street brawl, two car accidents, one of which was reportedly a suicide attempt and declaring bankruptcy – in part due to $400,000 a year spent on maintaining a flock of pet pigeons – and an arrest for cocaine possession.

In 1991, Tyson was accused of rape by Desiree Washington, a contestant in a beauty pageant he was judging in Indianapolis.

He was convicted on 10 February 1992 and served three years and one month in a federal penitentiary. On release Tyson regained his heavyweight belts and then planned a bout with Evander Holyfield, a clean-living, religious, former heavyweight champion.

In the third round, Tyson spit out his mouthpiece, bit off a chunk out of Holyfield's right ear and then spit it on to the canvas. Though Holyfield was in obvious pain the fight resumed after a brief stoppage, and then Tyson bit Holyfield's other ear. With ten seconds left in the third round, he was disqualified. His $30 million purse was withheld.

In 2013, the GAA had its own 'bite-gate'. The GAA's Central Competition Controls Committee initiated an investigation into the allegations made that Donegal forward Paddy McBrearty was bitten in a Division One clash with Dublin in Ballybofey. McBrearty subsequently required hospital examination in Letterkenny and was said to have had a number of precautionary injections that night. Donegal officials reported the alleged incident to referee Padraig Hughes at the interval. That detail made its way into the official report on the match and that triggered the probe.

McBrearty himself was not keen to press the matter. Dublin chairman Andy Kettle confirmed that a member of their medical staff was invited into the Donegal dressing room to examine McBrearty. Kettle said the medic had suggested that, in his estimation, it was 'a bruise, not a laceration'.

Subsequently, the Central Competitions Controls Committee (CCCC) proposed a three-match ban for the Dublin player involved after concluding their investigation into the allegations. However, the player chose not to accept the ban, for what the CCCC deemed a Category Three offence, and appeared before a three-man panel. A statement released by the GAA afterwards said: 'It was decided that on the basis of the evidence provided and the submissions made on behalf of both parties, the infraction against . . . as alleged was not proven.'

## GET AN EARFUL OF THIS

Then GAA Director General Páraic Duffy strongly criticised Dublin and Donegal in the wake of the controversy. In his annual report, Duffy wrote that it was 'reprehensible' that no one was held to account for the incident. Donegal were also criticised by the then GAA President Liam O'Neill for not seeing the case through although then county boss Jim McGuinness subsequently strongly defended McBrearty, insisting that the Central Hearings Committee had been furnished with all the necessary information.

Duffy's comments on the issue came as the Leinster Council were surveying another biting allegation against a Dublin player following an O'Byrne Cup match against DCU. Looking through the blinkers of morality Duffy described biting on a football field as 'primitive behaviour' and 'shocking and dangerous'. Duffy added that the controversy was one of the 'the low points of 2013' and added that the bite mark sustained by the Donegal man had been 'severe'. He said:

'That was a disgusting and shocking incident in itself but what is just as reprehensible is that no one could be held to account for what happened. The Central Competitions Control Committee investigated the matter as thoroughly as possible but was greatly hindered by the absence of video and other evidence. The CCCC, therefore, was reliant on the integrity of those involved to play their part in ensuring that justice was served. However, no one was proved to have inflicted the bite simply because no one admitted to having done so and because the player who was bitten decided not to attend a hearing on the case. The counties involved may have chosen to deal with this incident solely in terms of their own interests . . . they did not emerge with any credit and succeeded only in damaging the reputation of the Association.'

# 4

# HIGHWAY ROBBERY

*The 2010 Leinster Final*

A good soldier does not leave the field until the last shot has been fired.

If Séamus Darby scored the most famous goal in the history of Gaelic football when he sensationally deprived Kerry their five-in-a-row in the 1982 All-Ireland final, Joe Sheridan's goal is the most infamous.

When three minutes of extra time were indicated, Louth were a point in front of their closest neighbours and rivals, Meath, in the 2010 Leinster final. Louth were seeking their first Leinster title since 1957.

Then in the seventy-fourth minute Meath's Graham Reilly launched the ball into the square. It fell to Séamus Kenny who aimed for goal. Paddy Keenan, who had been stupendous throughout for 'the Wee County' (and who won a richly deserved All-Star at midfield later that year), threw his body in front of the shot and blocked the ball. Neither Dessie Finnegan nor Andy McDonnell could hold the rebound and it was grabbed by Joe Sheridan. He stumbled, fell and was almost prostrate on the goal-line before throwing the ball in the net.

A number of Louth players then surrounded the referee, Martin Sludden, who appeared to have noted the score in his book, even though the umpires' flags stayed down. Aaron Hoey urged Sludden to speak to the umpires and the Tyrone man went towards one of them. The television replays showed the umpire cupping his ear, Sludden saying something and the umpire raising his flag.

After the ensuing kick-out, the referee blew the whistle to finish the game. Sludden remained on the pitch, and, in the eyes of Louth fans, added to the injustice by booking a number of Louth players, including Aaron Hoey. The anger came from them like the rustle of leaves in a forest.

Then some upset Louth fans confronted Sludden. The Louth manager Peter Fitzpatrick (who would subsequently become a T.D.) and some Louth players stood around the referee to protect him as he was approached by other fans. A garda started to escort him off the pitch. Two years later two Louth fans were convicted and each fined €1,000 for attacking Sludden.

After the game Peter Fitzpatrick claimed Sludden was: 'Dick Turpin without a mask. It was pure daylight robbery'. On *The Sunday Game* Pat Spillane condemned the actions of a small number of Louth supporters but felt that their team were robbed. He raised the stakes by calling for the Central Competitions Control Committee to grant Louth a replay.

The fallout from the game dominated the media that evening and on Monday morning. GAA HQ issued a short statement on Monday evening saying they condemned the scenes. Sludden admitted in his match report that the goal was a mistake. Pressure was piled on Meath ahead of their county board meeting in Navan on Monday night. After meeting for over three hours, the county board declared no decision on a replay would be made until the next day when the players would decide. The Louth County Board stated that they would welcome a replay. None would be forthcoming.

## A MOTHER'S TEARS

Subsequently, Joe Sheridan revealed how the hate mail he received brought his mother to tears:

'I probably took the brunt of the abuse being the person that was involved. I got letters sent to the house and messages sent to me on the phone. It was pretty dire stuff for people to write down. They didn't even sign it off which was the annoying thing.

'I remember my mother got a letter in the post one day and started crying. To actually think that someone could sit down and write that kind of stuff on a letter and send it across anonymously as well. Emotions bring the worst out in people sometimes.'

Sheridan was unhappy with the spotlight on the Meath players at the time:

'The way it was handled was probably the worst thing. It was put back on the Meath players and what we were going to decide to do regarding a replay. It shouldn't have been. It had nothing to do with the players. It should have come out that the players had nothing to do with it. That would have been the biggest issue I had with it and the way we were portrayed as players. It was left to drag out. It should have been nipped in the bud simple as that and then everyone moves on. It was a bit much and the crack of Marty Morrissey up outside our meetings looking for white smoke for this and that. It was on the 6 o'clock news, it was blown out of proportion. It was hyped up completely just for the entertainment side of things but probably a bit of thought should have went into it.'

# 5

# THE BATTLE OF OMAGH

*Tyrone and Dublin's Bruising Battle*

The GAA has produced many great days. This was not one of them.

Tyrone manager Mickey Harte properly caught the essence of the contest: 'If Paddy Russell had been God Almighty he couldn't have refereed the game today.' Tyrone legend Owen Mulligan gave another invaluable insight claiming that 'for four or five minutes' it was 'dog-eat-dog'.

Dublin won 1–09 to 1–06 on 5 February 2006. However, after the game, nobody was talking about the result. Instead, they were discussing the series of incidents that led referee Paddy Russell to send off four and flash fourteen yellow cards in what was an unsavoury Allianz Football League opener at Healy Park.

It was clear that Dublin were out to make a statement. The previous summer Tyrone had beaten the Dubs in the All-Ireland quarter-final replay, a game that will always be remembered by Owen 'Mugsy' Mulligan's wonder goal. He won a 50:50 ball, leaving his opponent's face flat on the grass via a blistering hairpin turn. He sold two dummies before burying the ball into the corner of the net.

In his *Laochra Gael* episode, Mickey Harte revealed that he saw it differently to most fans who were spellbound by the Mugsy magic: 'I would like to bring people's attention to the fact that that goal actually started with a free kick for Dublin. Alan Brogan turned to kick a point, Brian McGuigan came across and blocked him. Ryan McMenamin picked up the breaking ball. He fisted it to Davy Harte. He was on the line. McGuigan was on the ball again, a centre half-forward in his own D. He kicked it up to Stephen O'Neill, who turned and kicked it to Mulligan. But the reason why those dummies worked was because Enda McGinley and Brian McGuigan were now up beside him heading for goals. It was very much a team goal, a really quality team goal.'

The Dublin management and players were determined that their intensity would be superior to their Red Hand opponents in Omagh. Their manager Paul Caffrey had highlighted areas from both games for the squad where they had been physically bullied by Tyrone. The third time was going to be different. For those keeping score: Dublin had eight players booked, Tyrone six, and others were lucky to miss out on any sanctions. The referee was escorted off the field by stewards as furious fans expressed their anger at the end of the match.

## BLOW BY BLOW

It began with a fourth-minute melee involving more than fifteen players. Punches were clearly thrown by a number of players, but the referee initially opted to be lenient, simply showing yellow cards at Brian Meenan and Alan Brogan.

Tyrone's Colin Holmes received a straight red card, with Dubs midfielder Denis Bastick; Dubs forward Alan Brogan and then Footballer of the Year Stephen O'Neill were dismissed on second yellows. One of the defining images of the game was the spectacle of Brogan being hauled off the pitch by then Dublin manager Paul 'Pillar' Caffrey, with the star straining against his manager's grip seeking to run back into the thick of the action. With the benefit of hindsight Brogan was grateful for Pilar's intervention: 'I was kind of glad he held me back all right! I took a yellow card and it was my second one so I got a red. It was one of those games. We were sick of losing to Tyrone at that stage; they had beaten us a couple of times before that and they were the one team we couldn't get off our back at all.'

In total nine players were later charged but only Holmes served a suspension as he was the only one to have been issued with a straight red card. The leniency did nothing to placate the critics of the GAA's often controversial rule book.

On RTÉ television, Denis Bastick would subsequently dismiss it as 'handbags'. A few years later, though, details of Dublin's 'Blue Book' were leaked, including a reference to the Omagh affair as, 'a day when we crossed the line together like a Dublin squad hasn't done in years.'

# 6

# FROM A JACK TO A KING

*Jack Lynch Splits Glen Rovers*

The characters were familiar to me, but this version of the story was new to my ears.

At the time I met Jack Lynch he was the only man to have won All-Ireland medals in six consecutive years, so for a few hours in his company I was trapped in a state of imaginary grace. While I was intrigued by his sporting career, I had to ask him about his involvement in one of the most controversial events in Irish history: the Arms Trial. It is indicative of his sensitivities around the topic that he said he would only speak about it on the condition that I would only publish the piece 'long after' he died. He was standing on the edge of the past that was terrifying as he recalled with a studied eloquence:

'The North was to be my major preoccupation as Taoiseach. Very shortly after I took office in 1966, I travelled to Stormont to see the Northern Premier, Captain Terence O'Neill – this was the time when my car was snowballed by a handful of Ian Paisley's supporters.

'I had enthusiastically supported Seán Lemass's initiative in seeing Captain O'Neill a few years before, for it introduced an element of rationality to what was, essentially, an absurd situation. From my childhood I had come to regard the division of our country as a blight on the land. That division was mirrored in splits and dissensions within almost every other national organisation – we had two trade union movements for a while, there were two athletic boards, two soccer authorities and two Chambers of Commerce in Cork, etc.

'I was never brought up to feel any antagonism to the Northern unionists, nor did I feel that their legitimate rights and aspirations should, or indeed could, be ignored. I had little personal contact with the North, however, although Éamon de Valera did send me to a meeting in Coalisland in 1948 or '49, for a debate on unity. In spite of this, however, I always wanted to advance the cause of Irish unity by agreement and, indeed, I referred again and again to this concept of unity by agreement, even before any of the troubles broke out in the North, in the autumn of 1968. It had been suggested that unity by agreement was not always Fianna Fáil policy, but rather, unity by peaceful means. However, I have always failed to see how unity by peaceful means could mean anything other than unity by agreement and I think it was helpful to be explicit about this.

'Although I had not travelled to Stormont for Seán Lemass's first meeting with Captain O'Neill, I did attend the follow-up meeting at Iveagh House and afterwards had a meeting with Brian Faulkner, who was then Minister for Commerce in Northern Ireland. It was obviously our hope that under the O'Neill conciliatory policy, the old attitudes in the North would soften and that gradually the Northern unionists would recognise that their future lay in a united Ireland, or, at least, that the discriminatory practices towards the Catholic minority would cease and that there could be an end of animosity and bitterness on the island. This was not to be. The civil rights movement in the North, which demanded ordinary democratic civil rights for Catholics, evoked hard-line unionist opposition, leading to violence first of all from the loyalist side and then, when the situation was in turmoil, from the IRA, which leaped in to exploit the situation for its own ends. I was unhappy from the outset about the introduction of British troops on to the streets of Northern Ireland, but their presence there soon became a political reality and there were obvious dangers in their immediate withdrawal.'

As he relived those troubled times his voice became lower and more intimate. He talked in the same tone people speak at a funeral, hinting at the emotional and psychological strain he was under at the time.

'I expressed my initial unhappiness in my speech in 1969 on RTÉ, immediately before the introduction of the troops. While I think that my fears about their involvement in the six county area have been borne out by events, I acknowledge that once they were there and, more particularly, once they became part of the political geography of Northern Ireland, a peremptory withdrawal of the troops would have caused even further chaos. The Northern situation gave a new dimension to the position of Taoiseach because for the first time, at least in our generation, the words one spoke could have resulted in the loss of lives of fellow countrymen in the North. It imposed a great strain on the office and made one circumspect about all one said and did, while at the same time there remained an obligation to spell out the basic political realities of the situation, without the resolution of which, there could be no permanent peace.

'I was careful to pursue a consistent political line throughout on my handling of the Northern situation. At the Fianna Fáil

Ard Fheis in 1969, I said, "the first aim of Fianna Fáil today is to secure, *by agreement*, the unification of the national territory". Later that year, I said in response to the Downing Street Declaration, "The government agree that the border cannot be changed by force. It is, and has been, their policy to seek the reunification of the country by peaceful means ... Nothing must be left undone to avoid a recurrence of the present troubles, whether in five or fifty years, but to continue to ignore the need for constitutional change, so clearly necessary, could only have such a tragic result."

'In Tralee I said, "It will remain our most earnest aim and hope to win the consent of the majority of the people in the Six Counties, through means by which North and South can come together, in a reunited and sovereign Ireland, earning international respect for both the fairness and efficiency with which it is administered and for its contribution to world peace and progress."'

For a few moments silence settled between us like snow on frosty ground. I wondered if he was recalling the screams of fervent fury back then.

'At the Fianna Fáil Ard Fheis (on January 17, 1970), I said: "Until the ugly blooms of mistrust and suspicion which poison the atmosphere have died and the ground is planted with the fresh, clean seeds of friendship and mutual confidence, reunification can never be more than an artificial plant, rather than a burgeoning, blossoming flower. And so I have said our course is clear: amity not enmity is our ideal; persuasion not persecution must be our method; and integration not imposition must be our ultimate method."

'I indicated that we should contemplate constitutional and legislative change in the south in advance of any negotiations about unity, to encourage the Northern unionists, to look favourably at our overtures. However, the reaction to our removal of a section of Article 44 of the Constitution, which gave special recognition to the Catholic Church, was very discouraging. This initiative was completely ignored in the North as of absolutely no consequence, while previously Northern loyalists had repeatedly pointed to this section, as evidence of the denominational character of the southern state. Shortly after the general election of 1973, and the Presidential election the same year, a Northern Ireland politician came to see me and I alluded to my disappointment with the Northern reaction to the constitutional change. He agreed it had almost no effect on Northern opinion. I then pointed out that we had just elected a Protestant President (Erskine Childeres), asking if that had any impact on unionists. He replied that it had little, if any, but said that had we not done it, then there would have been a reaction. I appreciated then that it was futile making any constitutional changes in advance of unity, and that any further changes should be made in an all-Ireland context.'

## IN THE SHADOW OF THE GUN

Lynch's attitude to the IRA was controversial. His gaze did not waver from mine as he trawled through the memory bank:

'I was bemused about Northern unionist suspicions concerning my personal attitude, and that of my government, towards the IRA. We introduced a plethora of measures designed to clamp down on them, we spent very much more on security on a per capita basis than the British government, and we repeatedly expressed our abhorrence for all the IRA stands for. By attempting to force a united Ireland on the Northern unionists, against their wishes, the IRA was acting not only contrary to what the vast majority of the people in the Republic and throughout the island would wish, but they were actually doing great damage to the cause of unity, which they allegedly espoused. There can be no unity through force or coercion – the unity we seek can come only through agreement, and the IRA was making that unity immeasurably more difficult.

'This is quite apart from the revulsion which we all feel towards their repeated acts of barbarity. The catalogue of such barbarism is a long one but one incident sticks out in my mind. This was the bombing of the Abercorn restaurant in Belfast (on Saturday 4 March 1972). No warning of the bomb was given and two young women died and 130 people were injured, many losing limbs and otherwise being maimed for life. One young woman lost both her legs and an arm and many others suffered similar injury.

'I was absolutely appalled to realise that, on this island, an organisation claiming to act in the name of the Irish people should perpetrate such an atrocity. What is the point of a united Ireland if this is the price to be paid for achieving it?

'It was later that year that we passed the Offences Against the State (Amendment) Act, which empowered senior garda officers, of the rank of chief superintendent and higher, to state in evidence in court their opinion on whether an accused was a member of an illegal organisation. That measure had a very significant effect on the IRA and it meant that, for a while, leading members of the organisation were safer in the North than they were in the south. This was an indication of our determination to deal with the organisation that has brought shame on all of us Irish people. I was perplexed by the doubts that have persisted about our determination to wipe out the IRA, by all legitimate means, within the rule of law.

'The debate on that Offences Against the State (Amendment) bill, was the prelude to the calling of the 1973 general election. I was naturally very interested in the developments then within the main opposition party, Fine Gael, which was deeply divided on the issue. Quite obviously, this would have been a good time for us to go to the country and offer ourselves as the alternative to a deeply divided opposition. However, I didn't want to curtail the debate on the bill and it dragged on longer than I had originally assumed. It was my intention to call a general election immediately after the debate concluded, but this became impossible once the debate dragged on, because it would have had to be held either on Christmas Eve, or the day after Christmas, neither being suitable for obvious reasons. I was also anxious not to be seen to take advantage of the public outrage following the bombing of Dublin, on the evening of Friday 1 December, in which two busmen were killed and eighty-three people were injured. I therefore decided to wait until the new year before advising the President to dissolve the Dáil and, in retrospect, it must surely have been agreed that had circumstances permitted us to go to the country in the pre-Christmas period, we would have won the election.

'In the event, we lost by a mere handful of votes. Had about 2,000 votes spread throughout key constituencies swung to us, then we would have ended up with the two-seat majority, instead of a two-seat minority. I think that 1973 election result was probably Fianna Fáil's greatest electoral achievement with me as leader, although the party was the loser. Never before had a political party, or combination of parties, won such a high vote and lost the election.'

## THE ARMS TRIAL
Things would escalate for Lynch with the Arms crisis:
'There was a time during that period when it was widely believed we would be decimated at the polls, whenever an election took place. This was, of course, due largely to the

dismissal of ministers on 6 May 1970 and the resignation of another minister. Naturally, this was a very trying period for me personally. Although I was not close socially to any of the people involved, I had grown up in politics with them and a bond of camaraderie had developed between us. To have had to dismiss them from office was a very painful thing to do, as was the subsequent recrimination.

'History will adjudicate on the rights and wrongs of that period, but I felt I had no option but to act as I did, given the information placed at my disposal by the security forces. There have been suggestions that I orchestrated the prosecutions throughout the affair, but, again, the fact of the matter is that I had no involvement whatsoever in anything to do with the prosecution, or with the conduct of the case, once I handed the papers over to the Attorney General.

'Almost overnight in May of 1970, we lost four senior members of the government – Charlie Haughey, Neil Blaney, Kevin Boland and Michael Moran. These were difficult ministers to replace, especially given the fact that a Taoiseach really has only a one in two choice from which to make government appointments. In the circumstances, I don't think we did badly, in spite of continued, opportunistic harassment by the opposition. The growth rate for those years in the early seventies was very high. We dealt competently with the security situation and we began to make substantial progress with the British on a solution to the Northern Ireland problem.

'One of the difficulties I experienced in dealing with British Prime Ministers or ministers on the North, is that they often were not very well acquainted with the issue and didn't rate it high in their order of priorities. This is understandable, given the relative importance of the Northern Ireland issue in the context of the overall British political situation, but it did mean that the Northern problem was allowed to drag on, sometimes unnecessarily.'

## A GAA CONTROVERSY

There is no doubt that Lynch's great achievements on GAA fields helped kick-start his political career. However, there was a major controversy which threatened to prevent him from claiming his place in the political arena:

'Having played with Glen Rovers, I was identified very much with the Blackpool area, where there was a strong nationalist tradition dating back to William O'Brien. Glen Rovers decided they would conduct a campaign for me. The Fianna Fáil organisation was not happy when the Glen put out special polling cards and did a personalised canvass for me. I asked Glen Rovers not to do it, but they argued that it was purely a private matter for them and didn't involve the Fianna Fáil party. I went so far as to impound the personal canvass cards, but they got another supply.

'There was some tension for a while as the other Fianna Fáil candidates, quite rightly, didn't approve of what was happening. The tension died down, however, when Tom Crofts, the director of elections, personally intervened and suggested that, when canvassing, the Glen Rovers members should ask for support for the other Fianna Fáil candidates and this they agreed to do.'

# 7

# HOUSE OF CARDS

*The Black Card*

Say yes to the redress.

Whenever I hear people talking about Jack Charlton I think of Eugene McGee.

Tony Cascarino was playing cards with some of the Irish lads early in Charlton's tenure as Irish manager when he noticed that Burt Reynolds was on the television. He ridiculed him because of the wig he was wearing. Immediately Big Jack went up to him and berated him because his brother Bobby had lost his hair at a young age and had been constantly mocked about it which had caused him much hurt. Cascarino was shocked to see that caring side of Jack. He would see it many times in the coming years. Big Jack protected Paul McGrath the way nobody would.

As a result, the players forgave him his trespasses. Before Ireland played Holland in his last game, Charlton did some video analysis. When the players realised they were watching the Dutch under-20 side rather than the senior team they turned to Jack with quizzical glances. He sighed in exasperation and said, 'Just f**king watch it. They all play the same.'

The high point of Jack's time with Ireland was when they qualified for the World Cup quarter-final at Italia '90. The bonus was that the team got an audience with the world's most famous goalkeeper Pope John Paul II. Less than a week later Ireland lost 1–0 after the team's goalkeeper Packie Bonner had spilled a shot. In the dressing room afterwards Charlton said to Andy Townsend: 'The f**king pope would have saved it.'

The nation owes Big Jack a debt. Arguably his greatest achievement was that he allowed the Irish people to reclaim the tricolour from the IRA.

Jack was awkward and gruff but we loved him because he was authentic. He suited us and we suited him. The same could be said for Eugene McGee and Offaly.

Even though there were times when he had looked as if he could scare away the plague in some of their training sessions, when Eugene died it was like the Offaly players who played under him had lost their second Dad and the county's fans who could remember 1982 had lost their grandad.

After he stepped away from football management, McGee continued to be one of the most influential voices in Gaelic football as a pundit. He chaired the GAA's Football Review Committee which recommended the introduction of the controversial 'Black Card' rule to deter cynical fouling in the game.

Motion 4 proposed that a new 'black card' be introduced to deal with a specific category of foul, relating to 'cynical behaviour' and was passed with an eighty-two per cent majority at the GAA Annual Congress in Derry in 2013. The motion proposed that an offender shown a black card would be ordered off the field but would then be replaced by a substitute.

Dublin chairman Andy Kettle was the first delegate from the floor to back the new proposals and described cynicism as 'a cancer on the game'. Referees chief Pat McEnaney said that yellow cards were not a sufficient deterrent against cynical play: 'The onus must be put back on the player, not the referee.' The black card, though, had a number of high-profile critics including Tomás Ó Sé and Bernard Flynn. Eugene McGee responded to their criticisms by saying:

'The main one that attracts the attention is "deliberately", and that's the crucial word, "deliberately pulling down an opponent to the ground". You could elaborate more than that but that's fairly idiot-proof for most people. When people talk about variations from referees, the interpretation of a referee – one referee, whether it's deliberate, and the other referee, whether it's not – that's a matter of opinion, the same as all the other topics in all refereeing around the world. It's the same in the Premiership, in Australian Rules, American Football. A big issue is made of that but "deliberate" is the crucial thing. The rule is carefully contrived not to embarrass people and punish them for making decisions which are purely accidental. The idea is to stop the fouling and make the game more free-flowing.'

Jim McGuinness, though, continued to protest loudly about it. Eugene McGee replied that McGuinness, 'Thinks because he won one All-Ireland he is the high priest of football. If he is that good, why didn't he win a second or third All-Ireland?'

The black card was not like marriage in a fairy tale and the end of all problems.

### HURLING EXEMPTION

The black card was only intended for football. The hurling fraternity was vehemently opposed. Cork's Patrick Horgan has a strong claim to be considered the greatest current player never to have won an All-Ireland, especially since becoming the all-time leading scorer in hurling Championship history. It is fair to say he was not a fan of the idea: 'I think we're trying to change way too much about it, the game that we all fell in love with, there was nothing wrong with. So, I don't understand why we're trying to bring in this yellow, red, black, pink, there's all sorts of every card now. You'd have to have a double take to see am I sent off for five minutes: "Am I sent off?" Or whatever. So I just think we just get on with the game. Obviously, if a foul is worthy of a red or yellow card then fair enough but I think introducing any other sort of sin bin would be out of the question for hurling. I just wouldn't change it.'

Kilkenny legend Eddie Keher wrote to Croke Park to outline his objection to black and yellow cards claiming they were 'a pompous and triumphalist exercise causing humiliation to our great players in front of their families, friends and supporters'.

However, the 2021 Congress witnessed a change in hurling. Pat Spillane, not known as a hurling expert, was pleased:

'Played properly, hurling is the greatest field game in the world. When we witness a bit of magic from the likes of Joe Canning or Richie Hogan it creates the wow factor. But hurling is no different from any other sport – it has issues. Like those who are devoted to rugby and horse racing, hurling aficionados are a close-knit group and all seem to know each other. They are cheerleaders for their sport. The analysts don't do negativity and rarely criticise. And, of course, the favourite catch cry of the hurling fraternity is the guffaw – followed by the line "we don't want to go down the same road as Gaelic football".

'To them, football is the ugly sister in the GAA family. It drives them bonkers when football guys comment about the game of the Gods. Referees are already overburdened. But here's a few home truths about hurling. As a spectacle, hurling is in decline. Ground hurling is almost extinct, as is the overhead strike. We will probably never see a goal again like John Fenton's famous effort against Limerick in 1987. Furthermore, there has been a decrease in the number of goals scored in Championship hurling. Due to the lighter sliotar, points are being scored from the "next parish". There is far more hand-passing than striking the ball with the hurley. Worse still, most of the so-called hand-passes are blatant throws. Hurling referees adopt an *à la carte* approach to their job – blowing up about one in five fouls.

'And there are other issues. Some of Gaelic football's worst tactics have infiltrated hurling. Possession is ninth-tenths of the law – teams operate in pods and play in triangles, and there are more mauls and rucks for the sliotar than ever seen in a rugby international in the Aviva Stadium. And, of course, we were constantly told there was no cynical play in the game. It was a case of move on, nothing to see here. Thank God for David Hassan and his playing rules committee. His evidence-based presentation proved the exact opposite. Out of the twenty games he analysed between 2017 and 2019, almost half the fouls committed were cynical. In 2020 the delegates simply ignored his excellent presentation, but in 2021, common sense prevailed.

'I'm equally pleased that cynical play will be penalised in a similar way in Gaelic football. There could be issues down the line, however. The new rule increases the workload on the already-overburdened referee. Deciding whether a clear-cut goalscoring chance has been denied is very subjective – particularly when the call has to be made in real time. *The Sunday Game*'s panel will have endless cases to mull over.

'My other concern is that a small minority of football referees who have prima donna tendencies will see this rule as an opportunity to take centre stage.'

In fact, the new laws in hurling created the first major controversy of the 2021 Championship. Referee James Owens's decision to sin bin Clare's Aidan McCarthy and award

# HOUSE OF CARDS

Tipperary a penalty in the Munster SHC semi-final stirred up the proverbial hornet's nest. Owens's call was incorrect as McCarthy's foul on Jake Morris did not deny a goalscoring opportunity. Though he was furious afterwards with Owens's decision, Clare boss Brian Lohan argued the rule as it stands was a satisfactory deterrent to cynical play. His problem was with the way the rule was interpreted.

# 8

# GPS-GATE

*Mayo's Distracting Tactic*

The Bard of the Banner, Anthony Daly, offers a parable of the GAA at its best: bitter rivals becoming the best of friends:

'The first time I had a run-in with Johnny Leahy was when Clare and Tipp met in the 1995 League in Ennis. Ger Loughnane had us pumped. Fights were breaking out everywhere. At one stage, Leahy and I went at it. I questioned the extra pounds around Johnny's hips. "Have you had your Mars bars?" I enquired.

'His response was that I'd got the handiest All-Star ever given to anyone the previous year. "At least I played in the Championship anyway," I said to Leahy, who missed our Munster semi-final after getting injured with the Tipp footballers. "They gave you one for sitting on the bench."

'Johnny didn't take too kindly that afternoon to being accused of buying boxes of Mars bars and he was always looking to have his say anytime we met afterwards.

'We had some heated words in the 1997 Munster final. When the sides met again in 1999, Liam Doyle and I were goading

Leahy at every opportunity trying to get a hop out of him. Nicky English had him completely focused, but I had an angle for the replay. After the drawn game, some Tipp supporters had set fire to curtains in one of the carriages on the train back to Clonmel. When a shemozzle kicked off early in the game and Leahy was stuck in the middle of it with Doyler, I let him have it. "I see you got the train home the last day."

'Leahy started roaring laughing. So did Tommy Dunne and Brian O'Meara. I got a fit of the giggles then. As the shemozzle was breaking up, four or five lads were falling around laughing in front of nearly 50,000 people. By that stage, we could have some fun with Tipp at our expense because the wheel had turned full circle. And we were no longer the butt of their jokes.

'When Tipp finally took us down in 2000, the first person I shook hands with afterwards was Johnny Leahy. "Fair play Johnny," I said. "My war is over now." I was listening to a podcast where Tommy Dunne spoke about the first half of his Tipp career. Tommy said that Tipp measured everything they did off what Clare were doing. While we ran up the hill in Shannon, Nicky English had Tipp running up the Devil's Bit. It put a smile on my face.

'After Johnny Leahy missed his late goal chance in the 1997 Munster final, I whispered in his ear that he had bottled it as he lay on the ground. It was all part of the feelings at the time, but that bad blood ended.

'In Clonmel many years later I was down for the coursing. A group of six of us were inside in a small pub in the town, full of the joys of life, when I took a notion to do a party piece. I completely acted the clown because we thought we were the only ones in the place, but it was some craic. When it was all over, this fella hit me a tap on the shoulder. "Hi Dalo," said Johnny Leahy, "there's a bed out in Cahir for you too if you want it."'

### LAST THROW OF THE DICE

Rivalry is at the heart of sport. Manchester United's rivalry with Liverpool is among the most high-profile of the species. Former United star Gary Neville retains a deep antipathy for Liverpool as was evident when he was interviewed on Sky Sports after Thiago was transferred to the Merseysiders from Bayern Munich.

Martin Tyler: 'His dad won the World Cup with Brazil. Thiago was born in Italy but represents Spain because he grew up there, and he speaks and understands English perfectly.'

Gary Neville: 'That will be no use to him where he's going.'

The most keenly contested GAA rivalry in recent years has been between Mayo and Dublin. In the fullness of time, both sets of players will develop the type of supportive relationships now enjoyed by Anthony Daly and John Leahy. But they are not there yet. In February 2022 Dublin's Philly McMahon observed: 'Truth is, Mayo were more concerned with being seen to stand up to you than sticking to what they were supposed to be doing.'

Players cope in different ways. Cillian O'Connor, in preparation for one of the big games between the sides, practised his frees with headphones on and had the song 'Come on ye boys in Blue' blaring out to get ready for the hostile environment that was awaiting him.

In a pulsating 2017 All-Ireland final, Dublin and Mayo were tied at 1–16 each. Dublin were awarded a free. Dean Rock placed the ball. Mayo were playing in their eleventh game of the Championship and were not going to surrender easily.

In a desperate last-ditch attempt to save the game, Lee Keegan removed the GPS from the back of his jersey and tossed it over the ball. It did not distract Rock. Cool as an iceberg, he scored the free. Of course, if he had missed, the controversy would have escalated to a whole new level.

## TWEETS FOR MY TWEET

On social media, public opinion was divided. Dublin fans saw it as evidence of the collapse of civilisation. Outside the Pale, though, there was much more support for Lee Keegan where he was depicted as a great warrior. In one post it was claimed that he had shouldered the tower of Pisa and afterwards it needed its name to be changed.

For his part, Joe Brolly saw Mayo's defeat as further confirmation that they were 'celebrity losers' with a unique flair to win 'every game that didn't matter and lose every one that did'.

## I FEEL IT IN MY FINGERS, I FEEL IT IN MY TOES

The gods of love are clearly untroubled by GAA controversies. In August 2022 it was announced that Joe Brolly was to marry . . . a Mayo woman!

Not only that, but Laurita Blewitt, a cousin of Joe Biden, would marry the green and red's most virulent critic in Mayo.

Could this be what that well known GAA savant Rihanna meant when she sang about finding love in a hopeless place? And if so, was she thinking of the bride or the groom?

# 9

# THE NOTEBOOK

*Paul Galvin Slaps Away Referee's Notebook*

The chimes of time rang out the news.

The image of Kerry's Paul Galvin knocking the notebook out of referee Paddy Russell's hand, against Clare in the 2008 Munster Championship after he was booked, created a strong reaction. Galvin had got into trouble initially for a 'coming together' with Clare defender John Hayes. Russell picked up his notebook and showed Galvin a second yellow card. Galvin received a six month ban shortly after, but the ban was subsequently reduced to three months which enabled him to play in the All-Ireland final later that year.

Before he passed through sleep's dark and silent gate Eugene McGee spoke to me about his feelings about the incident:

'Of course, he shouldn't have done it, but people often don't realise the verbal provocation, not to mind the physical, that a player may endure. The other thing that I don't like is players diving. Think of the way Aidan O'Mahony went down after he got a little slap in the 2008 All-Ireland semi-final against Cork. Donncha O'Connor was sent off as a result. Cork argued that there were procedural issues in referee Joe McQuillan's reporting of the episode and their player was reprieved. That is not the Kerry way.'

Away from the game former Dublin manager Pat Gilroy is one of the most reflective people about the sport he loves so well. His big frame gives him a huge physical presence but when he speaks to you, he does so with gravitas. Rather than speaking directly about the Paul Galvin incident he wanted to frame the discussion in a wider context:

'I think we could learn a lot from rugby because of the culture they have in relation to referees in particular. In rugby nobody dares to question the authority of the referee, but that is far from the case in Gaelic games when referees are often treated with nothing short of contempt. The GAA is an incredible organisation but the one thing we need more of at all levels of our games is respect.

'I remember hearing Ireland's Olympic icon Ronnie Delany speaking one day. He said: "Respect is an enormous attribute for the younger athlete. Respect for the colours you wear, respect for your club, your county, your country, your province."

'These are two things we don't want in our games, and I would like to see them addressed. I think Gaelic games are one of the few places left where fellas are playing for the love of the game. "Sledging" or trying to get a fellow player sent off are not part of our wonderful tradition and we must ensure that they are not allowed to bring discredit to our games. Players are role models. What they do young kids imitate – the good and the bad. Coaches have a big role to play in this.'

Being in the managerial hot seat compelled Gilroy to examine his own conscience:

'When I was manager of Dublin I was forced to reflect on my own role in terms of the instructions I was giving to the team and in particular asking for more physicality. I did not want to be responsible for sending someone out to play for me who was going to cause a serious injury. When I talked about more physicality one player would have taken that to mean to get much tighter on his man and put him under pressure when they lost the ball, but maybe one of the other lads would have taken it as incitement to go out and decapitate somebody. Yes, I wanted to win but no, I did not want to win at all costs.

'One of the most unethical things I see in the GAA is pushing young people into situations too early in life. Because a manager wants to win an under-20 final he plays a fifteen-year-old. Other things I see are pushing young people into a situation where they are playing with a top team and they are just not able for it, and they are cut down because they don't make it and they are cast adrift.

'We in Ireland are all experts in one area: the blame game. I am not just talking about the media here but all of us in our clubs and talking in the pub, we all do it. I made mistakes as a manager and I know that I have to take criticism in those situations but there has to be a line that we don't cross. When a team loses there is always a rush to judgement and some poor unfortunate – the manager or the referee or the freetaker who has an off day and misses the frees – will be slaughtered to bits. Since social media has come into prominence players and managers are subject to the most savage criticism, but the people responsible for these often nasty and vicious comments do not have the guts to put their names to it.'

Media scrutiny also brings potential problems in Gilroy's eyes:

'The media spotlight has changed dramatically. There is certainly a fair bit of negativity in the media coverage. What particularly annoys me is what I consider the blight of radio phone-ins. It also creates a much more difficult environment for players and managers to operate in. You have to remember, these players are amateurs but often people under the cloak of anonymity ring in and make very personalised comments about players. We can all have a view on a pundit's comments on TV but at least they're putting their name to their comments. I don't have any time, though, for radio stations who give credibility to comments from a caller who has not the guts to put their name to their opinion. And, of course, on the internet you can say absolutely anything and sometimes these comments can be very destructive.'

Gilroy offers a parable about the way the game should be played:

'The 2013 All-Ireland football final did produce a great moment of sportsmanship. When the final whistle went you would have expected Jonny Cooper to have celebrated but he did not. His first instinct was to run over and console one of the Mayo players, Rob Hennelly, who is a friend of his from college. They won a Sigerson together with DCU. There was a picture taken of Jonny trying to console Rob and whoever said a picture tells a thousand words could have been thinking of this photo. It speaks volumes about Jonny and the way the game should be played.'

## GALVIN V DAVY

In 2020, Paul Galvin surprised the football world when he stepped down as Wexford manager after just over a year in the job. However, a year later he upped the ante when he spoke about his experiences co-existing with Davy Fitzgerald who was managing the county hurling team at the same time:

'I had no difficulties dealing with the hurling manager until such a time as he just started to interfere a little bit with my operation, to be quite honest. Davy wanted the training ground to himself. Some of the things he did made it clear to me that we weren't welcome in Ferns, basically. I took it on the chin because he's around a long time and Davy's a wily old fox and he's gained a little bit of soft power there in the media that he uses quite cleverly. And I took it on the chin because we needed results and I just had to keep my head down, but the thing that really annoyed me about that was the fact that he kind of made a big man of himself in the media on the back of it. He started talking about all the respect he had for me in the media and making a kind of virtuous man of himself on the back of it, but the reality was, behind the scenes, that wasn't the case at all. It was actually, I felt, trying to put me in the ha'penny place a little bit and put football in the ha'penny place a little bit.'

In July 2021 the feud erupted again. Davy's Wexford crashed out of the Championship to another adversary, Brian Lohan's Clare, for a second consecutive year. In his post-match interview Davy claimed in a cacophony of words that the previous year had been the toughest of his life and that the treatment of himself and his family on social media was 'an absolute disgrace'.

Galvin tweeted almost immediately: 'David Fitz loves to play the victim when it suits him. He's far from a victim in how he behaves behind scenes while fronting to the media & I can personally attest to that. Hope someone in the media has guts to ask him hard questions now. Always the victim, never your fault David.'

Pat Spillane's verdict was:

'Davy Fitz is our José Mourinho, for there are so many similarities between the pair. There's usually a brilliant first year, it goes downhill . . . after that – and it is all about Davy and José, and no mention at all of the team.'

# 10

# HILLGATE

*Dublin v Mayo*

In 2005, on a damp, dreary evening in Ennis, Anthony Daly told me: 'Timing is everything in life.' Typical of Dalo he had a brilliant story to illustrate that:

'It was definitely the shortest speech Loughnane ever made, but it was certainly the most memorable. Ger preferred to say his bit down around the town goal of Cusack Park on the Friday evening before a Championship game and in the hotel on the morning of the game rather than in the dressing room. Having said that, when we found ourselves four points down to Tipperary at half-time in the '97 All-Ireland final, we were expecting – and counting on – Ger to hit the right note before we went back out on the field. But he wasn't saying a word. He stood by the door, and he had absolutely nothing to offer.

'After three or four minutes of silence, I started talking. (Brian) Lohan and Mike Mac also spoke, but still Ger said nothing. Next, your man began knocking on the door, it was time to go. I have to say that I was getting annoyed that Ger hadn't contributed anything.

'As I was heading towards the door, Ger put up his hand like a garda stopping traffic. The players were nearly above on my back at this stage, all pent up to go out. There followed another twenty seconds of silence.

'Ger broke the silence with three words. "Men needed now." You could see everything in his eyes in that moment. I looked back at the lads and a roar went up. Afterwards was the best thirty-five minutes of hurling we ever played. We were four down, conceded two goals in the second half, and still beat them.

'It was Ger's timing. He had that gift where he could smell that now was the right time to speak. His three words left me in no doubt but that we were going to win – and we did.'

Twelve months later I thought of that conversation again. Sometimes, though, management teams don't always get their timing right. A case in point was Dublin's decision to flex their muscles before the 2006 All-Ireland semi-final against Mayo.

The Westerners were first out on to the pitch, they lined up for the team photo and then, to everyone's amazement, headed to the Hill 16 end of the pitch to warm up. According to folklore it was because their midfielder David Brady, after hearing that Dublin were to warm up at that end, said: 'Ah f**k it, we will go down to that end.' The atmosphere suddenly electrified. Everyone turned to see how the Dubs would respond when they ran onto the pitch.

Dublin delayed coming out and then headed for the bench over at the Cusack Stand for the team photo. Then, like a mighty military general, Ciarán Whelan led the panel to the Hill. They applauded their fans. Neutrals held their breath and waited for the outcome.

Then mayhem.

## MILL UNDER THE HILL

In the ensuing turf war both squads refused to budge, and altercations broke out among both sets of players and management teams. Both sides bombarded the goal with practice shots and with so many footballs flying around, the Mayo dietician Mary McNicolas was left sprawling on the ground and in need of medical attention. The most high-profile incident captured on camera was when the Dublin manager Paul Caffrey clattered into Mayo trainer John Morrison. Meanwhile there was nobody home at the Canal End. The conflict finally ended when both sides had to line up for the parade behind the Artane Band.

History is written by winners. If the Dubs won, their defiance would have been portrayed as a master stroke. But, instead, they managed to snatch defeat from the jaws of victory and surrendered a big lead, and a stunning point from Ciarán McDonald gave Mayo an unlikely win.

# 11

# THUGGERY

*2006 International Rules*

*'Silence becomes cowardice when occasion demands speaking out the whole truth and acting accordingly.'*

MAHATMA GANDHI

The French have a saying: dogs do not make cats.

International Rules football, sometimes called 'Compromise Rules' is a hybrid code of football which was developed to facilitate international representative matches between Australian Rules footballers and Gaelic footballers.

The first games played were test matches between Australia and a touring Meath Gaelic football team which took place in late 1967, after Meath had won that year's All-Ireland Senior Football Championship. Following intermittent international tests between Australia and an All-Ireland team, which began in the centenary year of the GAA in 1984, the International Rules Series has gained a unique place in the GAA landscape.

The most controversial incident in the series happened in 2006. I do not want to climb too high on my morality mountain but, in the classic cadence of the sporting vernacular, this crossed the line.

Having managed an earlier incarnation of the Irish team, Eugene McGee watched on with interest:

'A lot of people spoke out of both sides of their mouths when it came to the International Rules. They took the moral high ground and complained that the play was too robust, but secretly loved watching the games because of the physical contact. The controversies over the violence brought the games to public attention. The greater the violence, the greater the public interest. Having said that, what happened in 2006 was a bridge too far and did huge damage to the series.'

It started tamely enough in the first test. In poor weather, Ireland won a low-scoring affair 48–40. There were a few scuffles but nothing major though the Aussies seemed aggrieved. There were a few things in the papers from the Aussie players that intimated that they were going to bring serious physicality to the second test.

The game will be remembered for a first-half tackle by Australian Danyle Pearce on Graham Geraghty, knocking the Meath star out cold. The image of him being stretchered off the field, looking in a bad way, shocked those watching in the stands and on television.

In his interview afterwards, the Irish captain Kieran McGeeney famously said: 'If you wanna box, say you wanna box and we'll box. If you wanna play football, say you wanna play football and we'll play football.'

The normally calm Irish manager Seán Boylan was incandescent with anger, describing the match as 'thuggery':

'All week it's been highlighted what they were going to do to him (Geraghty). So don't go to a press conference with me and say that you're not going to do it. You know some of the decisions that were made out there today were absolutely disgraceful.

I've been involved in team management for twenty-three years and, as far as I am concerned, what happened out there in that first quarter is not acceptable in any code of sport. It's not acceptable on the street. In all my years of being involved, I never was as vexed in my life.

'Let me tell you why I was vexed. I don't mind being beaten. I never minded being beaten. But, when somebody has been done – and then to pride yourself at the end of the first quarter, saying "yeah, well, we softened them up a little" – don't give me that as sportsmanship. Don't give me that as trying to promote a series. That's thuggery. That's all that is.'

One critic observed: 'The players that participated in this Australian team were not an anonymous, nomadic bunch of wandering Ned Kellys. They were representing their country. But they disgraced themselves. They debased their sport. They embarrassed their hosts. They shamed their nation. They betrayed the sponsors. They defiled the esteemed memory of the late Cormac McAnallen in whose honour the International Rules Test Trophy is named and whose family must be gutted by the spectacle presented.'

The fallout from the controversy was the articulation of a code of conduct for future tests and falling popularity and crowd numbers.

# 12

# 'A DIRTY TEAM'

## *Armagh Demonised*

Enda McNulty was looking back not in anger but with regret. Everything had gone right for his Armagh team when they won the county's only All-Ireland in 2002. A wave of exultation swept over him:

'It was total euphoria when we won. The first thing that happens is hundreds of supporters jumping on top of you. I remember my little brother Patrick coming into the dressing room afterwards and that was very important to myself and my brother Justin. It wasn't about that I had realised my lifetime ambition, it was more about seeing the impact it had on the fans. I also remember the next morning it wasn't: "We're the men here." It was: "How can we win another one?"

'I remember feeling this drive to become the first Ulster team to win back-to-back All-Irelands since the great Down team of the 1960s. Going on a tour in south Armagh with all the bonfires lit was very powerful. The disappointing thing was that we only had one chat as a team without any hangers-on on the Wednesday afternoon in Paddy McKeever's bar in

Portadown. There had been a bottle of whiskey which had not been open since 1953 – when Armagh had been beaten in the All-Ireland final – and we all had a drink out of it. It was very powerful because it was just us. There is a time to meet the supporters, family and friends but we had too many of those and not enough with just ourselves. Again, there were too many hangers-on when we were presented with our All-Ireland medals. Any team I am ever involved with in the future I will always get the boys together on their own, whether it's a win or a loss, have a few drinks and decide what happens next and have closure.'

The following year, though, his Armagh team would be shrouded in controversy. His look hardened like wet cement solidifying as he recalled that episode for me:

'There's a lot of regrets about 2003. Probably on reflection we played better football in 2003 than we did in 2002 but we made a big mistake. Two weeks before the All-Ireland final we changed a few critical things. We changed the way we played the whole year which was a critical mistake. We picked some players in different positions which was a big mistake in hindsight. Not only the game plan and the positional changes, and I have spoken to Kieran (McGeeney) about this many times, but even more importantly was the change in our attitude. In all the games up to the final we had a take no sh*t attitude. We got stuck in and used our physical capacities, not in any dirty way, but harnessed the physical strength of the team: Francie Bellew, Kieran, the McEntees, Paul McGrane.

'In the run up to the final there were a lot of articles in the press saying that not alone were Armagh a dirty team but over the top dirty. One of the articles stated that somebody was going to be left in a wheelchair because of the way we played. I remember reading that article, which was written by a Fermanagh player, and thinking to myself: "Oh dear, what's going to happen if some of our players are affected by this?"

'We probably subconsciously decided not to be as physical as we were in the previous games which was an absolute disaster. Armagh's game had been built on our physical nature and, in a lot of games in 2002, we crushed teams just by our physical exertions and because we were so well conditioned we could easily deal with anyone else in that respect. Against Tyrone in 2003 we decided we were going to show the whole country that we could win by playing nice football. We tried to play less tough football and more champagne football. We needed to marry the skills with the physical dimension. We could also have been more intelligent on the day on the pitch – I'm not talking about management. For example, I was marking Peter Canavan and he wasn't fit to walk, and I marked him man to man. I should have come out in front of him and covered off Owen Mulligan as well. So, I am taking the blame for my own performance. The player I always knew I had to be unbelievably focused on when I was marking him was Peter Canavan. You knew you had to be incredibly switched on for every single ball because if you even blinked, he would stick the ball in the net. We must all shoulder the blame. I wouldn't blame the management for any of our defeats.

'We don't despise Tyrone though we have a great rivalry with them. You have to respect any team that wins All-Irelands. They were probably smarter than us in the games they beat us. I think the media have not picked up on the fact that winning Ulster so often has been a big disadvantage. We won way more Ulsters, but Tyrone won more All-Irelands. Playing in the qualifiers gave them more games and, above all, the opportunity to iron out their weaknesses when they lost. When we lost, we were knocked out and learned our weaknesses too late. It's not the only reason Tyrone have won more All-Irelands, but it was an advantage to them. I would say the rivalry has been a positive thing for football.'

Regrets I have had a few are as much a sentiment for Enda McNulty as they were for Frank Sinatra.

'I think Armagh were like Dublin. We needed to focus less on physical conditioning and go back more to skills. Dublin got carried away with the media hype in those years.'

Like many Armagh players, McNulty was less than happy with the media portrayal of his team:

'Even Kerry in the noughties while they played nice football pulled more men behind the ball than Armagh ever did. As I was watching Kerry play Cork in the 2008 All-Ireland semi-final, I got texts from my brother Justin and Kieran McGeeney both saying they couldn't believe how many men Kerry had behind the ball. Yet when Armagh pulled men behind the ball it was negative. It's all about perception. In the media, perception is reality.'

# 13

# TAKING NO PRISONERS

*Meath v Tyrone*

He lives his life as if his motto is not to look down on anybody unless it is to admire their shoes. Yet Seán Boylan's team did not mind treading on toes.

You do not have to be strong to survive in Gaelic football, but it certainly improves your chances. The Tyrone fans looked at the Meath team with the same suspicion as Thomas doubting the risen Christ.

In 1996 after the All-Ireland semi-final, Tyrone fans were loud in their condemnation of the Meath team, particularly of their alleged ill-treatment of Peter Canavan. After the Meath game Canavan spoke of 'the nasty wee men'. Later, he would recognise the clash as an important part of the evolution of his Tyrone team as they realised that skill was not enough. They needed a harder edge.

## HARD STATION

Not for the first time Pat Spillane found himself dragged into someone else's controversy. His state of mind played across his features like a newspaper headline:

'People often say Meath footballers are dogged, determined and stubborn – and that's only the nice things they say about them. A lot of players have the attitude of never going for a 50–50 ball unless they're 80–20 sure of winning it. Meath players never had that problem.

'The jury will always remain out about when Meath were regarded as "tough" and "hard". One could never put the finger as to who was responsible for Meath's at times "over robust" tactics. Was it Boylan or his senior players? It is something that I have never been able to get an answer to.

'Colm O'Rourke and I were analysing that match that night for *The Sunday Game*. There was an incident when I found myself in that very rare position for me of not knowing what to say. John McDermott knocked over Peter Canavan. The more you looked at it, the more you could find a reason to argue vehemently that he did it deliberately, but equally you could claim with the same conviction that it was an accident. An even more controversial incident occurred when Martin O'Connell was alleged to have stamped on Brian Dooher when he was on the ground. I could not be sure of O'Connell's intent, so I gave him the benefit of the doubt.

'There were a lot of calls into the programme about the incident and the producer decided Colm and I should discuss it. The problem was that we were watching the incident on a small monitor and were a little bit further away than usual and I wasn't fully sure, so I was very wishy-washy and gave the benefit of the doubt to O'Connell. Being wishy-washy is not something I make a habit of. Colm was not very critical of his former teammate. Afterwards most people said that's all they would expect from O'Rourke when it came to Meath but that I had chickened out.'

## POSTSCRIPT

Spillane feels that another incident needs to be considered in the interests of balance:

'Fast forward to the Leinster semi-final in 2004 when a Meath player stamped on a Laois player. In the analysis afterwards, O'Rourke, without any prompting, said immediately that the unsavoury episode was a "disgrace to the Meath jersey". Everyone would agree that Colm is a top-class analyst, but he went up still further in many people's eyes on foot of that refreshingly honest comment.'

# 14

## OUCH

*The 1998 Munster Final Replay*

When the ship is leaking water, you do not jump off. You grab a bucket.

Ger Loughnane was kicking himself.

He had missed a trick. Clare faced the Munster final against Waterford in the wrong frame of mind: 'There was nothing there to give us an edge against them. All of us went down there with the nearest thing to a casual attitude in my time as Clare manager. The same drive wasn't there.'

In marked contrast Waterford were really pumped for the game. Their diehard no-surrender mentality was evident before the match even started when the mentors occupied the Clare dugout before throw-in. The Waterford boss Gerald McCarthy was very animated when calls didn't go their way. Had Paul Flynn's last-minute free not tailed wide, the Déise would have been worthy winners, but the match ended in a draw.

### STAR FORWARD

Loughnane had some of the finest backs in the history of the game to call on in those years, but he had only one true jewel in the crown when it came to forwards. When I walked up the famous hill of Shannon which had been the Clare players' torture chamber during their brutal training sessions, Jamesie O'Connor recalled mainly great memories of his time under Loughnane. However, there were a few less happy ones also.

After the 1998 Munster final Ger Loughnane's mood was foul all week, as Jamesie recalled: 'There was a real edge to Loughnane and you could sense he was ratty and he was going to set the tone from the off. When Loughnane was cranky, you were keeping your head down and bracing yourself for the acidity that he could create with what he said to you.'

Jamesie himself was not going to take any prisoners:

'I went to go shake Brian Greene's hand before the replay and he shook his head. The next thing he hit me a belt and I went to shove him away with my hurl and broke it clear off his shoulder before the ball was thrown in. I'm waving the hurley running to the sideline for a replacement as the ref is throwing in the ball.'

The referee did not seem to notice, largely because there was mayhem breaking out all over the field and on the sideline. In fact, given the feverish atmosphere Willie Barrett even marched over to the sideline to caution the respective management teams. Within minutes Brian Lohan was given a red card, after he was involved in a skirmish with Waterford's Michael White.

More altercations would follow as Jamesie acknowledges: 'I remember at one stage in the second half, I think Fergal Hartley had given David Forde a clip off the ball. I spotted it and ran in thinking to hit Hartley a shoulder. Greene came in and hit me, and the next thing Ollie Baker arrived and skinned everybody. Certainly, there was a lot of stuff going on off the ball.'

Although many players were guilty of all kinds of swinging and pulling, it was Clare's Colin Lynch who was singled out for special attention. Despite no mention of him in the referee's report, the Munster Council charged him with 'repeated striking with the hurley', which prompted a three-month suspension. There was an irony in this for Jamesie:

'Lynch struck Ollie Baker probably more than he connected with Tony Browne and Peter Queally from Waterford. Listen, Colin was no saint in terms of what happened, but Tony Browne had a fine game the first day and was man of the match. Colin probably felt that he under-performed and Loughnane had probably raised the stakes. There was nothing about Colin in the referee's report, and he was suspended basically on the evidence of some guy sitting in the stand where you probably could have found another guy in the stand who would have seen something else.'

## REFEREE'S REPORT

The other man at the centre of the storm was referee Willie Barrett:

'The criticism of my performance did get to me, and I wasn't appointed to any other inter-county games that year. I got letters from people who were very angry. I stopped answering the phone for a while and my wife started taking the calls and she got the brunt of it. Someone said to me once that it was nice to have your picture in the paper, but I saw my picture every day twelve or thirteen days in a row and it didn't add to me, I can assure you. It did affect me, and I didn't know at that stage if I would have the confidence to referee a big game again. My daughter was in France at the time, and I felt under siege, so I brought the family to France until things settled down a bit.'

## LYNCH-ING

Colin Lynch's three-month ban spawned a new controversy. Having unsuccessfully tried to halt the disciplinary meeting with a High Court injunction earlier in the day, Lynch was not present when the Munster Council considered his case against him because his grandmother was ill. The Munster Council refused to allow him to be represented by a solicitor. Marty Morrissey went live on television and erroneously reported that his grandmother had died. On hearing this, Ger Loughnane stormed out of the Limerick Inn Hotel where the meeting had been taking place and confronted one of the RTÉ producers in the car park where there was an outside broadcast unit, surrounded by up to 200 Clare fans who had gathered outside to register their support. It was drama on an unprecedented scale in the world of Gaelic games.

So how does Loughnane feel about it all now? His answer is to quote Shelley: 'Fear not for the future, weep not for the past.'

# 15

# THE BRAWL

*Meath v Mayo 1996*

*Hai voluto la bicicletta e mo' pedala*

This Italian phrase literally means: 'You wanted that bicycle, now pedal it.' Essentially, it means that we must face the consequence of our desires. This is not a concept the Meath team had problems with.

When Dublin faced Meath after their 1983 All-Ireland victory Gerry McEntee said in the Meath dressing room, 'Let's clap them on to the field. We have to do that and then let's kick the living sh*te out of them.' The culture of Seán Boylan's Meath team was not to back down.

Billy Keane, son of the much-missed John B., once observed, 'The Munster final had more fouls than you would find in a turkey farm the week before Christmas.' Yet when Gaelic football fans think of real aggression, one Meath game looms large in the memory.

Former Mayo star and mentor in 1996 Peter Ford was very disappointed by the turn of events which led both teams to get involved in an unedifying mass brawl.

'I am convinced that we were hard done by and I'm not just talking about the sending off of Liam McHale. Pat McEnaney (the referee) had come down to the team before the final and had talked about what might happen if there was a shemozzle. I found his comments very strange and was convinced that there could be a very serious incident in the game. People may think this is sour grapes, but I still believe that the referee's decisions influenced the outcome of the game.

'With fifteen minutes to go I could only see one result. Mayo had a comfortable lead but we tried to defend it and pushed back too far and allowed Meath to pick off their points.'

It is very evident that Ford feels a strong greviance about the replay:

'The sending offs were a complete mismatch. Liam McHale was our best player and while Colm Coyle was a fine player, his loss to Meath in no way compared with the loss of Liam to us. I've heard it back since from informed sources, shall we say, that the referee had intended to send off one of the Meath midfielders but the umpire changed his mind.'

It was a case of so near and so far for Mayo's star Liam McHale. '1996 was my greatest year and my worst year. They say you make your own luck, but we were unlucky.'

The old wound must be reopened and the interview cannot progress without reference to his sending off in the All-Ireland final replay.

'I will never get over that. I felt I had no choice but to get involved. Fellas on my team were getting hit with haymakers and I was their leader and had a big bond with those guys. There was no way I could just stand back and watch and leave them to their own devices. If I had done nothing, I would not have been able to live with myself. If I was presented with those circumstances again, I would still do the same thing. I have a clear conscience because I didn't shirk my responsibility.'

McHale's regret about the sending off is tied in with his view of the way that game unfolded.

'Well, I believe the outcome would have been different if Meath had a midfielder sent off. When I went off, we had to get another midfielder on which meant that we had to take Ray Dempsey off. Ray had scored 1–2 in the All-Ireland semi-final and was in great form so losing him was a blow. You have to remember we could only use three subs then. If Meath had lost a midfielder too, we wouldn't have had to replace Ray.'

Many people were surprised when McHale stated that getting sent off was akin to hearing that your mother had died.

'Losing an All-Ireland final is far worse than losing any other game. When you get that far and lose, especially to lose by a point in those circumstances, it was sickening. We put in an astronomical effort, working very hard but had nothing to show for it.

'No matter what he (Colm Coyle) did, or I did in that melee, there were fellas doing the same thing. All the referee had to do was pull the two captains together and say: "Listen lads, the next man that steps out of line is gone." I don't think there is a referee in the country that would do that again. If he said his linesmen said this and umpires said that, it still doesn't make a difference. When it comes down to it, if there are twenty guys in a melee you don't send off two.'

Fifteen players got a total of thirty-eight months in suspensions. Meath's Jimmy McGuinness got six months, Colm Coyle (four), Enda McManus (three) and two each for Graham Geraghty, Trevor Giles, Darren Fay, Conor Martin and McDermott. For their part, Mayo's Ray Dempsey got a three-month ban, with two months for McHale, Noel Connelly, David Brady, Colm McManamon, Anthony Finnerty and John

Casey. Both county boards were fined £5,000.

Tensions were not alleviated at the traditional Monday reception for All-Ireland finalists in Croke Park, with rumours of a frosty encounter between McHale and his midfield rival John McDermott.

# 16

## CHARLIE'S NO ANGEL

*Charlie Redmond Is Sent Off Twice*

When you climb to the top of the ladder you have to remember the people who helped you build it in the first place.

In the roll of heartbreak, Charlie Redmond has known the 'dark night of the soul'. Pain's long duration has done nothing to take the harsh edge from it.

The Erin's Isle star played with Dublin for more than a decade. As a forward he did his scoring with chilling efficiency. He is perhaps most famous for scoring what would be the winning goal in the 1995 All-Ireland final. Less happily he also got sent off in the game – not once but twice.

Eleven minutes into the second half Charlie was given his marching orders by Paddy Russell after he reacted to a challenge from Tyrone's Feargal Lohan. The only problem was that two minutes later Charlie was still on the pitch, forcing the referee to stop the match and this time to make certain that the Dublin star actually left the field.

To add to Tyrone's woe, Seán McLaughlin's late equaliser was disallowed by Paddy Russell. He ruled that Peter Canavan had touched the ball on the ground.

Dublin won the game but there were questions asked about whether they had broken rules by having a player who was sent off remain on the pitch. Could it be that the Dubs would even have to forfeit the game and their title? Despite a short-lived frenzy of speculation, no further action was taken.

## UNFORGETTABLE

Charlie looks back on the events of that through a particular prism. He has since faced bigger battles off the field. Tragedy would cast a dark shadow on his life when he lost his beloved wife, Grainne, to cancer. Grainne lost her courageous battle to the condition on 3 December 2016, the result of a brain tumour she was diagnosed with back in 2013.

The problem first surfaced when the couple were on holiday when Grainne began having severe headaches and bouts of forgetfulness, so they went to see former Meath footballer and surgeon Gerry McEntee in the Mater Private for a scan. Charlie looked at him with the intensity of an expert inspecting a diamond for a hidden flaw. There was apprehension and agitation in his face.

McEntee's words are forever etched on Redmond's consciousness: '"Charlie, it's bad. She has a 5cm tumour." And he said something which is still ingrained in my brain today, he said, "You've got to go to Beaumont and you've got to go now."'

Grainne lived for twice as long as her prognosis. 'She got three years, cause she was such a strong person, she fought it all the way,' Charlie said, and he remembers her passing with crystal clarity. 'St Francis' have a night up in Blanchardstown, it's a carol ceremony. They have it outside the front door. It was the most beautiful experience I've had in my life. We were on the first floor. I couldn't see anyone. It was a cold, cold winter's night, a clear sky, I could see every star in the sky. All I could hear was "O Holy Night" coming over. The air was really thin, you didn't have to struggle to hear it. It was a surreal experience. I was there on my own, the door was slightly ajar, Grainne was asleep inside, and I know she could hear it. But she never woke up after that.'

Despite the sadness which always lingers on the periphery of his consciousness Charlie somehow finds the strength to bring some humour into the situation. It feels like a small, silent act of resistance to give him the strength to face whatever lies ahead. He describes how Grainne, who did not really have much understanding of the rules, watched him getting sent off in their clash with Meath in 1987.

'When is Charlie coming back on?' she asked Charlie's sister, her eyes fired with defiance.

'In about three months,' came the immediate reply.

## CORK'S RULES

A variation of the controversy came in the 2000 All Ireland Minor semi-final. Cork's Kieran Murphy picked up two yellow cards, but somehow, he never left the field. Cork would go on to win the All-Ireland and rejected calls that they offer Derry a replay. Cork claimed that the rule book was in their favour.

# 17

# THE BATTLE OF THE FOG

*Mickey Quinn Starts a Bust-up*

Defeat is a temporary condition. Giving into it is what makes it permanent.

Mickey Quinn never gave in:

'We went on a fourteen or fifteen unbeaten game run, which was very unusual for Leitrim, and won an All-Ireland B final in 1990. I won an All-Star that year and it was the first one in Leitrim. It caused a lot of excitement in the county and gave me a new lease of life even though I had two or three trips with them as replacements at that stage. It meant everything to me because it was always my burning ambition. Winning an All-Ireland with Leitrim was too much to hope for. We were playing Leinster in the 1984 Railway Cup in Ballinasloe when the journalist David Walsh told me that I had missed out on an All-Star the year before by just one vote.'

1994 was a never-to-be-forgotten year for Leitrim. Their nearest neighbours had to be dealt with first:

'Roscommon had been the biggest bogey team for us. We had great battles with them in previous years but no matter what we threw at them they always seemed to have the upper hand. That spring, though, we relegated Roscommon from our division in the National League in Carrick-on-Shannon. We knew then we could beat them, and we did in the Connacht Championship. In previous years we should have beat them but that year they should have beat us! We went on to take Mayo in the Connacht final. Although we made a dreadful start, we had great belief and that was in large measure due to our manager, P.J. Carroll.'

Quinn admits to playing a leading role in the infamous 'battle of the fog':

'Aughawillan were playing Clann na nGael in the Connacht club Championship in 1989 but the match shouldn't have gone ahead. The fog was so bad you couldn't see the goalie kicking out the ball. Things heated up when two of our players were hit. I think it was me who really started it off! I "had a go" at Jimmy McManus and soon the whole set of players, subs and supporters were involved. The referee had a hard time getting law and order back, but the game was a great battle in every sense.'

The match did have an amusing postscript though.

'Jerome Quinn played for Aughawillan against Clann na nGael that day and really dished it out to some of the Clann lads and developed a reputation as a hard nut. That was one of the reasons why Aughawillan versus Clann was renamed "the Provos versus the Guards". We were playing Roscommon in the Connacht Championship in 1990 and before the match P.J. Carroll had an unusual mind game planned. He said: "Jerome Quinn, they all think you're fu*king mad in Roscommon. What you need to do is pick up a clump of grass, stick it in your mouth and eat it in front of your marker's face. He'll sh*t himself." Jerome was wing half-back and was marking a lovely, skillful player. Sure enough, Jerome did as he was told and you could see the Roscommon player's legs turn to jelly!'

# 18

# NO FAIRY TALE IN NEW YORK

*The Keady Affair*

He was a horse of a man.

This is our ultimate compliment in the West of Ireland for men who are strong, tough and brave. Nobody personified them more than he did. Inevitably in a discussion of Galway hurling in the 1980s, the name of Tony Keady features prominently.

In 1989, Keady was denied the chance to fight for a third All-Ireland title in a row with his side when he was banned for a year by the GAA for playing a game illegally in New York.

Galway enjoyed a three-month break between their National League and Championship that year and, after spending time in the Big Apple with the All-Star team, Keady decided to prolong his stay. During his time there, he lined out for the Laois team in an exhibition game against Tipperary under his brother's name. The GAA were appraised of this development and despite all the assurances that he would be fine, Keady was suspended.

The decision caused an outcry, as Cyril Farrell and Galway did everything they could to get their star player on the field for their All-Ireland semi-final against their bitter rivals, at the time,

Tipperary. Generously, the Premier County voted in favour of letting Keady play in the match, but the other counties in Connacht voted against his appeal. Galway were not impressed by their lack of solidarity.

### A FALLEN HERO

Sylvie Linnane still mourns the loss of his great friend whose death at such a young age shocked the nation in the summer of 2017:

'The '88 final as a unit was one of our best games. It was very close until Noel Lane came on and scored a late goal. *The Sunday Game* had cameras live at our celebratory dinner and there was a dramatic hush when Ger Canning announced on live television, "And now the moment you have all been waiting for. *The Sunday Game* Man of the Match is . . . Tony Keady." Suddenly everybody started looking around but there was no sign of Tony. We found out later that he was five miles away in a pub with Brendan Lynskey and their friends.

'Tony was Texaco hurler of the year that year. That was why he was such a big loss to us the following year with the infamous "Keady affair". After he was suspended for a year there was an appeal but he lost 20–18. Seán Tracey came in for him and he did well for us, but we weren't the same tight unit of six backs as we had been when he was there. Nothing would have come through the middle with Tony there and he would have scored two or three points from long-range frees as he always did. Before the game and the appeal there was a lot of discussion about whether Tony would play and that was very distracting for us. Our focus was not as good as it should have been for a team seeking three in a row. In the game itself there were a lot of decisions given against us. Somebody made a comment afterwards about the referee:

"He was either biased against us or he was a sh*te referee." Others said he was both.

'I think we all felt angry about the Keady affair because there were hundreds of footballers and hurlers going to play in America at the time, but Tony was the one that was made a scapegoat of.'

Babs Keating has regrets about that year despite leading Tipperary to the All-Ireland:

'Both All-Ireland semi-finals were played on the same day. Before the match we got the news that Antrim defeated Offaly in the semi-final. Both teams knew that our match was really the All-Ireland final and that upped the ante. It was a thundery day and there was a black cloud over Croke Park so there was kind of an eerie atmosphere in the crowd. It was an ill-tempered game and, although we won, the fact that Galway had Sylvie and Hopper McGrath sent off took a bit of the gloss off it.

'1989 was unusual in many ways. We beat Waterford in a horrible Munster final. The build-up to the semi-final against Galway was dominated by the Keady affair. What really hurt me about that was that Galway people blamed Tipperary for setting Keady up. Tommy Barrett, the county secretary, was the Tipperary delegate and he spoke in favour of Tony Keady having been allowed to play. He never remembers anyone thanking him for it. I thought it was a very noble thing and I don't think we could have done any more. We never got involved in the politics of it. At the end of the day Galway had delegates from their own province who didn't support them.

'Everybody knew the rules. The Galway people in New York knew the rules.

'The atmosphere was very bad before the game. There was a lot of aggression. It was a pity. Galway had beaten us in the League final that year and it was a superb game.'

## EARLEY RISER

Dermot Earley was annoyed by the Keady affair because he told me he saw it as a symptom of a deeper underlying problem:

'I am fiercely proud to be a member of the GAA but there are times I am left tearing my hair out trying to make sense of their disciplinary procedures. Sometimes they can descend to the laughable. I think back to the great Mayo forward Willie McGee who was probably the most lethal goalscorer I have ever seen in the game. Willie got into trouble with the county board about playing in New York without getting permission, and they suspended him. He told the county board chairman he was just ignorant of the rules. He told Willie to put it in writing, but Willie answered back that that they hadn't put it in writing when they suspended him, and if word of mouth was good enough for them it ought to be good enough for him! There was a stand-off position for a while, and when one day he was on duty, as a garda, in Grafton Street, a priest, Fr Paddy Mahon, met him. He followed him up and down the beat for an hour in order to persuade Willie to change his mind. Eventually Willie relented and wrote his piece to the county board on the back of a cigarette box. To borrow from Charlie Haughey, it was grotesque, unbelievable and bizarre but not unprecedented – and that type of farce is no way for a great organisation like the GAA to conduct its business.

'If the rules always seemed to be applied consistently it would help a lot but they don't. I think straight away of Tony Keady and his ban. He missed out on playing in an All-Ireland final but hordes of GAA players travelled to New York every summer and the GAA turned a blind eye. That kind of inconsistency I firmly believe is damaging for the GAA as a brand and they need to try harder to get these things right. Our game is more than just a game but, sometimes, trying to make sense not of the rules but of the way they are implemented is like arguing with Plato in Greek.'

# 19

## BOOT BOY

*Wicklow Referee Assaulted*

He was always scanning dark horizons for the guidance of lighthouses to reach the security of the shore.

The greatest champion of referees I ever met was John B. Keane. He soared into a near operatic standard of storytelling to make the case for them to me:

'There is a daring breed of men whose exploits never make the front pages of newspapers, whose heroics forever remain unsung, whose visages will never be seen on our television screens and about whom no songs are made. Be that as it may, what matters is that this breed of men is common to every generation and no matter what abuses or tortures the breed suffered in a previous generation, it will always bob to the surface in this present one. It will show itself to be unsullied and untainted by previous wrongs and it will carry on with the job regardless.

'I refer, of course, as if you didn't know, to that dauntless band of gentlemen, none other than those heroes who referee junior football matches. Now don't get me wrong. There are few of us who loved the game who did not at one time or another find ourselves with a whistle in the hand when the appointed referee failed to turn up. This is all very well but, while we may have acted the part once, nothing on this earth could induce us to do so again. We did it and we wrote it down to experience. We were grateful to escape without injury and those who suffered physically were even more resolved never to be caught again with a whistle in the hand.

'The hero to whom I refer is he who comes out Sunday after Sunday to do the needful in the matter of refereeing. Often his task is easy and pleasant but only when one team is so much better than another that a referee is not needed at all. His life is in danger, however, when there is nothing between the teams. Then, in the eyes of the partisans, his every decision is riddled with prejudice and no matter what way he points the finger he is greeted with a storm of catcalls and booing. To these he is impervious and he takes them for granted. It is when he makes the genuine mistake that he is in serious trouble. Nothing will convince the injured party but that it was deliberate. First the ball is flung at the referee. Then he is abused with a wide range of choice epithets.

'At this stage experienced referees go to where the ball is, sit on it and wait till the whole thing blows over. The worst he is likely to suffer if he chooses this course is a belt of a scraw. However, if he attempts to hand the whistle to one of his tormentors it is felt by one and all that he is stepping outside the part and is no longer, as it were, in sanctuary. Acts like this are regarded as impertinence. Once he ignores his enemies he is more or less ignored himself but once he takes them seriously he is asking for trouble.

'After the game is over is the worst time. There is no police protection and it is quite true to add that the game may have been contested in a village where there never were police. His best bet here is to pick out the biggest man in the vicinity and to open a conversation with him. Those who are out for his blood can never be sure but 'tis his brother or maybe his uncle he is talking to.

'A referee who togs out in white is taken far more seriously than a referee who does not tog out at all. Like a singer who appears on stage wearing a dress suit, he has a head start over those who treat the occasion lightly. The referee who merely stuffs his trousers inside his socks and hands his coat to his girlfriend is asking for trouble.

'Whatever way one looks at it, it is a hazardous occupation. Referees for the most part are even-tempered men who do not court trouble. This, however, is no protection and the good referee must know a few tricks if he is to survive.

'The best I heard of came at a junior semi-final. All went well and our friend staggered around without falling. What saved him was the fact that he did not blow the whistle. Then, following a long bout of booing, he blew and having blown he could not remember why. The pitch was invaded but, completely in command, our friend raised his hand and announced that he had blown the whistle in order that two minutes silence might be observed. Nobody asked who was dead. It wouldn't do to exhibit such ignorance.'

While John B. created humour out of these situations, he also recognised that there were times when it was anything but funny. Tipperary-based referee Willie Barrett was struck on the back with a hurley in 2010 by a supporter.

## DOWN WICKLOW WAY

In 1985 Johnny Price made national headlines following Blessington's one-point win over Annacurra in the Wicklow under-21 B football final in Baltinglass. Price walked to his car to change and get ready for his journey home to Roundwood from Baltinglass. His youngest son, David, was seated in the front seat when he heard a loud noise, the sound of the car's rear door slamming shut. During the game his father had sent off a player from Annacurra and while he was changing afterwards three men approached him and shouted abuse at him, before one forced him inside the car. Reports in the local media claim that it took the intervention of the county vice-chairman Liam O'Loughlin and Baltinglass secretary, Garda Séamus Kelly, to rescue Price from the boot of his car.

A week earlier in Arklow, Price had suffered a severe assault in the course of a League match between Aughrim and Barndarrig which left him out cold for a short time. He was punched twice and kicked in the ribs while on the ground. Showing remarkable physical and moral courage Price got to his feet and finished refereeing the match.

However, the story of a referee locked in the boot of his car created a media sensation. The Annacurra fan who attacked Price at his car was banned for life by the GAA. Mr Price died in 2005.

**A PEACEFUL PROTEST**

Occasionally, fans show their frustration using non-violent protest. In the 2008 under-21 Munster final Clare goalkeeper Donal Tuohy was deemed to have stepped out of his small square while taking a puck-out. A 65 was awarded to Tipperary, as a result, and Pa Bourke duly popped it over the bar for the winning point. This led to a sit-down protest from Banner supporters.

# 20

## TUFF STUFF

*Meath v Cork 1988*

He is a poet of the soul. He has a great intellectual curiosity. He lives as if we were to die tomorrow but learning as if we are to live forever. He was the man who pointed the boat in the right direction. Faith can move mountains and Seán Boylan can move the rest.

He is one of the kindest people I have ever met. There is no substitute for kindness. Acts of kindness are contagious, just like germs, only kindness does not make you sick but the very opposite. If kindness does not work for another human being, nothing else will.

Boylan lives his life as if he is in full agreement with Belloc's lines:

> 'In all my walks it seems to me
> the grace of God is found in courtesy.'

But when he managed Meath, kindness and courtesy was put on the shelf. For over twenty years Seán Boylan drank from a glass that continuously refilled itself; the last long, cool swallow as necessary as the first, his thirst unquenchable.

Some managers have a strained relationship with their players. When Tony Book became Manchester City manager, he fell foul of star player Rodney Marsh. It got back to Book that Marsh frequently called him useless. He called in Rodney and invited him to take back the comment. 'Actually,' Marsh answered, 'I don't think you are as good as that.'

Seán Boylan was cast in a different mould. He created a new culture. It was based around a real sense of collegiality. To take one example, Mick Lyons described Robbie O'Malley as 'a Rolls Royce corner back'. It was also built on brutal honesty. Witness Liam Harnan's close observation: 'I was as slow as a fu*king boat.'

Roscommon legend Seamus Hayden tells a story of having a drink with Mick Lyons. A few fans approached them and were shocked by how friendly and easy-going Mick was compared to what he had been on the field. Eventually someone plucked up the courage to say: 'Do you know you're a lot different in real life than you were on the football pitch?'

Lyons replied: 'If the jersey didn't change me, what was the point of wearing it?'

Lyons and his colleagues did not hold back once they wore the Meath jersey. Their philosophy to opponents was that of Gandalf in *Lord of the Rings*: 'You shall not pass.'

## AGGRO

In a repeat of the 1967 final, Meath won their fourth All-Ireland in 1987 when they beat Cork by 1–14 to 0–11. In the 1988 All-Ireland both sides drew in an entertaining game played with fierce intensity. Meath were very lucky to get a replay. It was the first draw in an All-Ireland final since 1972 and it took a controversial free in the dying seconds for Brian Stafford to equalise.

In the days that followed that drawn game, Meath's mood had darkened and McEntee was agitated up by a huge hit from Liam Hayes during a ferocious training camp in Louth. Six and a half minutes into the 1988 All-Ireland final replay, on foot of claims Meath were bullied around Croke Park by Cork in the drawn game, their midfielder Gerry McEntee 'clashed' with Niall Cahalane and was red-carded. McEntee would say, 'We played a game among ourselves and nearly killed each other. The people from Cooley came out of Sunday Mass and were looking at us. They thought we were gone mad! There were three, including myself, hurt. I got a knock from Liam Hayes during the game. He gave me a dead leg – and it was only the Sunday before the All-Ireland final he would have got one back. I deserved to get sent off in the replay. Nothing on the field really led up to the incident. It was more to do with the three weeks building up to it and I went out on the field in the wrong frame of mind.

'There was nothing personal between Niall Cahalane and myself. For me, 1988 was not as enjoyable as the previous year. The whole saga of getting sent off ruined it. But, then again, for others it was wonderful. For the fourteen fellas who stayed out on the field it was even sweeter than the first year.'

### 15 ANGRY MEN

Meath won 0–13 to 0–12. The match was overshadowed by events of the following days and months as the back-to-back All-Ireland winners were demonised for apparent rough-house tactics. In accordance with long-established tradition, the following day the Meath and Cork players came together for lunch at the Royal Hospital and were addressed by GAA President John Dowling who said he was 'disturbed' by the events and promised an investigation. It was one of the few times the Meath manager Seán Boylan was publicly incensed.

Two months later, Dowling arrived in Meath to hand out the medals, but McEntee and Liam Harnan refused to get up on stage. Three other players accepted their medals but declined to shake hands. They were annoyed that the battering Colm O'Rourke's head and chest had taken in the drawn game had seemingly been forgotten, as well as the five stitches Brian Stafford needed on his lip after a challenge, and a collision between a Cork elbow and Mick Lyons's jaw.

Cork star of that era Conor Counihan stated, 'Failure is the fuel for success'. In 1990 the sides met for the third All-Ireland final in four years but this time it was the Leesiders that emerged on top. Meath full-back Mick Lyons went to his manager Seán Boylan after losing that game to Cork, with a badly bruised face. He said, 'I'm awful sorry Seán.'

'Why?' Boylan inquired.

'When X gave me that blow into the face I should have started an almighty row and that would have galvanised us.'

It was a revealing comment and it said so much about the rivalry between the two counties during those years.

The tragic death in 2001 of John Kerins, the Cork goalkeeper for the 1987 and 1988 finals against Meath, finally brought the two groups of old foes together. Up to then, hostility reigned supreme and P.J. Gillic, who dropped into midfield after McEntee's dismissal in that '88 replay, admitted, 'It was just very hard to accept being branded as thugs.'

## THE MILLENNIUM MAN

The player from that side who was selected on the team of the Millennium was Martin O'Connell. He has gone public about how the mood changed: 'There was a bit of bad blood between the teams. We both went on holidays to the Canaries the following January and they'd be sitting on one side of the swimming pool and we'd be sitting on the other. I wasn't mixing with any of them, for some stupid reason, just because of the bad blood from the All-Irelands. You'd see them and just look at them and keep going. The thing that changed it all was John Kerins's death. Gerry McEntee was actually treating John for his illness. Then he rang me when John died to say that a few of the lads were organising to go down to the funeral.

'There were eight or ten of us that went. A lot went down on the plane on the Thursday night for the removal, and myself and Mickey McQuillan drove down together on the Friday morning. Gerry McEntee was down, Liam Hayes, Bob O'Malley, I think Bernard Flynn as well, Joe Cassells and Colm O'Rourke. Unfortunately, it took a death to break the ice between Meath and Cork. That puts it all in perspective.'

## ROYALTY V ROYAL

The GAA rejoiced when Sligo won only their second Connacht title in 1975 because it was a fitting reward for the supremely gifted Micheál Kearins. The legendary forward put Sligo football on the map. He played in seventeen successive Championship seasons with Sligo from 1962 to 1978.

After his retirement from playing, he became a referee. His career with the whistle is probably best remembered for the time he sent off Colm O'Rourke:

'It was an incident after half-time and he got a heavy enough shoulder while in possession. It knocked the ball out of his hands but he didn't try to retrieve it but came after me. The play moved down the field and he followed me the whole way down sharing "pleasantries" with me! I had no option but to send him off.'

## THE SEQUEL

The two giants of the game had another heated exchange subsequently, in the 1988 All-Ireland semi-final when Kearins was a linesman.

'There was a line ball incident and he felt I gave it the wrong decision. I know myself now that I was wrong and he was right, having seen the replay on telly. I would have to say, though, he was a great player and actually made the Meath forward line while he was in his prime. He was their playmaker.'

# 21

# SEE NO EVIL

*The John Finn Incident*

During the battle of Copenhagen in 1801, Lord Nelson got a signal that he should stop attacking the Danish fleet and retreat. In response Nelson took a telescope to his blind eye and said, 'I did not see the signal'. He ignored the order and went on the attack. He won the battle. The episode created a new phrase: turning a blind eye.

The GAA have turned it into an art form.

Micheál O'Hehir is perhaps the person more than any other who was responsible for bringing Gaelic games to a mass audience. However, his tendency to describe acts of violence on the playing fields with stunning understatement as 'a right shemozzle' was anathema to Breandán Ó hEithir. In his acclaimed memoir *Over the Bar* he bemoaned the famous commentator's 'folksy technique which seemed to be aimed at providing entertainment for hospital patients rather than giving a complete picture of what was happening'.

When it comes to disciplinary matters in general it sometimes seems that the GAA's attitude is: see no evil, hear no evil. The

1985 All-Ireland semi-final between Dublin and Mayo is best remembered for the so-called 'John Finn incident' in which the Mayo half-back sustained a broken jaw in an off-the-ball 'challenge'. Despite a protracted investigation no action was ever taken against a Dublin player. Everybody knows who the culprit was, but he got away as free as a bird. It was heroic for John Finn to play on with a broken jaw. He deserved more from the GAA.

Despite much tut-tutting and wringing of hands no action was taken against the player in question. What makes many GAA fans' blood boil, though, is the GAA's penchant for selective justice. No Clare person will need reminding of the striking contrast, and I use the words advisedly, between the GAA's vigorous pursuit of Colin Lynch in 1998, after Clare met Waterford in the Munster final replay, and the way in which in the same year the GAA was prepared to turn a blind eye to Michael Duignan striking his hurley across Clare's David Forde. Duignan has admitted since that he was lucky not to be sent off for what he described as a 'desperate' challenge. Everyone saw it live on national television. It was captured in photographs in the national newspapers, but no subsequent action was taken. Clare fans asked: How can you have faith in consistent standards being applied by the GAA in those circumstances?

There have been so many anomalies. Clare's Ger O'Grady was sent off for fouling Kilkenny's Tommy Walsh in the 2005 Division One final but the ban only applied to the League, enabling him to play in the Munster semi-final against Tipperary.

Ryan McMenamin's yellow-card foul on John McEntee in the 2005 Ulster final was upgraded to a red by the Central Disciplinary Committee (CDC). The Disputes Resolutions Authority intervened and ruled that the now-defunct CDC did not have the authority to change the colour of the card handed out by the referee based on video evidence.

**HAWKEYE**

The GAA's answer to VAR, Hawkeye was introduced to make the referee's life easier. It has not always been entirely successful in that respect. Tipperary and Kilkenny had played a thriller in the 2014 All-Ireland final. The match came down to a long-range free from John 'Bubbles' O'Dwyer. When the sliotar hit the back net behind the goals, the umpires were uncertain. The newly introduced Hawkeye was consulted. The GAA nation held its breath. The technology declared the ball was wide, and the teams headed for a replay. To this day many fans in Tipperary think Hawkeye got it wrong.

# 22

# THE TWELVE APOSTLES

*Dublin v Galway 1983*

They were unwilling disciples.

It has become known in the GAA vernacular as the dirty dozen final.

In 1983 Galway showed all the signs of a good team when qualifying for the All-Ireland final. They won without playing well, as their midfielder Brian Talty recalls:

'I remember waking up on the morning and being very disappointed that it was such a wet and windy day because I knew it was going to spoil the match a bit. The game ended with us having fourteen players and Dublin only twelve but it could have been six versus six there were so many belts flying in. Despite the extra men, we still lost because we missed so many easy chances. The Dubs manager Kevin Heffernan got his tactics right. He withdrew everyone else from the full-forward line and left Joe McNally up on his own. With the wet and windy conditions, it was the sort of day you could crowd your opponents. We didn't have the tactical variation to respond to the circumstances or even the conditions.'

The boil must be lanced. It is time to hear what really happened with Brian Mullins. I felt a distinct change in the atmosphere between us as I moved into uncomfortable territory:

'From a personal point of view it was a massive disappointment to become embroiled in the worst controversy of my career. That was the hardest part for me, not that Brian nearly took the top of my head off! If you look back on it on TV you will see he really made contact with me! Brian was one of my heroes when I went to Thomond College and played with him. When I got married in 1980 Brian was at our wedding. I was on my honeymoon when he had that terrible car accident. As he started to rehab, I played soccer with him, so I knew at first hand how far he had to travel to get back to the level he did. Nobody else would put themselves through what he did to get back to the very top. I'm sorry that his achievement in getting back was tainted a bit by him being sent off in an All-Ireland final and especially because it was for striking me. I think what Dublin did that day was incredible but it is such a pity for their own sake that the controversy took away from what they did. It was heroic stuff.'

Many years on, the story of what happened in the tunnel continues to be shrouded in mystery. Talty will take the full truth to his grave:

'There was a bit of pushing and shoving and I was struck. The real damage to me was not that one, nor Brian's one, but, after the sending off, I was charging through to the Dublin goal when P.J. Buckley caught me in the head. Having said that, after Brian and P.J. I could have done without the one in the tunnel! In the dressing room Billy Joyce asked me if I was okay to continue and, while I said I was, the selectors saw it differently.'

There was unfinished business to be resolved afterwards:

'There was a lot of tension the next day when the two teams met up for the meal which was the tradition at the time. A few words were exchanged! Joe McNally got up to sing "The Fields of Athenry". I remember thinking, "Jesus Christ, wouldn't I love to kill you!"

'Brian and I went outside in the car park to have a conversation. What sticks in my memory is that when Brian was coming towards me I was thinking, "I hope he's not going to strike me again!"'

# 23

# AH REF

*The Séamus Aldridge Saga*

It seemed the world was on his shoulder.

After Séamus Darby's sensational last-minute winner for Offaly against Kerry in 1982, Mikey Sheehy's goal in 1978 is the most famous ever scored in an All-Ireland final. Paddy Cullen's frantic effort to keep the ball out was memorably described afterwards by the legendary Con Houlihan, who wrote it was like 'a woman who smells a cake burning'.

Pat Spillane recalls the goal with a wry smile: 'I was just watching the tape of the goal recently and I heard Micheál O'Hehir describe it as: "the greatest freak of all time". You would have to take him to task for that comment. It was a moment of pure genius in the speed of thought and the execution of a very difficult skill. Absolutely magnificent. Of course, it wasn't a free. But that's beside the point.'

Spillane's comments give a tiny indication of the storm of controversy that referee Séamus Aldridge's performance generated in that game. The Dublin camp were very annoyed after their defeat by Kerry, with Sheehy's cheeky goal the main talking point. With his razor-sharp brain, Sheehy's quick free and his deft lob, as Paddy Cullen was caught out of his goal, completely changed the complexion of the game, after the Dubs had raced into a big early lead. The goal appeared to knock the stuffing out of them.

Events took a dramatic turn when the Dublin captain, Tony Hanahoe, gave a substantial interview to *Magill* magazine which had a huge readership at the time and often set the agenda in the national discourse. Hanahoe made the startling claim that he had objected to the appointment of Aldridge as referee for the match, having earlier done likewise for the Leinster semi-final fixture with Offaly. The Dublin captain claimed that he was unhappy with Aldridge's 'interpretation of the rules of the game'.

In the wake of a rash of criticism of referees by prominent players and personalities, the GAA had issued dire warnings that such attacks would be met with suspensions. After Hanahoe's interview the GAA wanted to flex their muscles and, equally importantly, to be seen to be doing so.

Hanahoe was the first 'victim' of this new policy, and he was duly given a one-month ban. There followed a controversy within a controversy. The suspension was issued on a Saturday but nonetheless Hanahoe played a League game for the Dubs against Kildare the following day. Dublin claimed that because an appeal was pending, their captain was eligible to play. To those hostile to Hanahoe this was a red rag to a bull and he faced a possible six-month ban for playing while suspended.

A will they/won't they stand off continued for the following month and was the subject of endless articles and comments throughout that time. As if temperatures were not already hot enough, they reached near boiling point when it was suggested that the Dublin squad would strike if their leader was banned for six months.

All politics is local and as Aldridge was a prominent figure in Kildare GAA circles, the Kildare County Board publicly praised Aldridge for his 'competent and first-class handling' of the All-Ireland final. In late November, the GAA's Management Committee upheld the one-month ban but took no additional action against Hanahoe for playing after the initial suspension was imposed. To many outside the capital it looked as if the GAA did not have the stomach to take on one of the most powerful counties in the Association. The affair only confirmed the prejudices of those who felt there was a widening gap between the 'haves' and 'have nots' in the GAA.

# 24

# TOUGHER THAN THE REST

*Páidí's Punch*

In Paul Simon's famous song, *The Boxer*, the protagonist is simply a poor boy 'whose story is seldom told'.

The story of the GAA's most famous boxing controversy is often told – largely because of the fame of the two pugilists.

He was tough as teak. In his own words he was a *fear crua*. The best words I can find to describe him are 'rough as a saw-edge, and hard as whinstone'. This was Emily Bronte's description of Heathcliff. Páidí Ó Sé won eight All-Ireland medals as a player and as a manager led the Kingdom to two All-Irelands.

The classic Páidí story, which I stress is apocryphal, was told to me by a man with a flush of a face which hinted at an acquaintanceship with drink. It involves the referee who decides that he has to make a quick getaway after an All-Ireland final between Kerry and Dublin in Croke Park in which he sends off three Kerry players and awards two controversial penalties. He drives too quickly, crashes coming round a bend and is thrown through the windscreen on to the road. By coincidence, the car following him is driven by one of the players he sent off, Páidí, and he stops to see if he can help. He finds that the referee is in a bad way and makes a 999 call on his mobile.

'I think the referee's dead,' he shouts down the phone in panic. 'What can I do?'

'Calm down,' says the operator, used to dealing with emergencies. 'First of all, go and make sure the referee is dead.'

The operator hears a choking sound and the cracking of neck bone. Then Páidí returns to the mobile: 'Ok,' he says. 'I've made sure he's dead. Now what should I do?'

## EVERYBODY LOVES GOOD NEIGHBOURS

Páidí joked that he had a love-hate relationship with Cork fans. He loved them and they hated him!

Dinny Allen was also a great character. He captained the Cork team to win the All-Ireland in 1989. I always thought he contributed very well but his critics said he did very little. As a result, Dinny christened himself 'the non-playing captain'!

For those of us of a certain age, the defining image of the Cork-Kerry rivalry saw Páidí Ó 'Sé knocking Dinny Allen on to the seat of his pants in the 1975 Munster final after Allen had thrown the first punch. Then came a moment of classic comedy when the referee, running in to admonish the two bold boys, slipped on the wet ground. To add to the sense of incredulity, neither player was sent off.

Years later when I spoke to Páidí about it he couldn't believe he was not sent off especially as the incident was shown on TV. 'If it happened thirty years later I would probably have got a long suspension for bringing the game into disrepute! I am so thankful that there was no internet or mobile phones back then because otherwise I would have been crucified in the court of public opinion. Mind you, there was still a real storm of controversy about it.'

## I CONFESS

According to legend, Páidí went to confession a month after the game and confessed to the priest, 'I lost my temper and said some bad words to one of my opponents.'

'Ahhh, that's a terrible thing for a Kerry player to be doing,' the priest said. He took a piece of chalk and drew a mark across the sleeve of his coat.

'That's not all, Father. I got mad and punched one of my opponents.'

'Saints preserve us!' the priest said, making another chalk mark.

'There's more. As I got out of a shemozzle, I kicked two of the other team's players in the . . . in a sensitive area.'

'Oh, Jesus, Mary and Joseph!' the priest wailed, making two more chalk marks on his sleeve. 'Who in the world were we playing when you did these awful things?'

'Cork.'

'Ah, well,' said the priest, wiping his sleeve, 'boys will be boys.'

# PART II

# Controversies for All Seasons

*'My mistakes are my life.'*

SAMUEL BECKETT

Sheila, a friend of mine, phoned a utilities company to close her partner's account and explained that he had passed away in the previous year. The young woman on the phone asked if she could speak to him to verify the request! Sheila explained that that would not be possible as he had been cremated. Sheila stated that she was the executor on his will and the assistant said Sheila would have to prove it. She patiently enquired what reason she might have to be trying to close an account fraudulently, but the assistant just kept repeating that it was procedure. She didn't think it was funny when Sheila suggested holding a seance so that she could communicate with him directly – she did not get sarcasm!

Sometimes I get the same level of bemusement in the world of Gaelic games. In 2022 Ciarán Whelan described the GAA's Suspension Appeal system as a 'farce'.

If there are fifty shades of grey, there are a 100 shades of GAA controversies.

Joe Brolly, who knows a thing or two about GAA controversies, claims that the world has been taken over by stupid confident people. That may be part of the reason.

One of my most memorable Saturday afternoons came in 2008, on a typical Irish summer's day where the rain came down so heavily that even the puddles had puddles in them. It was spent in the company of Joe Brolly and his late father Francie and for a few hours of my life I was transported to Anecdote Central as they shared some of their memories with me.

False modesty was not one of Francie's characteristics. When it came to arguments, though, they both appeared to share the same philosophy: ensure you equalise before the other team scores.

When I asked Joe if he ever regretted the controversies he created, he turned to his dad first and then turned back to me to observe: 'As my father said one time, I won't be apologising to the likes of you.'

Diversity is a buzzword in many walks of life today: in politics, the media and education to name just some.

There have been many different types of controversies. This section documents some of the most dramatic ones.

# 25

# THE HARTE OF THE MATTER

*Mickey Harte v RTÉ*

There is the way things look and the way things are.

The Swiss psychiatrist Carl Gustav Jung (1875–1961) believed that aliveness comes down to one thing – consenting to rise, to be dented, impressed, pressed in upon, to rejoin, to open, to ponder, to be where we are in this moment and see what happens, allowing the breath of not knowing to be taken, wanting to see what is there and what is not there. Aliveness springs from our making something of what we experience and receiving what experience makes of us. This is the wonder of the child the New Testament always recommends us to return to, what the philosopher Paul Ricœur calls our 'second naiveté'. In such a space we allow ourselves to depend on something greater than ourselves, to take what it gives us and respond to it.

However, Jung also believed that wanting to protect ourselves from psychic pain, we limit our imaginations, our ability to play around with ideas, our bodily sensations. We take someone else's words instead of fumbling for our own. We neglect giving attention to our dreams. We fear to go down into the depths of one relationship and instead substitute ever new ones. We avoid saying the hard truth to the ones we love. We may sacrifice whole parts of ourselves in order to protect against pain, but then the whole of us loses some of its essential vitality.

This struggle to live all we can in the face of death, illness, loss of relationship, unbearable grief, acts of injustice, is a struggle we share in all our different circumstances of life. In the New Testament words, the pearl of great price [Matthew 13:45–46] is what we sell all we have for the sake of; riches, fame, security do not ensure simple happiness in being, only this precious aliveness. What, then, is that pearl of great price? It is feeling alive and real, vibrantly the aliveness that belongs to each of us.

What we all want is pretty simple, really. We want to be alive. To feel alive. Not just to exist but to thrive, to live out loud, walk tall, breathe free. We want to be less lonely, less exhausted, less conflicted or afraid and more awake, more grateful, more energised and purposeful. But sometimes when we feel a threat to our sense of who we are, we respond by putting on our metaphorical boxing gloves.

### THREE TIMES A CONTROVERSY

Jung would have loved to study Mickey Harte – in particular his thorny relationship with the national broadcaster. The three time All-Ireland winning manager has had no less than three controversies with RTÉ.

The first came after Mícheál Ó Muircheartaigh stepped down as RTÉ radio's main commentator. Harte wanted his close friend Brian Carthy to succeed him. When he did not the then Tyrone manager sent a letter to RTÉ about their choice of commentators.

The second came after the tragic murder of his beloved daughter Michaela when she was on her honeymoon in January

2011. A clinging sense of coldness clasped the nation tightly at the shocking news. Harte has revealed that RTÉ were unhappy Michaela's funeral would not be broadcast. When it was decided that big screens would be erected outside the chapel showing the images inside, it was suggested that they would point their cameras at one of the screens. One popular RTÉ figure wanted Harte to do an interview. He called him up to sixty times over a single weekend and when all those calls went unanswered, drove straight up to the family door.

The third came when RTÉ broadcast a radio sketch that used the song, 'Pretty Little Girl From Omagh' while mocking a visit Harte and his bereaved son-in-law John McAreavey made to the Dalai Lama as one strand of their grieving process. Harte has never given an interview to RTÉ since.

# 26

# 'AN EMBARRASSMENT TO THE GAA'

*The Seánie Johnston Saga*

In 2017 Shane Lowry was doing an impromptu twitter question-and-answer session as he was waiting in an airport and took questions from fans on a broad range of topics. One question was: who was Kildare's best-ever footballer? Lowry replied: 'Don't know, but Seánie Johnston is defo their best-ever hurler.'

The exchange was a reminder of the most controversial transfer saga in the history of the GAA. In 2012, rainforests were destroyed all around the world to cover all the column inches that were written about it. Despite his many accomplishments with Cavan, to many GAA folk Seánie Johnston will always be the footballer who went to Kildare.

Richard Burton claimed that fame does not change who you are, it changes others. It is like a sweet poison you drink of first in enthusiastic gulps. Then you come to despise it. Seánie Johnston would empathise.

In 2003 Johnston joined the Cavan panel and over the next eight years built up a reputation as a high-scoring forward on the inter-county scene. In 2011, though, Cavan suffered a crushing disappointment to Longford in the qualifiers. Team manager Val Andrews decreed that radical surgery on the panel was required and Johnston found himself surplus to requirements.

Then the news emerged that he was transferring to Kildare. He did not work there but he had an address there. At an appeal, the Central Appeals Committee (CAC) upheld Johnston's appeal against the decision of the CCCC (Central Competitions Control Committee) to block his move from Cavan Gaels to St Kevin's of Staplestown.

Their decision was upheld, 'on the basis that there had been no objection by either Cavan Gaels or Cavan County Committee within the ten-day time limit prescribed in the Official Guide.' Previously his transfer had been turned down on regulations of residency and ethos.

After surely the briefest hurling career in the history of the GAA, Seánie Johnston became eligible to play for the Kildare footballers. In 2012 Johnston had to feature in a Kildare Club Championship match before he was eligible to make his Kildare debut. With that opportunity not arising for his new club, St Kevin's, before Kildare's clash with Meath the next day, Johnston lined out with the hurlers of Coill Dubh, St Kevin's sister club. Having started at top of the left Johnston was substituted almost immediately.

Given the scale of the controversy a clip of his appearance was shown on *The Sunday Game*. The programme editor Eamonn Donohue tweeted a picture of Johnston in the warm-up as well as coining an official hashtag for the occasion, #Seániewatch.

Johnston's hurling prowess did not impress the giants of the ash. Michael Duignan pointed out that his technique was all wrong and tweeted: 'Wrong hand on top Seánie.'

Ciarán Whelan on *The Sunday Game* described it as 'an embarrassment to the GAA' and argued that 'many GAA people in

Kildare would be embarrassed by it'. He pointed out that there had been many precedents of players who had transferred to other counties once they started to work in that county, but Johnston was continuing to work in Cavan.

On a separate edition of the programme Colm Parkinson said he had plenty of experience of falling out with managers, but it would never have occurred to him to transfer to another county. Tony Davis had three concerns: that it blocked the pathway of a young Kildare player to get a place on the team; that it was against the ethos of the GAA and that there was a question about residency. Needless to say, on social media some of the criticism of Johnston was more virulent with words like 'glory-hunter' and 'traitor' being thrown around with wanton abandon.

The sporting gods decreed that Johnston's debut for the Lily-whites in 2013 came against Cavan in his home county in the qualifiers. He came on as a sub and scored a point. Whether it was because of the huge media scrutiny on him or all the additional pressure it created, Johnston's career with Kildare never really took off and in 2016 he returned to play in the Cavan colours. The prodigal son scored six points in a League fixture against Meath. He reflected:

'It wasn't a nice experience, clearly [coming on against Cavan]. It was very, very difficult. It's one that you try and . . . look, you can dwell on things as much as you like but I'm trying to move on and look to the future rather than the past. I'm trying to focus as much as I can and trying to perform as well as I can for the team. I've probably tried to leave that in my past – if you constantly dwelt on it, it would put you in bad form.

'In life, you're learning all the time. You look back and there are things that maybe didn't work out as well. I felt in a very difficult situation. I said this openly at the time that I always wanted to play with Cavan. It was never that I didn't want to play. Since I was six or seven and I went on the development squads at thirteen or fourteen. I always wanted to play for Cavan.

'People have their own opinions. I learned very quickly that you can't please everyone and, when you try to please everyone, you end up annoying more people. For me, football was every-thing for a lot of years but, as you get older, you see a different side of things and there are more important things.'

A similar controversy spawned in 2022. After scoring nine points in the All-Ireland final loss to Kerry, Galway ace Shane Walsh transferred to Dublin giants Kilmacud Crokes from his own club Kilkerrin-Clonberne. It is fair to say not everybody was happy as a result.

# 27

## GETTING A RED CARD

*Man Off the Line*

Necessity is the mother of reinvention.

In 2019, Dublin's Greg Kennedy brought the role of the *maor foirne* into controversy. Kennedy effectively marked a Kilkenny player during their Leinster Championship clash at Nowlan Park when he intercepted a pass, which, if completed, would have created a clear goal-chance.

Referee Cathal McAllister had awarded a Kilkenny free in and was talking to Dublin defender Chris Crummey when he allowed play to restart. Spotting that Kilkenny's Billy Ryan was standing on his own in a dangerous position, Kennedy basically went to cover him and then cut out the pass from Reid's free. Kennedy should not have been on the pitch at the time, and he certainly was not entitled to interfere with the play.

Willie Barrett, Chair of Croke Park's Referees Development Committee, articulated the concerns that referees in both hurling and football felt over the role of those runners who were allowed to run on the field:

'A referee obviously wants to adjudicate on a game. You could be refereeing a match, you may not see an encroachment on the field. Your whole focus is on the game as a referee, absolutely. You're not going to be looking around the field to see if there's someone on the field. I don't think any of us want people on the field of play, to be honest about it. We would have said throughout the League that we don't want encroachment.'

The role was introduced in 2007 to regulate the congested sidelines at county games and mirror the AFL 'runner'. The rules stated a *maor foirne* was only allowed on the pitch during a break in play after a score or wide or when the referee has stopped the game to allow medical attention for a player. However, it was not uncommon to see runners moving into the field while the ball was in play or remaining on after the play had restarted following a break. Some teams used this as a tactic to slow the game down. Former All-Ireland winning Kerry manager Éamonn Fitzmaurice observed:

'While the Greg Kennedy incident has brought matters to a head, it was no huge shock to me as the *maor foirne* role has been exploited for some time as every team (including ourselves) have sought to push its limits. Tony McEntee (former Mayo selector) was a great man to spot and fill space on an opposition kick-out, as he slowly withdrew from the pitch, disrupting goalkeepers' appreciation of space. Jayo (Jason Sherlock, Dublin) is a good man to drag his backside when required also.'

However, Limerick hurling manager John Kiely was not keen on the motion to ban the *Maor Foirne* role at the 2020 GAA congress:

'Why is it being done? Why has the proposal gone forward for the *maor foirne* to be done away with? It's because of another problem and the other problem is some people aren't leaving the pitch in the designated fashion that is required. In other words, "get off the field and don't be loitering around preventing a goalkeeper from kicking or pucking a ball into that space". That's why it's happening. Let's call a spade a spade. We see it every single weekend where certain individuals are staying on the pitch and/or exiting the pitch through a space. In my opinion, in a circumstance such as that, the fourth official should be given the power to yellow card the (team) official who does go in and stand (on the field). And if he does it a second time, it's a red and he's up in the stand and that's the end of it. If that was done on a couple of occasions, the mentors who are persisting in this type of behaviour would quickly adjust their behaviour and exit the field in an appropriate fashion. There are plenty of mechanisms for them to be dealt with. There is no need to be introducing some other daft notion.'

### NOT MISSING YOU ALREADY

The 2021 Congress consigned the *maor foirne* to the dustbin of history. Pat Spillane believes that the GAA should live by the adage that if what you did yesterday seems important, then you haven't accomplished anything today. Success comes before work only in the dictionary. That is why he always wants the GAA to do better, prising open vistas of experience and avenues of growth:

'I was delighted to see the *maor foirne* – or runner – get its P45. I never understood why they were allowed in the first place. Soccer and rugby manage nicely without them. Why is football and hurling so different? Too often they ended up being mischief makers. There was no end to the illegal activities they got up to. Take your pick from sledging opposing players, attempting to influence referees, getting involved in skirmishes, blocking the line of vision of goalkeepers and occupying space before kick-outs and puck-outs. They behaved like preening peacocks. Good riddance.'

# 28

# TORN BETWEEN TWO LOVERS

*Club v County*

We must embrace the challenge rather than run away from it.

In 2020 the coronavirus struck the world with the ferocity of a tsunami. It left a trail of death and destruction in its wake but one unexpected outcome out of it was that it was the catalyst for the resolution of one of the longest running controversies in the history of the GAA. For many years club players saw themselves as the poor relation because of their schedules that gave no certainty to the ninety-eight per cent of players who are outside the inter-county fold.

In 2017, Declan Brennan of the Club Players Association called for All-Irelands to be over by the August weekend to give more space on the GAA calendar for the club player. Many critics smiled benignly at his naivety. Nobody could have predicted that four years later the GAA congress would agree to finish them by the end of July.

Liam Griffin, who was the most high-profile member of the Club Players Association, stated: 'The fixture system in the GAA is definitely in need of a massive overhaul to make the inter-county game better and the club game better. The club game is suffering greatly. We need a better plan for how we're playing our games at the moment because the club player is suffering greatly under the present system. Because we have two leagues in effect. There is a National Hurling League and then the All-Ireland Championship is essentially a league as well. We should be seriously examining where we're going and come up with a proper blueprint to start with a whole new brand looking GAA that's fit for purpose for everybody if we're sincere about it. We can well afford maybe to take a few hits on big games just to give the club player a better chance.'

Even before the pandemic, the GAA had been moving in the direction of the club player such as 'result on the day' fixtures at inter-county level. April was designated as a club-only month but with limited success. The calendar was seen to be heavily tilted in favour of the inter-county season. However, the pandemic achieved what years of work groups and committees could not do by illustrating perfectly how club and county fixtures could exist separately while complementing each other. Club Championships were played first and then the inter-county season.

After the decision by Congress to have a 'split season', the Club Players Association announced that they were dissolving. Liam Griffin explained their relationship with the GAA: 'I didn't get too many hugs and kisses when they were going about the place, I'll tell you that. That's okay now, there were little jibes passed by everybody, let's be honest about it. When there is nothing left to be said, some fool will always say it and that happened in one instance at least. We were only talking about a shade of difference; we are all GAA people. We are all kissy-kissy now, we have made up and, hopefully, it will move on. There is no triumphalism here, everybody came to the same agreement, that's what happened. It is very important that we keep it with the integrity attached to it and just change the goalposts a little.'

## THE SPLIT SEASON

Pat Spillane gives much of the credit to the resolution of the issue to a former GAA president:

'When reflecting on Liam Horan's three years as GAA president: in the negative column he did nothing to tackle the monster that Dublin GAA has become. But a born-and-bred Dub was never going to touch that hornet's nest. On his watch, high-profile rows erupted over Liam Miller's testimonial match in Cork and the "Newbridge or Nowhere" issue about the venue for Kildare v Mayo in the 2018 qualifiers. Really these were minor kerfuffles compared to the unprecedented crisis which hit the GAA during the final year of his presidency.

'Maybe, like Napoleon, he was a lucky general. The pandemic was awful, but it enabled the GAA to solve three thorny issues which heretofore it had struggled with. It helped enormously that Horan spent a lifetime in teaching. I know their *modus operandi* – after all I, too, was a teacher. We're conservative, cautious, slow to change and always adopt a safety-first approach. And that's how Horan dealt with the Covid-19 crisis. He kept his head down, avoided antagonising anybody and didn't do sound bites. Instead, he adopted a safety-first approach which yielded an excellent dividend.

'Furthermore, Horan's decision to appoint an expert advisory group on Covid-19 early in the pandemic was a wise move. Behind the scenes he cultivated a close working relationship with the government which enabled the GAA to tap them for €15m – which allowed the All-Ireland Championship to go ahead. He resisted the urge to criticise the government for not including senior inter-county activity in the list of elite sports exempted under Level 5 restrictions. My gut feeling is that the outgoing president wanted to stay on side with the government, because he knew the GAA would need financial assistance again in 2021. All told, he can be happy with his legacy.

'Spending on inter-county training has been curtailed and, better still, it will be centrally monitored from now on. And the GPA's wings have been clipped because their financial dig-out from Croke Park has had to be curtailed. We now have a split season, thanks primarily to 2020's successful roll-out of the concept.'

However, Spillane was concerned about one implication of this new fixture list: 'The 2022 Championship is the GAA's version of speed dating – blink and you'll miss it. It is a complete joke.'

Many fans struggled to come to terms with the shock to their systems of the intercounty season finishing in July. The GAA's unique splitting headache hasn't gone away, you know.

# 29

# SHRINE OF DUTY

*Bríd Stack Gets a Broken Neck*

It was supposed to be a fairy-tale end to her career. But the glorious last chapter was over almost as soon as it began.

An eleven-time All-Ireland winner with Cork, Bríd Stack had taken a career break to move to Australia in 2021 with her husband Cárthach and her young son Cárthach Óg to play in the AFLW season for the GWS Giants. There she would link up with Irish sporting royalty Cora Staunton.

Her debut was against the Adelaide Crows. The match began well for her. She was out to prove that she belonged, and the head coach praised her at quarter-time for the intensity with which she was playing. Then one of her opponents Ebony Marinoff 'made contact' with her and left her with a broken neck and needing to wear a neck brace.

Stack described the tackle: 'As soon as the impact occurred, I got an immediate surge of excruciating pain down my neck and my right arm. I actually thought I might have broken my arm. I never experienced pain like it.'

When she first met with the head spinal consultant, he was

initially very worried. He told her that the fact that she was not paralysed came down to a matter of millimetres.

A new layer to the controversy began when the initial three-match ban handed to Marinoff was overturned on appeal. As Stack watched a match on television, the news came up on a strapline across the bottom of her screen that Marinoff had been cleared. She was gutted: 'My heart just sank. I broke down in tears.'

Stack described the result of the appeal as leaving her 'trapped in this vortex of disbelief because I suddenly felt like a scapegoat'. An additional burden for her to carry was that much of the commentary, mainly on social media, had suggested the injury was down to her own lack of experience in the code.

However, the tribunal had access to a camera angle, which conclusively proved that Stack's feet were planted, that she had her head over the ball, and that she did not have any forward momentum. In addition, the footage showed how Marinoff took three steps forward from when Stack planted her feet until she made contact with the Cork woman's head.

Under AFL protocols, the duty of care lies with the player who chooses to tackle, no matter the opponent's position. AFL legend Heath Shaw agreed the tackle did not follow duty of care.

Matt Busby said football is about supporters not money. Stack was gratified by all the fans in Ireland and Australia who sent her messages of support including former Gaelic footballers who had made it big in the AFL such as Colin O Riordan, Setanta Ó hAilpín and Nicholas Walsh.

# 30

# NEWBRIDGE OR NOWHERE

*Kildare Hold Firm*

An image of a gable proclaiming 'Newbridge or Nowhere' became one of the defining images of the 2018 Championship.

Nobody could have foreseen that it would be Kildare who would create the story of the year. In Spring they were relegated to Division 3 and then their humiliation was confirmed with a crushing loss to Carlow in the Leinster Championship in Tullamore. Their manager Cian O'Neill seemed set for his P45. The Lilywhites gained some respite with wins over Derry and Longford in the early rounds of the qualifiers. Then they were drawn to play Mayo in Round 3 of the qualifiers. Stephen Rochford's men had come within a whisker of toppling the Dubs and winning a famous All-Ireland less than twelve months earlier. Even diehard Kildare fans were struggling to generate any optimism for the fixture.

They had come out first in the draw and would have home advantage in St Conleth's Park after two games on the road. However, for health and safety reasons, as the ground was too small to accommodate the expected crowd, the GAA formally fixed the Kildare-Mayo match to Croke Park, as part of a double header with Cavan-Tyrone. Kildare's fate had been decided – or had it?

Their manager Cian O'Neill appeared live on the *Six One News* that evening having been coaxed into doing so by the irrepressible Marty Morrissey:

'I don't think anyone saw it going to the level it did. It literally was a phone call from Marty. It was that simple. I was in work at a quarter to six and he just rang. And Marty being the wily old reporter that he is, he probably knew he had something. And he said, "Do you want to go on the *Six One*?" This was never considered. I was just trying to put a written statement together. And I said, "I'm here in work." He said, "Can you get into the studio in Cork?" I didn't even know there was a studio in Cork. He said, "You have to be in there by twenty past six or it won't make the *Six One*." It wasn't pre-planned, there was no script. It just happened. Jacket on, in the car, into Cork. I'd say between walking in the door and being in the room, it was about six or seven minutes. It just happened organically and grew legs from there.'

O'Neill started a crusade and the mantra 'Newbridge or Nowhere' spread like wildfire through the county and captured the public mood on a national level. Such was the force of popular opinion that within days and Kildare insisting they would hand Mayo a walkover rather than compromise, the GAA, caught badly on the backfoot, capitulated, and sanctioned the game for Newbridge.

Three days later, the Lilywhites, surfing a wave of popular support, beat Mayo. It was the first time the Westerners had failed to reach at least the All-Ireland semi-final since 2010.

O'Neill reflected on the events: 'We probably wouldn't have got the traction as a group of players or a management or a county board unless the groundswell of support had come from across the country. That was powerful and it was something no one could have anticipated – for something that was relatively small. It was a fixture argument. But it blew into something far bigger than that which I think did represent at that time a feeling within the grassroots of the GAA.'

## PAPAL APPROVAL

The affair did have an amusing postscript. The other main story of that summer was the visit of Pope Francis to Dublin and Knock. After Cian O'Neill's campaign, social media was buzzing with the news that the pope had cancelled his trip to Knock. When asked why, he was said to have replied: 'It's Newbridge or Nowhere!'

# 31

## STAR OF SCREEN

*Tyrone Footballer Appears in Adult Film*

*'If you don't read the media, you're uninformed. But if you read the media, you're misinformed.'*

DENZEL WASHINGTON

We are not prisoners of fate but prisoners of our minds.

He made headlines:

'GAA porn star avoids prison term.'

'Red Hand Star Caught Red-Handed.'

'IRA Threat to GAA Gay Porn Star.'

'Fears for Gay Porn GAA Ace Cathal.'

'GAA Gay Porn Star back in Tyrone Squad.'

The headlines miss out on the context. Tyrone footballer Cathal McCarron had a gambling addiction. There were issues in his family life and he was struggling in school. He was addicted at sixteen. He will battle it for the rest of his life. Like most gamblers, people often love them, but they do not like them when they are gambling.

Gambling released him from the anger deep in his soul. When he had money and was gambling all was well. That happiness only went away when he had no money. It started off innocently enough with a small bet on a horse. Within a short time, he was stealing from his parents to feed his addiction.

In 2007, McCarron won a County Championship with Dromore – their first title in history. Within twelve months he was on the bench for the All-Ireland final when Tyrone beat Kerry. But his gambling was deteriorating and it was rupturing important friendships. A meeting was arranged with Oisín McConville and it was agreed that McCarron needed rehab. Two days later, on 9 November, 2009, he journeyed to the *Cuan Mhuire* centre near Athenry.

Mickey Harte visited him and presented him with a small velvet box. It was the All-Ireland medal Celtic Cross. Harte also had a rallying cry: 'If you focus on life, and on living life well, just think of all the possibilities out there. Look at the football you were playing, with all the hell that was going on in your life. Imagine, just imagine, what you really could do if you got all of this sorted out.'

After he emerged from rehab he coped well initially, but eventually he slid back into familiar patterns. The debts started to mount. He was on the tube one morning and saw an advertisement looking for male models. He sent a scantily clad picture of himself and received an email a few weeks later to come in for an interview. They offered him £3,000 to play 'Fergus' in a movie and assured him that nobody would see it – they dealt exclusively with US hotels. He needed the money.

A month after the shoot, the details of his acting career went public and he found that he had 'gone viral'. It was humiliating but the Tyrone team welcomed him back into their intricate web of relationships, released him from his cell of shame and he went on to play the football of his life.

## MIND FULL

Sometimes the most important lesson we have to learn in life is that we are good enough as we are. GAA stars are not insulated from the problems of the wider society. We have a mental health crisis in Ireland. Against that background it is no surprise that GAA players would experience mental health issues. A number of prominent personalities have bravely talked about their struggles in this area. Dublin manager Dessie Farrell was among the first when he ended his playing career: 'As my depression deepened, my mind was a constant blur and I felt I had reached a dead end. The fear and stress of my situation engulfed every waking hour. Sometimes, I would pace the kitchen floor until dawn trying and failing to find a way of hauling myself out of this crisis. Other times, I would sit in the car and drive aimlessly around the city. In my darkest moments I even considered ending it all. The outcome terrified me, yet the thought that I could end this remorseless misery held some grizzly appeal. All of a sudden, I was giving the idea of ending my life more and more consideration. I was in big trouble. I needed help. But I was afraid, horrified and ashamed that I, a Dublin footballer, a man, a father, with everything in the world going for him, was unable to cope.'

Farrell appreciated the then Dublin manager Tommy Carr's support: 'Tommy said: "I will support you in any way I can. We all have skeletons in our cupboards." I realised that Carr cared about me, the individual, not just about Dublin or the captaincy, not even about the pressure on him.'

Farrell did seek help. 'I contacted a counsellor and made an appointment. As soon as I started to discuss my problems, the bleakness of the previous few months slowly evaporated with every conversation, with every new day.'

Often our choices reflect our fears rather than hopes. Moral courage is often more challenging than physical courage.

Addiction is a huge social problem in Ireland today. Cathal McCarron is not the only prominent GAA personality to fall victim to it. Niall McNamee, Davy Glennon and Oisín McConville have all courageously spoken out about their struggles in this area. In this way they serve an invaluable service to the GAA family and the public at large by reminding us that when we ask for help, we are not giving in but, instead, refusing to give up.

## NO MINOR STRAIN

While the GAA to its credit has shown greater concern for mental health there is still room for improvement. In May 2022 Tipperary claimed a dramatic Munster minor hurling title with a 3–0 shootout victory over Clare in the TUS Gaelic Grounds. Thankfully no single player on the Clare side was responsible for a miss that cost his side the title. But what if one had? What a burden that would have been for a teenager's mental health. We have to do better to avoid these situations. A 'golden score' is an obvious solution when a minor match finishes level rather than a shootout.

# 32

# THE UNFAIR CITY

*Splitting Dublin*

Jim McGuinness was stroking the flames.

In the build-up to Donegal's 2014 All-Ireland semi-final against Dublin, he argued that Dublin's advantage over the rest of the leading contenders for the Sam Maguire was 'a worry'. Not concerned about rocketing up the emotion, he compared their rise to dominance with Chelsea's ownership by the Russian billionaire, Roman Abramovich:

'I think the divide is becoming bigger and bigger. Dublin are way out in front of everyone. I suppose if we were having this conversation ten years ago you'd have said Kerry was the team with all the resources, that really looked after players with jobs, Kerry Group supporting them and that type of thing. The level they (Dublin)'ve taken sports science to and nutrition, strength and conditioning, the number of coaches they have; it's a professional set up in every sense. They're getting the benefits of that now.'

It was a unique take on the controversy about Dublin's supremacy which culminated in a call to split the county in two from a GAA perspective. There were a number of different strands to the controversy.

In 2020 former Westmeath footballer John Connellan elicited a huge response when he wrote an open letter about Dublin's much-debated funding issue. He wrote to every county secretary outside of Dublin outlining a motion which he sought to be tabled at the 2022 GAA Congress which would require all games development funding to be allocated based on the number of registered GAA members in each county. He claimed that this 'disproportionate funding' creates an uneven playing field:

'The current GAA player experience and pathway of a child in a school or club in Dublin is so far superior. They are disproportionately funded per head compared to a child in a school or club in Athlone or Tullamore. Why is that acceptable? All we're asking for is that no longer are the Dublin schools funded so disproportionately at the expense of the clubs and schools down the country. It's as simple as that. It should be like pushing an open door but, for whatever reason, the powers that be don't want to look at it that way.'

## DESPERATE MEASURES?

As Dublin steamrolled their way to the six-in-a-row in 2020, Colm O'Rourke claimed radical surgery was required. After Dublin thrashed Cavan by fifteen points in the All-Ireland semi-final he observed:

'I suppose it shows the gap that there is in class between Dublin and the rest. They're like the grim reaper when anybody comes here. They just put them away with ruthless efficiency. This is the future. This isn't going to stop this year or next year. We could be looking at Dublin going for ten in a row. Dublin have created a monster and the GAA at central level need to decide what's going to be done about it. But the only answer for the future has to be that Dublin will have three or four teams. Otherwise, everybody else is wasting their time.'

Pat Spillane agrees that it is time to finally face the problem but not in such a radical way:

'The "money" matter sticks out like a sore thumb and must be addressed. Let's take Croke Park's coaching and development fund, for example. Between 2007 and 2019, Kerry received €1.2m from this fund, whereas Dublin got €19.2m. Between 2010 and 2014, the payout worked out at €19 per registered player in Kerry, whereas it was worth €270.70 per club player in Dublin. Dublin's average annual grant from the fund between 2007 and 2019 was €1.4m. Next on the list was Cork, who received €186,561 per annum. Mayo, Sligo, Leitrim, Donegal, Longford, Down, Fermanagh, Monaghan, Tyrone and Armagh all received less than €70,000 per annum. In 2019, the grant was worth €652.82 to every registered juvenile team in Dublin, whereas, in Cork, it was worth just €143.89.

'Analysing the problem is the easy bit; coming up with workable solutions is far more challenging. Forget the mad idea of splitting Dublin into two or, worse still, four. It could be a case of being careful what you wish for. Would the Leinster Championship benefit from having two or four Dublin-based teams? Like hell it would. Equally nonsensical is the idea of the weaker counties amalgamating. It would destroy what makes the GAA unique.

'Lots of issues, such as the population imbalance, cannot be resolved by the GAA. However, there are things the GAA could sort out. Number one is distribution of the coaching and development grants. Surely now, Dublin has sufficient financial resources to fund their own coaching programme. The grants should be awarded to the rest of the counties based on registered players with designated weaker counties receiving extra help.

'Ten of Stephen Cluxton's first 111 Championship games were not played in Croke Park. This needs to change, but, if it did, the GAA would have to cut the prices they charge for the corporate boxes and the long-term premium seats in Croke Park. All success in sport is cyclical and Gaelic football is no different. Dublin were eventually beaten in 2021. I don't see them dominating forever. The issue is that the other Leinster counties have raised the white flag, opting for damage limitation when they face Dublin, instead of trying to beat them. So, my message is to reform finance, and sport's cyclical nature will take care of the rest.'

In early 2022, much of the heat was taken out of the debate as Dublin's form dipped alarmingly. After their third consecutive League defeat against Mayo, Joe Brolly's report on the game began: 'In Croke Park, Brian Fenton, Ciarán Kilkenny and Dean Rock bore the expressions of lads who had been transferred without warning from Real Madrid to Wycombe Wanderers. I watched the game with a crowd of Knockmore men. Before the throw-in, a Westport man said, "How did the Leinster game finish up?" Damien Martin said, "I thought the Railway Cup was abolished."'

# 33

## 'THE MESS'

*Galway v Cork 2020*

Abeona is the Roman Goddess for safe passage.

The Galway ladies' football team could have done with her in 2020.

In March 2021, Helen O'Rourke, CEO of the Ladies Gaelic Football Association, accused former Galway manager Tim Rabbitt of attempting 'to destroy the integrity of the Association and the people involved'. O'Rourke's annual report dealt in great detail with events surrounding the 6 December, 2020 All-Ireland semi-final between Cork and Galway, a fixture that was moved from Parnell Park to Croke Park on the morning of the game. It had its throw-in time brought forward from 1.30pm to 1pm as Croke Park was hosting the All-Ireland men's semi-final between Tipperary and Mayo later in the afternoon.

Shortly afterwards, Rabbitt described the situation as a 'mess' after his side had just seven minutes to warm-up following the late venue/time change of their All-Ireland semi-final meeting with Cork. Given the scale of the furore, the fact that Cork won 2–17 to 0–13 seemed incidental. The former Galway manager described the decision to move the tie to Dublin as 'absolutely crazy':

'This shouldn't be happening. When we talk about equality in the game, these kinds of incidents should not be happening and the LGFA has to make sure this doesn't happen again.

'We were treated like something you'd find on the bottom of a shoe. The whole experience was a joke. These are things that just wouldn't happen in the men's game. If we're going to talk about equality, there has to be some substance to it, not just pushing things under the carpet like they're not happening. They are happening, every year. The ladies' game is probably one of the fastest growing sports in the country, but we don't seem to have the officialdom in the Association that can keep pace with it and to bring the professionalism that is required.

'We agreed that we would play it, that we would get there as early as we could, once we were given assurances that we were given sufficient time. Whether the game threw in at 1pm or 1.10pm, we weren't concerned about that once we were given assurances that we could do a proper warm-up and we were properly prepared. But the minute we took to the pitch, LGFA officials, referee, straight away in our ear: "Six minutes, you've got six minutes to warm up." I don't want it to sound like sour grapes but that's the time we should have taken a stand. We should have just walked off the field. We shouldn't have continued on until we had a sufficient warm-up in place. The disrespect that was shown once we hit Croke Park was completely unacceptable.'

The controversy followed the rumblings earlier that week when Cork and Galway were forced to travel huge distances – with Cork incurring massive costs after booking fifty rooms in a Dublin hotel to stay over on Saturday night because of the Covid crisis – after their last-four clash was switched from the

LIT Gaelic Grounds (to facilitate the Limerick hurlers' training) to the capital.

In fact, the Galway squad were still en route in their cars on the M6 in Kinnegad when the game was changed. To compound the embarrassment, TG4, the competition's sponsors, were unable to air the game live due to the late venue change.

## EPHIE'S ELEGY

Cork boss Ephie Fitzgerald was 'disgusted' when informed by the LGFA at 11.30 that morning that Parnell Park's pitch was frozen, and he questioned the direction which women's sport is going in after the game was switched to Croke Park and brought forward by half an hour.

Fitzgerald regretted the long journey back to Cork which many of his squad faced and reckoned that they were not getting 'the same treatment as the guys get':

'You'd have to say it is a bad week for ladies' sport, wouldn't you really? My wife just rang me there and said, "Twitter is lighting up with what's going on here. Why is this happening?" It is a bit of a kick in the teeth. You'd have to say this has been a negative step for ladies' football, for women's sport in general. I find it hard to get into my head what happened, we were so rushed. It is unacceptable.

'I actually feel more disappointed for the families and supporters of Cork ladies' footballers that it wasn't on television. My father is in hospital and he had arranged to get a television into the room to watch the game. They are the people I really feel sorry for. We were here, we could see the game, but where are we going with ladies' sport if this is going to happen, where are we going in an All-Ireland semi-final? This is a logistical issue, but I think it's a women's issue as well.

'Maybe I'm in a stronger position to talk about it because we were victorious, but I was disgusted and I felt very sorry for Galway, they were rushing on to the pitch after us. There are no words really, what can I say?

'All I want for them is that they get the same treatment as the guys. My argument was, and has been from the start, why are we making things difficult for us? We talk about lifting the spirit of a nation. There was nobody that saw that today. I would have just thought that if we could have got a pitch where we could have travelled in the one day, then that would have made it a lot simpler.'

In her Annual Report Helen O'Rourke was speaking about the All-Ireland semi-final controversy publicly for the first time, and remarked it was 'unfortunate' that both Cork and Galway were 'inconvenienced in terms of their pre-match preparations'. She claimed the subsequent media fallout was 'severe'. She added:

'The Galway manager was particularly aggrieved in his post-match comments and his dealings with the media over the coming days, by not having enough time available to them to warm up . . . It is regrettable that a manager who was so gracious earlier in the day for the efforts that were made to have the game played and who had his requests for additional time met would then turn and try to destroy the integrity of the Association and the people involved after the game.'

The comments by LGFA President Marie Hickey, on national radio the day after the All-Ireland semi-final, also created controversy. During the interview, Hickey said: 'Galway arrived in Croke Park at 12.30pm and they then proceeded to the dressing room, so they spent quite a bit of time in the dressing room and then emerged out on to the pitch. They would have had the opportunity to get out on to the pitch earlier had they not spent so much time in the dressing room.'

## BURKE'S BITE BACK

Galway wing-back Sinéad Burke was interviewed on RTÉ after Hickey's comments. She said: 'It is very disappointing and disheartening to hear that. I have so much time for the LGFA and have had amazing days with the Association, and to hear that being said, it is a punch in the guts. The most disappointing thing is the question was never asked could the men's game be pushed back thirty minutes. That's the killer blow. The question wasn't even asked. All we were asking for was ten minutes to get a sufficient warm-up done to get us to match intensity to be prepared going into that game yesterday and we weren't allowed.'

The viciousness of the comments directed against Ursula Jacob about her performance as a pundit on *The Sunday Game* during 2022 suggests that there is still a journey to be travelled before there is full equality between women and men in the GAA.

# 34

# 'LUDICROUS'

*Camogie's Coin-toss*

'There are no words in my vocabulary that convey the hurt, the disappointment, the absolute feeling of betrayal.'

Bríd MacNamara, PRO of Clare Camogie, was speaking about the actions of the Camogie Association, and the hurt they caused the Clare Camogie panel and those working with them in 2015. Clare and Dublin had finished their Championship group tied on points in third place. Both sides had played out a 1–8 to 1–8 draw earlier in the campaign. Under the competition rules, teams which finish level are ranked by the higher number of goals scored in games between the two, and then by the higher number of points in the games, before proceeding to the drawing of lots.

Only one of the teams could progress to the quarter-final stage, and the Camogie Association decided for the draw to be broadcast live on YouTube. Thus began the controversy of the 'camogie coin toss'.

The procedure was described as 'ludicrous' by Dublin manager Shane O'Brien and both counties lodged appeals minutes after Clare's final group game was completed. The Dublin County Board and the management, after hearing the thoughts of the players, met in the Red Cow Hotel to discuss their response. They decided that they would withdraw their name from the coin toss. Clare opted to take the same stance with both sides agreeing that neither should lose out over the toss of a coin.

Initially, a statement issued by the National Transfer Hearing and Disciplinary Committee (NTHDC) claimed that it could not reconsider a decision taken by Ard Comhairle and: 'Confirmation of the team that progresses to the All-Ireland Senior quarter-final on 1 August to play Wexford will be announced tomorrow (Wednesday, 29 July) after a draw to determine this, is carried out.' Given the scale of negative comment across the media, the Camogie Association back-tracked, agreeing for there to be a play-off match between Dublin and Clare.

Dublin secured a narrow 1–11 to 0–12 victory. Two days later Dublin played against Wexford in the resulting quarter-final and it is fair to say that the two-day turnaround and controversy contributed to Wexford winning the match. The Camogie Association revised their rules in light of the coin-toss controversy.

There are those who believe that such controversies are good for camogie because they create rare moments when the nation turns its lonely eyes to the sport. There have been some other controversies which have helped in this regard down the years.

### IT'S NOT OVER UNTIL THE LADY SINGS
In 2018, Cork and Meath's camogie sides contested a thriller in Croke Park in their All-Ireland Intermediate final clash, but the main talking point was referee Liz Dempsey's decision to

blow up for full time, with Meath having a clear chance to score. The Rebelettes had built a good lead, but Meath reeled them in and were pushing on to win the title for the first time in their history. Their midfielder Megan Thynne burst through the Cork defence and set herself up with a chance of the winning score, but just as she was about to take her shot for the decisive score, referee Dempsey blew for full time.

## DUAL STARS

Cork considered withdrawing from the 2020 Championship if a solution could not be found to the fixture clashes impacting on the county's dual players. The situation arose because of the controversy that dragged on over the schedule facing Cork's dual players Hannah Looney, Fiona Keating, Meabh Cahalane, Ciara McCarthy and Libby Coppinger. Both Cork teams were due to face group-stage games on Saturday, 7 November with other potential clashes in store over the course of that month. There was sustained criticism of both the Camogie Association and the Ladies Gaelic Football Association for their communication over fixture programmes.

Tipperary's Aishling Moloney went public in criticising the scheduling of two county finals in ladies football and camogie within twenty-six hours, involving her club Cahir, leaving the club now opting not to field a team in the camogie decider:

'We have to take a stand; we have to raise awareness. It's hard to fathom really. It probably comes down to lack of communication. Back on the weekend of the 12/13 September we played the Junior A camogie semi-final followed by the football semi on the Sunday. We feel like we are not being accommodated. The issue of player welfare is a real concern. I'm exhausted and the whole thing has taken its toll. It's an awful lot to ask for my colleagues and I to play both games this weekend. We did it on the 12/13 September. We kept it quiet and said nothing. We survived that weekend, we were down nine points in the football with five minutes to go. The knock-on effects of all that were felt the following week. I don't know what we have to do. It can be so easily solved. Simple communication and these issues could be solved.

'It's upsetting that we have to do this. There are girls on the camogie team who don't play football. Sport is there to be enjoyed and you don't want to be engaging in this kind of controversy. Growing up I was encouraged to play camogie and football. With this going on, dropout will occur. We have raised awareness and we hope it won't happen again.'

## EQUALITY OF THE SEXES

There has been ongoing controversy about the lack of equality between camogie players and their male counterparts. In 1967, a man wrote to a national newspaper calling on the GAA to ban women from attending the upcoming All-Ireland finals, claiming that the sight of women, outside the home, in Croke Park, was revolting and unnatural to him.

In 2021, Dublin camogie star Ali Twomey went public about the challenges she and her teammates confront to line out for their county:

'Still, we don't get any expenses for going to training. We don't always get food after training. We got gear last year, but the year before I don't think we got much. What you see the lads getting and what we get, there is still a huge difference.

'Girls are starting to put their foot down. In terms of expenses, I've been paying €90–€100 a month in tolls just to go training, before Covid. That's without petrol or buying food for meal prep or all the other expenses that go with it. It is a very expensive hobby, and when you compare it to the lads, it is very disheartening.

'To be honest, as time goes on, it is tough to stay motivated. Obviously, you do get times where you're low on motivation, or you get years where you say, "Oh, I can't go back, it's too much commitment." But, at the end of the day, you just love the sport; you want to play; and that's what always brings me back, that I just absolutely love playing and it's all I want to do. It is hard to keep motivated, to keep really upbeat about the situation when you do see what the lads are getting compared to what we're getting. But that's kind of out of our hands, as such. It's something that . . . higher up something needs to be done, there needs to be more respect for what we do as players and as people.'

A few weeks later this issue came before the Department of Tourism, Culture, Arts, Sport, Gaeltacht and Media. It was revealed that male players in the GAA receive over €3m in government grants while their female counterparts are given just over €700,000 annually. Galway camogie captain Sarah Dervan observed: 'You want to see that gone, that's Stone-Age stuff. We want to see women in sport coming to the fore and being seen as equal to the men. And that someday, not too far in the future, we'll just call it sport. I suppose I don't really think about it too much in terms of I just get on with it because it's so normal which is shocking, I think. It's just become the norm that we do that, that we pay for our own hurls, we look after ourselves. Players pay for their own gym. In this day and age, it's not good enough. Camogie and ladies' football are at such an elite level now, we want to make sure they get the showcase they deserve and be able to put their best foot forward.'

In 2021, the government announced that female Gaelic games players will receive the same amount of funding as their male counterparts. One other small sign of progress. It was a significant moment when the most recent series of *Reeling in the Years* included highlights from both the camogie and ladies' football All-Irelands for the first time.

# 35

# SPYGATE

*Donegal v Kerry*

One of the sports stories of 2019 was the news that the Leeds United manager Marcelo Bielsa sent people to spy on upcoming opponents. 'Spygate' provoked some noteworthy responses. First there was a bizarre interview on Sky Sports News about Bielsa.

Peter Shilton: 'He's Italian.'

Jim White: 'No, he's Argentinian.'

Shilton: 'Oh, is he?'

White: 'Yes.'

Shilton: 'Oh, it makes it even worse then, doesn't it?'

However, for a slice of cutting humour it was hard to top the exchange between Leeds' official Twitter account and Pizza Hut.

Pizza Hut: Hi, @LUFC, we've just seen a suspicious-looking man peering through our chef's window. Can you let us know if you're planning to put Pizza on the menu in the club canteen?

Leeds: Prefer @Dominos thanks! They don't take a week to deliver a tweet.

Pizza Hut: Bit rich for a club that hasn't delivered since 1992.

## MISSION IMPOSSIBLE

Before the 2014 All-Ireland football final the GAA had its own 'spygate' when Donegal civil servant Patrick Roarty was rumbled up a tree apparently trying to spy on the Kerry training session a few days before the All-Ireland. The Kerry background team heard the noise of rustling branches coming from the grounds of St Finan's Hospital, the now vacant psychiatric unit adjacent to Fitzgerald Stadium.

Kerry-based Mr Roarty is from Donegal manager Jim McGuinness's hometown of Glenties and both men played together for the local club, Naomh Conaill. According to media reports at the time, Mr Roarty said he and the Donegal manager had attended each other's weddings. They also stated that Mr Roarty is heavily involved in the Donegal Association in Kerry, where he doubles as chief entertainer and is a well-known guitar player.

When asked what he thought of Mr Roarty, former Donegal player John Gildea, who played with him at Naomh Conaill, said: 'Patrick is a great fella, a really decent and lovely lad.' When pushed about what he thought Roarty was doing up a tree, Mr Gildea said: 'Sure, it's September. He was probably just looking for apples.'

Mr Roarty was confronted by a member of the Kerry back-room team. He ran off but dropped a card on the ground that disclosed his identity. The Kerry County Board confirmed it was aware of the incident.

The war of words escalated with claim and counterclaim and a James Bond feel. Sources in the Donegal camp claimed that they believed that their training sessions were 'observed' at least four times. Each time people with camcorders drove

off when challenged. When queried about those alleged incidents, Mr Gildea calmly replied: "Maybe they were looking for
apples, too. The good thing about the (Donegal GAA) centre
of excellence in Convoy is that there isn't a tree for three miles
around the place. It's not fertile ground for apples.'

# 36

## TALK TO JOE

*The Garth Brooks Fiasco*

*Liveline* went into meltdown.

Joe Duffy could barely cope with all the moral indignation from seemingly thousands of callers. The last saga to create this level of controversy was Roy Keane and Saipan.

The GAA's most infamous link with music came in 2014 with the shambles over the cancellation of the Garth Brooks series of concerts in Croke Park because of a dispute over licensing laws. It hurt all the more because, like Bruce Springsteen and David Gray, we had made him one of our adopted sons.

In 1994, Brooks started his world tour in Dublin where almost 70,000 people attended his eight concerts at the Point Depot. It was largest audience for an event in Dublin since the Pope's visit in 1979. The conquering hero returned to Ireland in 1997 to play three nights in Croke Park.

In June 2008, Prince had cancelled a concert with 55,000 ticket holders at almost the last minute. But this cancellation barely created a whimper compared to the level of outrage by the Brooks controversy.

In a 2019 documentary Garth claimed: 'I never wanted to be the guy that ever was in a controversial anything.' Five years earlier, though, the saga of his concerts and the will they/won't they storm of controversy they created convulsed the country.

Brooks himself criticised the handling of his five concerts in Dublin after they were cancelled. Dublin City Council granted permission for only three of the gigs to go ahead at Croke Park stadium. As a result, all five, scheduled to take place from 25–29 July were called off.

The concert drama rumbled on throughout the summer before the planned concerts, estimated to earn the Irish economy €50m, were cancelled. The five concerts were due to take place in Croke Park before the local residents protested in opposition to them taking place. A judicial review blocked the staging of the five concerts, instead allowing for a maximum of three.

The controversy took another twist when Brooks announced he would stage five concerts or none, and eventually announced he was cancelling all his Croke Park gigs with 'great regret'. The US star claimed that if the Taoiseach Enda Kenny wanted to speak with him to try and find a resolution, he would 'crawl, swim and fly over'.

More than 400,000 ticket holders were left crestfallen, while the GAA lost out on a windfall, not to mention all the pubs and hostelries in the vicinity of Croke Park. The controversy had some bizarre subplots. Dublin Lord Mayor Christy Burke claimed the Mexican ambassador had offered to intervene in the Garth Brooks saga.

## FRIENDS IN LOW PLACES

Some cynics were very unsympathetic to the huge loss of

revenue for the GAA with the news of the cancellation of the concerts – on the basis that they had agreed to three concerts a year but then went for more. Hence, the new name, the NGAA: The Not Great Arithmetic Association.

Cynical fans are part of the furniture of the GAA. Another illustration of this came in August 2022 when Davy Fitzgerald was appointed as Waterford hurling manager for a second time. It is fair to say that there was a mixed reaction among Déise fans. One disgruntled supporter took to social media to suggest: 'Davy brings more baggage than Louis Vuitton.'

# 37

# PAPERBACK WRITER

*Kevin Cassidy Is Booked*

The French use the term amour fou. It means an obsessive love. Many of us have an obsessive love for Gaelic games. So many Irish people have an obsessive love for literature. That is reflected in our four Nobel prizes for literature. The cocktail of books and the GAA has occasionally been explosive.

Bernard Flynn offers an example: 'I'm a big admirer of Mickey Harte, but I was taken aback when he wrote in one of his books about Seán Cavanagh's inability to start against Cork in the 2009 All-Ireland semi-final. Cavanagh nearly single-handedly won Tyrone the 2008 All-Ireland. Seán Boylan wouldn't dream of criticising one of his players in public like that.'

Kevin Cassidy infamously missed out on an All-Ireland medal in 2012 because of his involvement in a book. The previous year, Donegal won the Ulster Championship and Cassidy won an All-Star after a series of stunning performances, culminating in one of the finest points ever scored in Croke Park, against Kildare. However, his involvement in a book about a series of Ulster players by Declan Bogue led to manager Jim McGuinness axing him from the Donegal panel. The Donegal manager felt that Cassidy's sharing of insights about the inner workings of the squad constituted a breach of trust. This included the revelation that on the morning of the All-Ireland semi-final against the Dubs, McGuinness asked them to hand over their phones for the day before disclosing his plan that involved positioning fourteen players behind the ball when they lost possession. McGuinness also took umbrage that Cassidy had not informed him that he was collaborating in a book.

The controversy sparked a further controversy when McGuinness insisted that Declan Bogue should not attend his post-match conference after he led Donegal to their second All-Ireland.

In 2021, in an episode of *Laochra Gael*, Cassidy revealed:

'In April (2012), Jim and I had a meeting. He said, "Listen, you're welcome to come back to the panel." I didn't think it would benefit Donegal if I was on the panel. I knew they were close to winning the big one, but at the same time, it just wasn't right for me, and that's the decision I made.'

## BOOKED

In 2015, Jim McGuinness published his own book. It created a controversy of its own within Donegal. McGuinness was unhappy with the county board who he felt sabotaged Donegal's 2013 season when they opted to go ahead with club Championship fixtures during the summer. As a consequence of injuries picked up in club matches, McGuinness felt the odds were unnecessarily stacked against him: 'To my mind, there were people on the county board who wanted me to fail, and if that meant that the Donegal team failed in the process, so be it.'

# 38

# FROM CLARE TO HERE

*Davy v Loughnane*

Not for the first time Davy Fitzgerald created controversy.

In his second autobiography in 2018, Davy Fitzgerald departs significantly from his first by having harsh words for both his former teammates Brian Lohan and Jamesie O'Connor. However, he goes perhaps surprisingly gently on Ger Loughnane given some of the critical comments Loughnane had written about him in his newspaper column. He does have a cut though at Loughnane for fuelling the rivalry between Clare and Galway to the detriment of the Banner in 2016.

After Kilkenny beat Galway in the Leinster final, Loughnane, with characteristic understatement, had described the Westerners as 'made of absolutely nothing' and of having 'no guts whatsoever'. With the peerless Joe Canning calling the shots, Galway were determined to crush Clare when the sides met in the All-Ireland quarter-final after Loughnane's incendiary comments, and they did. As the Clare manager at the time, Davy described himself as 'hugely let down' by Loughnane's 'diatribe'. Although Fitzgerald dismisses his critics as 'empty vessels making noise' he nonetheless expresses his frustration about 'one Clare man setting up another for a fall'.

For his part, since he retired, Joe Canning has gone public about his desire 'to play with a chip on my shoulder'. He cited Loughnane's comments in 2016 when he described the Galway team as having 'no guts whatsoever' and his comparison of the team manager Micheál Donoghue to the late Dermot Morgan's comic character 'Father Trendy' as part of their enhanced motivation to win the 2017 All-Ireland.

### DAVY 2

In 2020, Loughnane had another public squabble with Davy. Initially, Loughnane compared Davy to a Jack Russell dog who always needed attention. After Fitzgerald's Wexford team performed badly in the Championship, Loughnane was critical of the team and their manager in his newspaper column. In an interview on South East Radio, Davy hit back:

'He wouldn't really be up with what's going on in the GAA world, in my view. My honest opinion is I feel a bit sorry for him. Ger isn't involved with any clubs. He hasn't been involved with anyone since he went to Galway and did not have a good time. He actually couldn't read a game. If you read any of his articles, he can't read the game. He doesn't see what is going on. I don't hate Ger Loughnane. I feel sorry for him. Because every single week he is having a cut at someone.'

Davy claimed the hostility dated back to Fitzgerald's time in charge of Clare:

'I remember the night I asked him to present medals to the team in 2013. He actually said to them he did not rate them a good team until they won a second one, which I thought was a very nasty thing to say to them. Before we played Galway in 2015, the things he said about them were unreal, he gave them so much motivation. I remember a member of the Galway management team telling me only a year or two ago that Ger gave them so much motivation, they had things up in their dressing room. That tells its own story about Ger Loughnane. The only one who is "me, me, me" is Ger Loughnane.'

## DAVY 3

Davy has also fallen out with another Clare legend. In 2001, Ger Loughnane predicted that Brian Lohan would go on to manage Clare. In 2019, after a controversial and sometimes turbulent process, Lohan was appointed Clare manager. His first major test as a manager came in the League away to Wexford, managed by his former teammate Davy Fitzgerald. The media went into a frenzy beforehand about whether both men would publicly shake hands afterwards given the high profile spat between them. There was no grand reconciliation.

## DAVY 4

Davy has also been critical of Clare fans who criticised him on social media. In 2019 he said: 'The amount of good people that have come up to me and thanked me for what I've done for Clare, I appreciate that and I know you have people on social media out there and they are nobodies, they like to think they are somebodies but they are nobodies.'

## THE COUNTY BOARD

The controversial Centre of Excellence at Caherlohan has also divided the Clare hurling family. In 2021, Anthony Daly ventilated some of the issues:

'There has been an atmosphere of fear created around our county board. The whole country knows at this stage that we're going backwards but we've tolerated it for too long. Everyone in Clare knows that Caherlohan is not fit for purpose. There is no medical room and there is no defibrillator. The gym can cater for twenty people. How big are inter-county panels now?

'(Brian) Lohan has faced one obstacle after the next since applying for the senior job. In his interview, Lohan wasn't even asked about the make-up of his back-room team, which was a clear signal that he wasn't getting the job. Shortly afterwards, Lohan got a phone call to say that the board were appointing Louis Mulqueen. Lohan was out of the picture until a handful of club delegates put up their hands and shouted stop.

'Nobody should have been surprised because the way Donal Moloney was treated was nothing short of a total disgrace. Donal, who had been joint-manager with Gerry O'Connor, was interested in the job but the board kept stringing him along for three months. So, if a guy who had given his life to Clare hurling over the previous decade, joint-managing Clare to unprecedented Munster and All-Ireland success at U-21 level, and nearly guiding Clare to a senior All-Ireland, is treated that poorly, it's easier then to form a background picture of what Lohan has had to consistently put up with.

'The board clearly didn't want to give Lohan the job but when the clubs dictated otherwise, the modus operandi then has been to put as many obstacles as possible in his way. I know the HSE were using Cusack Park as a Covid Testing Centre, but the squad seemed to have limited access to Cusack Park during last year's Championship. If Cusack Park was out of bounds, surely some accommodation could have been sought when the squad had no alternative with Caherlohan not fit for use. Lohan was reliant on the good grace of the clubs for the use of their pitches.

'We've heard all the stories of Lohan's multitude of emails unanswered by (Pat) Fitzgerald (the Clare County Secretary and father of Davy), of Lohan having to pay S&C (Strength and Conditioning) staff, of him paying for meals below in Wexford after a League game. How is that right? Some of the details are disputed but how is Lohan having to deal with this stuff in the first place? I cannot understand how – in my opinion – our greatest ever player is not being supported to the hilt by the board.'

Former Banner forward Jamesie O'Connor acknowledged the challenges facing Brian Lohan:

'I'll hold my hand up here, my wife is an accountant. Brian asked her to come on board as treasurer of Club Clare. I see, first hand, some of the challenges that he's had and he's having to do things that I don't think John Kiely or Brian Cody are having to worry about. Just trying to give the Clare players a chance to compete and to have what any player wants, which is to feel that you have the best chance possible. And that's a challenge for Brian in the current environment. We continued to make the headlines right throughout the winter for all the wrong reasons but a lot of the issues that were raised are of concern I'd say to genuine hurling people, in particular, in the county. Caherlohan, the training facility, isn't up to standard.'

# 39

## THE SKY FALLS IN

*The Sky Deal*

Interviewed on *Off The Ball* in 2021, the Taoiseach Micheál Martin, a keen GAA fan, stated that he had been opposed to the GAA's controversial deal with Sky Sports. He expressed the wish that all GAA games should be shown on terrestrial television.

There was mayhem when the agreement was first announced in 2014: an initial three-year deal that gave Sky Sports exclusive rights to fourteen Championship games in addition to All-Ireland semi-finals and finals simultaneous with RTÉ.

Many traditionalists were horrified by the GAA 'selling its soul' or 'taking the shilling' and radio phone-ins were jammed with emotive calls and stories about the hardships it would cause to elderly relatives. Given the virulence and the hostility of the reaction, GAA President Liam O'Neill revealed he scarcely slept for two weeks afterwards, tossing and turning as he pondered if it was the right move for the Association. But, in the end, he was convinced they had. Fans remained unconvinced, pointing to how it would push some games beyond the less well-off and elderly who didn't have access.

Two critics were particularly vocal. Interviewed on *The Sunday Game* in 2017, the two-time All-Ireland winner Michael Duignan did not disguise his contempt:

'To me the biggest disgrace of the weekend was on Saturday evening, that that Waterford-Kilkenny wasn't shown on free-to-air television in this country. The Sky deal is so wrong on so many levels and it's not because I'm in RTÉ working for *The Sunday Game*. My parents are at home, my father is eighty-three years of age. A savage hurling man. Why should he go to the pub? He doesn't go to the pub to watch a match. They have enough money in the GAA. How much money do they want? What about the people who have supported it all their lives that can't watch it? I think it's disgraceful.'

Given his abhorrence to anything smacking of elitism against the Association it came as no great surprise when Joe Brolly came out strongly against it. His initial response, though, created a controversy of its own. He took to the social media platform to express his views but played the woman not the ball when he described their presenter Rachel Wyse, who was to be the face of Sky's coverage, as a '*Baywatch* babe'. Initially, he responded to the storm of controversy by stating what he described as a deliberate policy from Sky of hiring 'beautiful people' to present their Sports programs. Brolly did eventually apologise, sending a tweet to Wyse, and he clarified that his comment was not meant as any 'reflection on your abilities as a presenter'.

The GAA had justified the deal initially because it would lead to the GAA reaching an international audience. The numbers told a different story. Brolly joked that more people went to Mass in Donnybrook than watched GAA coverage on Sky Sports.

However, in 2020 Brolly finally gave up the ghost: 'We're ten years down the line now and eventually you have to come to the realisation that you're howling into the wilderness. The decision has been made by the GAA and there's no going back. I love the GAA and I'll defend it to the death to the outside world, even if I excoriate it on the inside and to the hierarchy. But, you look at it, even my own kids are saying, "What are you doing?" And I suppose increasingly if you're the only one out there with a pitchfork you're in danger of becoming irrelevant. A friend of mine said, "You're like f***ing Aontú." I would like things to be a different way but they're never going to be.'

## LIKE A PRAYER
There was an amusing postscript to the controversy. Rumours spread on social media that, after getting the rights for GAA matches, Sky was going to go head to head with RTÉ for the rights to another Irish national institution: the Angelus!

# 40

## HANGING ON THE TELEPHONE

*Claregate*

I learned a new word recently.

As a noun, respair means a return to hope. As a verb it means to be hopeful again. Respair is an obsolete word that is rarely used. There is a festival in London called Respair that celebrates stories of journeys from despair to respair.

Ger Loughnane took Clare from despair to respair. He recognised that after eighty-one years in the hurling wilderness despair was no longer an option – and that action was the best antidote to despair. On the way, he created all kinds of controversies. One of his most 'colourful' episodes came because he forgot to hang up the phone.

If a week is a long time in politics eleven years is a long time in hurling and, in 2006, a bizarre series of events involving an overheard phone conversation and a complaint to the guards created a virtual civil war in Clare hurling that entered the vernacular as 'Claregate'. The background was that the Clare hurling fraternity decided to honour their best team for the previous twenty-five years and confer an award for the person who gave 'special services to Clare hurling'. Given that he was the county's first All-Star and that was he voted 'Hurling's Manager of the Millennium' Loughnane might have expected to be the recipient. However, instead, the award went to Fr Harry Bohan.

Loughnane spoke with the then County Chairman Michael McDonagh on the phone and expressed his displeasure about the awards. He clarified that his issue was not that he had not received an award himself. He would later explain that there are no awards on display in his house. The only such photograph he has is of the 1995 People of the Year award with Maureen Potter.

Loughnane did not hang up properly and after finishing his call with McDonagh rang a friend on his mobile and joked about going hunting and imagining a certain person's head being the target. McDonagh had not hung up either and heard the entire conversation. His response was to report the incident to the gardai.

At its core was a row between Loughnane and what he terms 'the Clare hurling establishment'. How does Loughnane reflect on the bitter controversy? He lapsed into silence: the silence before a storm is brewing before replying:

'I believe there was an element in charge of hurling in Clare who wanted to rewrite the history of what happened in '95 and '97 because they wanted to keep things in their own hands. Essentially, they were bypassed in our glory years and they didn't want that situation to be repeated – even if it meant we were not successful as a county.'

The controversy reheated itself in '07 when Loughnane weighed in to back his old friend Tony Considine who was experiencing a turbulent time as Clare manager. What raised most eyebrows was the timing of his comments – shortly before his Galway team were playing Clare in a crunch game. Loughnane was bemused by the hullabaloo:

'I threw a pebble and everyone thought it was an earthquake. Christ, I got such criticism, some of it for words I never actually used, that I thought at one stage I was going to be blamed for global warming! I sometimes laughed when I turned on the radio and listened to sports shows and found they were talking about something I said as if it was more newsworthy than the Gettysburg address! What makes it all the more laughable is that they invited journalists on to interpret what I had said, and they talked about "Ger" as if they knew me well. Some of these guys were people I had rarely, if ever, spoken with in any meaningful way, and often they knew as much about me as I know about synchronised swimming.'

How does he react to the suggestion that he has an agenda? Loughnane gives a typical withering glance: 'To say that I've an agenda is the catch-cry of the clown.'

# 41

## TO B OR NOT TO B?

*Special Congress Defeats Proposal B*

For Hamlet the question was: 'To be or not to be?' For delegates at the GAA's Special Congress in October 2021 the choice was Proposal B or no change. They were voting to adopt the league-based All-Ireland football championship known as Proposal B.

Despite receiving the public backing of President Larry McCarthy, Director General Tom Ryan, the GPA and ex-President John Horan, a slim majority (50.6%) were in favour but that fell well short of the 60% threshold.

The Offaly GAA chairperson Michael Duignan was one of many disappointed with the outcome:

'I'm personally, and on behalf of Offaly, very disappointed in the result. I think it's an opportunity missed. When you hear Tom Parsons's view where eighty per cent of the players were in favour of change and you have fifty per cent of the delegates not representing that view, there's a mismatch there somewhere. I think a lot of the people that voted today were protecting their own interests. They are strong counties that don't want to change, and they are forgetting about a large number of players that are putting in the same effort and commitment.'

Former Armagh ace forward Oisín McConville was also disappointed by the outcome:

'A lot of weaker counties, more so the players in those counties, were more or less promised change in the summer . . . the momentum came to a shuddering halt this week because anybody who knows how Congress works, will know that in the last week or so, it was obvious that it wasn't going to pass, there seemed to be so many dissenting voices, mainly from Ulster. My argument was that this is for the greater good of all of the Association. I know. I'd be very worried that we are not going to revisit this again. I think a lot of players will vote with their feet.'

While conceding there were flaws with Proposal B, Pat Spillane had a typically unique view of it:

'I'm thinking of the words of former US President Theodore Roosevelt, that "in any moment of decision, the best thing you can do is the right thing. The next best is the wrong thing, and the worst thing you can do is nothing." Yet the elegates went for Proposal C, which was to go back to the All-Ireland quarter-final structure, without the Super 8s, that last applied in 2017.'

Former Kerry manager Éamonn Fitzmaurice said of the failure of Proposal B: 'We are reverting to a system that was officially deemed broken over four years ago and was dysfunctional for long before that. In fact, delegates were so anxious for change in 2017 that the Super 8s was heralded in with seventy-six per cent of the vote. This time round, the suits . . . selfishly prioritised the provincial championships that are a dead duck.'

Colm O'Rourke was characteristically blunt: 'The unspoken word from football strongholds is, "To hell with everyone else." The present feeling is that the Ulster block is likely to resist anything they feel mutilates their Championship, even if many loudly protest they are not against change. Yeah, right, as young people are likely to say. Another "Ulster says no". The argument is that the Ulster Championship is a land of milk and honey, and therefore no change is needed. Move on quickly, nothing to report.'

# 42

## THE MIGHTY FITZ

*Páidí v Maurice 2001*

Football management is not rocket science. It is a lot more complicated and demanding.

Gaelic football managers can be classified into two categories: those who have been sacked and those who will be sacked. There can be a fine line when a manager's admirable independence of mind spills over into self-destructive stubbornness. Think of Jack Charlton's treatment of David O'Leary.

The late Páidí Ó Sé's managerial record compares favourably with most. He did bring a National League and under-21 All-Ireland to Kerry and two All-Irelands in 1997 and 2000. Those people who doubted Páidí's credentials when he was appointed Kerry manager were proved wrong.

His former teammate Pat Spillane was a keen admirer of his good friend: 'He brought an All-Ireland to Kerry in '97 with what I have publicly stated was the poorest team to ever win an All-Ireland.'

The wheels came off the wagon in the 2001 All-Ireland semi-final when Meath beat Kerry by no less than fifteen points.

Kerry went through a twenty-nine-minute spell in the first half without scoring and then could only muster a single point from substitute Declan Quill in the second half.

Inevitably when a Kerry team loses by fifteen points in Croke Park serious questions were asked, particularly when Páidí refused to start Maurice Fitzgerald – a forward who could consistently promise to fill the minds of football fans with glittering memories and deliver on that promise with a series of sublime performances. He is destined to be forever remembered for the All-Ireland quarter-final in 2001 in Thurles when his magical long-range sideline drew the match. Mickey Ned O'Sullivan said of Fitzgerald, 'If he had played in the Kerry team of the 1970s, he would probably have gone in history as one of the greatest forwards of all time.'

Even as a boy young Maurice's exceptional talents were evident to all shrewd observers. His father Ned had played for Kerry and the family were close friends with the legendary Mick O'Connell. Maurice won the first of three All-Star awards in his teenage years in 1988, having scored ten points in the defeat to Cork in the Munster final. It would be nine years later before Fitzgerald won his first All-Ireland medal when Kerry beat Mayo, their first All-Ireland in eleven years.

You can train for all conscious eventualities, but a player's greatest moments are when their instinct takes over, and afterwards they cannot remotely explain why they did what they did. Maurice's career is peppered with moments of genius like that. His finest hour was the 1997 All-Ireland when he regularly broke through, with Mayo defenders falling around him like dying wasps, and kicked incredible points from all angles.

Pat Spillane has high praise for him: 'Along with Mikey Sheehy Maurice was the most skillful player I ever played with in the Kerry jersey.'

The later years of Fitzgerald's career were overshadowed by the controversy created by his relationship with the team manager.

Many GAA fans were looking forward to reading Páidí's autobiography because they thought it would be the perfect opportunity for him to finally reveal what his problem with Maurice was but, on the single issue that most exercised football people, he said absolutely nothing.

When I asked him about all the controversy Páidí gave me a long rambling answer that clarified absolutely nothing. He smiled sheepishly when I quoted Ernest Hemingway at him that the great fallacy of life is to think as we get older that we grow wiser. The reality is that we just get more cautious.

I asked him if that applied in this case. He favoured me with that familiar smile. He replied: 'Especially in this case.'

# 43

## ABSENT WITHOUT LEAVE

*Michael Donnellan Leaves the Galway Panel*

His was a talent that danced to music not yet written.

In the first half of the 1998 All-Ireland final, Kildare were in the ascendancy. Michael Donnellan produced a surging run, a little shimmy and scored a stunning point. In 2005, this run and score was voted 'the greatest GAA moment of all time' by a poll carried out for RTÉ television.

The first time I met John O'Mahony he was on the back foot. He was under pressure because Roscommon had crushed his hotly fancied Galway team in the 2001 Championship. But he was also reeling from the biggest controversy of his career. As we sat in his Ballaghaderreen home, savouring his wife Ger's beautiful hot scones, our conversation was interrupted a number of times as he fielded calls from a number of GAA correspondents all seeking a headline.

A fatal setback seemed to the sensational decision of Michael and John Donnellan to withdraw from the county panel in the middle of the Championship team. Youth, impetuosity and the intense will to win go together in a highly combustible concoction.

At the time, Michael Donnellan was universally recognised as one of the best, if not the best, footballer in the country – and certainly the most thrilling. The news of the Donnellans's controversy burst so dramatically, when so much of what seemed so stable was shifting unnervingly around them, that some of the Galway camp gave convincing impersonations of skiers in an avalanche, struggling to keep their feet as the old world crumbled beneath them. For O'Mahony, caught in the full glare of media attention, and with the fate of his team seemingly on the edge of the abyss, the possibility of anonymity, of assuming another identity entirely, was momentarily delicious. Despite the media frenzy, O'Mahony worked quietly behind the scenes and the brothers were soon back in the fold with the minimum of fanfare.

Over twenty years later O'Mahony continues to maintain a monastic vow of silence about the incident. A few months after the Donnellan brothers' controversy, he confounded his critics. A good team wins an All-Ireland, but it takes a great one to win a second All-Ireland. O'Mahony's Galway team achieved that against the raging hot favourites, Meath, in 2001. All O'Mahony will say is:

'Meath had demolished Kerry in the All-Ireland semi-final and we had been beaten by Roscommon in the Connacht Championship. At that stage people thought we were dead and buried but we had a great team and we came back. I would like to think there is a lesson there for everyone. It is not about the setbacks you confront in life that matters, but the key question is how you cope with these setbacks.'

In search of insight into O'Mahony's methods I sought outside counsel.

### FROM THE HEART

After Meath sensationally trounced reigning All-Ireland champions Kerry in the 2001 All-Ireland semi-final, Kerry manager

Páidí Ó Sé said: 'Meath football is honest-to-goodness football, it's from the heart, it's passionate. To succeed you need the two ingredients and you have both in abundance.' Ó Sé could just as easily have been talking about the Meath manager, Seán Boylan, a man who always wears his heart on his sleeve.

That year, his Meath side was hotly fancied to add another Sam Maguire victory to their collection but, in an amazing match, Galway ran out as easy winners. The football world was shocked and frantically searched for an explanation of this tale of the unexpected, but not the then Meath manager:

'It was very simple. Galway were a better team on the day. It was very tight for a lot of the game. Then a few things happened very quickly that changed the game. Firstly, Ollie Murphy broke his arm. Secondly, Nigel Nestor was sent off. People talk about Trevor Giles missing the penalty but that wasn't the reason why we lost the match. Galway won because they produced outstanding football. Nobody wants to lose an All-Ireland but if I had to choose to lose to another manager, it would be to John O'Mahony. A lot of the credit for that All-Ireland has to go to John.

'John was a wonderful manager. All you have to do is to look at his record not just with Galway but with Mayo and Leitrim. What he has done for football in the West is remarkable and he's brought it on to a whole new level. He's very professional in his approach and he has the most basic quality a great coach needs: the ability to get the best out of his players.

'John also played the media very well in the build-up to the game. He fed into the notion that Meath were red-hot favourites and Galway were really only there to make up the numbers. I never believed that for a second, but a lot of people did because of the way we had beaten Kerry in the semi-final. That was just a freak day. Everything went wrong for Kerry and right for us.

It would have been much better for us if we had only won by a point, but in a match like that you can't tell your players to take their foot off the pedal. What John wasn't saying in public, though, was that Galway had a great hunger to win, having lost the All-Ireland in a replay to Kerry the previous year. John was able to channel that hunger positively and get his team to produce wonderful football on the day. The best team won. We've no complaints. I salute him not just for winning that All-Ireland but for the quiet way he diffused the Michael Donnellan situation and, even though the world and his mother wanted him to tell the inside story, he kept it to himself.'

# 44

# WHO FEARS TO SPEAK OF '98?

*The Jimmy Cooney Lost Minutes*

In a summer like no other, his mistake would spark a huge controversy.

In the All-Ireland semi-final replay, Clare were leading Offaly by three points with two minutes to go and their forward Barry Murphy was goal-bound on the 21-yard line. The fallout for referee Jimmy Cooney was huge:

'After I blew the final whistle, I saw my umpire and he had his hand out with his five fingers up. I thought to myself "Oh Jesus". All the photographers were nearly pushing themselves out of the way to get a picture of me because I ended the game prematurely because I read my watch wrong. The umpires told me afterwards that I didn't tog in for two hours. I don't remember it, but I remember my wife eventually coming into the dressing room and she was crying of course. We went to the Aisling Hotel and 'twas news time and I was flashed across the screen. The waitress looked at the screen, then looked at me. Before she said anything, I said: "That's me." I just wanted to get home. We had a young family and I knew there could be phone calls.

'There were lots of calls. If one of the girls answered they asked if their Daddy was a referee. When they said yes, they were told that their Daddy was going to be killed and their house was going to be burned down and if they didn't pass on the message they would be killed as well. When I got to the phone and offered to meet the callers face-to-face they hung up quickly. It would have lasted till Christmas and after that.'

The Offaly fans staged a sit-down protest after the game and Clare agreed to a second replay.

## FURY

When the final whistle blew, Ger Loughnane was raging, but not with Jimmy Cooney:

'When the game was over there was no sense of elation, except a sense of anger. The question in my mind was: Why the hell did the ref blow as Barry was going through? I said to Colm (Flynn), "What's he doing?" Colm said, "It's over." He started jumping up and down. I felt no sense of exhilaration. I was preparing to give the team the most ferocious bollocking in the dressing room for taking the foot off the pedal and allowing Offaly back into the game. Jimmy Cooney didn't deprive us of the All-Ireland that year, but he did deprive us of getting there.

'When we learned there had to be a second replay after the Jimmy Cooney saga, I thought to myself: Jesus, that's the last thing we want. We were beaten by Offaly in a terrific game. If ever the mental toughness of Clare was tested, it was against Offaly in that third game.

'Offaly had the hangman's noose around their neck – the next thing they found they were free. They woke up in the next world and they were alive. All of the cards were in their favour. Clare had won and were in the All-Ireland, but now not in the All-Ireland. Offaly had a massive psychological advantage.

'We were devastated by injuries. P.J. O'Connell was injured. Ollie Baker was injured. Liam Doyle was injured. Brian Quinn had suffered a blackout the previous Tuesday, which I didn't know about. Barry Murphy was injured.

'I thought we'd be trounced by Offaly. What Clare produced in the second half that day was really out of the top drawer. They did everything you could do when your last ounce of energy is drained out and your back is to the wall. They fought like lions and only three great saves by the Offaly goalie and we'd be in the All-Ireland. Lucky enough we weren't because Kilkenny would have beaten us in the final, no question about it.

'It was the day I was most proud of them in every way – with all the odds stacked against them and all the media stacked against them. Their manliness and courage against tiredness and injury was something to be cherished.'

# 45

# THE LIFE OF BRIAN

*Whelahan Misses Out on All-Star*

It was a selection howler of monumental proportions.

The late RTÉ Gaelic games correspondent Mick Dunne was the founder of the All-Stars. The awards did not come out of nowhere:

'The famous John Kerry O'Donnell of New York was a wonderful character. Back in the 1960s I was involved in selecting the team that would travel to New York to play in the Cardinal Cushing Games to raise money for the Cardinal's mission in Peru. It was almost the precursor of the All-Stars. We tried especially to pick some good players from the weaker counties. In fact, the former GAA President John Dowling always maintained that one of the reasons why Offaly eventually made the breakthrough in hurling was because of the boost it got when players like Paddy Molloy got one of these trips.'

For many years Dunne was secretary to the journalists who selected the All-Stars. The fruit of their deliberations often generated controversy – for their perceived sins of omission as much as their actual selection. Selecting the best fifteen often provoked passionate disagreements among the journalists in question:

'When he was president of the GAA, Pat Fanning said after seeing us picking the teams, "The amazing thing is that they are such good friends after a night fighting like this!"

'The president and director general of the GAA sat in as observers. The only time they ever intervened was if there was a tie over a particular position when somebody abstained. They then, having listened to all the arguments, went out of the room and decided who got the nod.'

Controversy erupted in 1985 when Paul Earley was chosen at full-forward on the All-Star football team ahead of Monaghan's Eamonn Murphy. An article was written by a prominent GAA personality in Monaghan which claimed that Earley was awarded the honour because he was an employee of the sponsoring bank. Was there an informal canvassing will disqualify policy in operation by Dunne?

'The accusation that the bank interfered in Paul's selection was totally wrong and very unfair to his abilities as a player. If they had tried to persuade us to pick Paul, it would have ensured that he wouldn't get the All-Star!

'The only time I ever got "approached" was when I got a phone call from a manager of a team the day before the team was picked. After a bit of casual conversation, he blatantly started talking up some of his players with a view to influencing my selection. I simply said, "It would be much better for their chances, Brian, if you didn't interfere in this way."'

## THE OFFALY ROVER

To a contemporary eye it is incredible that they were sponsored for many years by a cigarette company. Throughout their history the All-Stars have generated many controversies – sometimes

© Sportsfile/Piaras Ó Midheach

© Sportsfile/Eóin Noonan

**GOING BRAVELY WHERE NO WOMAN HAS GONE BEFORE:** Maggie Farrelly became the first woman to referee a men's County Final in 2021.

**ARE YOU SURE?**
Glen Rovers keeper Cathal Hickey isn't altogether convinced that it's a 65 for Midleton as tensions rise in the Cork Premier SHC 2021 final at Páirc Uí Chaoimh.

© Sportsfile/Ray McManus

## DADDY'S GIRL
Mayo's All Star defender-cum-everything Lee Keegan and 14-month-old daughter Líle examine the prize after Mayo claimed the Nestor Cup with the 2021 Connacht SFC final win over rivals Galway at Croke Park.

© INPHO/James Crombie

## THE GALWAY GIRLS

Galway's Shauna Healy has her hands full with god-daughter Ellen Burke after their 2021 All-Ireland Senior Camogie final win over Cork at Croke Park.

© Sportsfile/Brendan Moran

## THE FAB FOURS

Limerick's All-Ireland winners Barry Hennessy (and daughter Hope), Graeme Mulcahy (with daughter Róise), selector Paul Kinnerk (with daughter Enya) and Nickie Quaid (and son Dáithí) after the 2021 SHC final victory over Cork in Croke Park.

© Sportsfile/Piaras Ó Midheach

## HEAD ON

Eoin Cody of Kilkenny runs past the flying hurl of Liam Óg McGovern of Wexford on his way to scoring his side's first goal during the Leinster 2021 Hurling Senior Championship Semi-Final match between Kilkenny and Wexford at Croke Park.

© INPHO/Morgan Treacy

## THE MAN FROM CLARE

Clare's Colin Lynch was at the centre of a storm of controversy in 1998.

© Sportsfile/David Fitzgerald

## *CATCH OF THE DAY*
Cora Staunton of Carnacon in action against Roisin Flynn of Knockmore during the 2021 Mayo County Senior Club Ladies Football Final match between Carnacon and Knockmore at Kilmeena GAA Club in Mayo.

## NOSE JOB
Denis Walsh of Cork catches Nicky English of Tipperary on the nose in the 1990 Munster final.

## THE BRAWL
An altercation ensues between Meath and Mayo players early in the game which resulted in Meath's Colm Coyle and Mayo's Liam McHale being sent off by referee Pat McEnaney in the 1996 All-Ireland Football Final Replay.

## THE THROW-IN

Meath's Joe Sheridan bundles the ball over the line for Meath's controversial goal in injury time in the 2010 Leinster final.

### MIGHTY MAURICE

Kerry's Maurice Fitzgerald jumps with Cork's Mark O'Connor in the 1995 Munster final.

## WET. WET. WET.

Galway supporter Des Casey from Ballybane, Galway, left, shelters from the rain before the 2021 Connacht Football Senior Championship Semi-Final match between Roscommon and Galway at Dr Hyde Park in Roscommon.

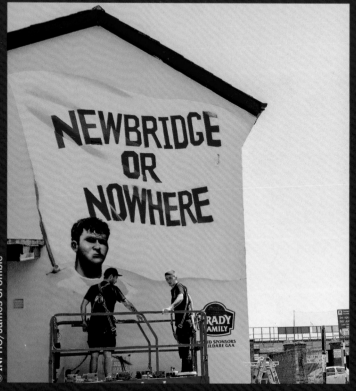

## WE SHALL NOT BE MOVED

A view of Newbridge ahead of the All-Ireland Senior Football Championship Qualifiers Round 3, St. Conleth's Park, in 2018.

for their inclusions, more often because of their omissions. The most jaw-dropping of all came in 1994.

Brian Whelahan was chosen as Hurler of the Year that year as Offaly won an unforgettable All-Ireland with a dramatic late flourish to beat Limerick. A few years later, Whelahan would be the only hurler of his generation to be chosen on the official Team of the Millennium. Yet, in the year of his life, he lost out on an All-Star award.

Amid an understandable concern to ensure that there were no 'leaks' and have the hurling selection announced 'live' on RTÉ's coverage of the All-Star night, the side was selected by secret ballot. Whelahan's main rival for the wing-back position was Limerick's Dave Clarke, but since both had played on the right, one of them would have to be accommodated in the left half-back position. Clarke was selected on the right-half slot, with presumably the selectors assuming Whelahan would get the number seven. While an Offaly player was selected as the number seven, it was Kevin Martin not Whelahan.

# 46

# NOT HAVING YOUR CAKE

*Shane Curran's Penalty*

His inter-county career began and ended in controversy.

Throughout the long history of the GAA few things have generated as much controversy as referees. People understand that referees will make mistakes but what really annoys them, though, is their inconsistencies. While the standard of refereeing has improved considerably in recent years there is still a long way to go. The GAA could stop worrying about minor offences and concentrate instead on ensuring that the rules of all the game are applied consistently by all referees.

Sometimes, though, it is not the referee's fault. There is nothing in their manual to prepare them for the stunts that some players will produce. A case in point was former Roscommon goalkeeper Shane Curran.

## A TALE OF THE UNEXPECTED

The GAA needs characters. Shane 'Cake' Curran is certainly one of them.

Curran first exploded on to the national consciousness in the

1989 Connacht minor football final. Roscommon trailed Galway by two points when they were awarded a penalty in the last minute. Peadar Glennon, corner-forward with the Rossies, placed the ball on the spot and stepped to take the kick. Out of the blue, Shane raced forward and blasted the ball past the Galway goalie. There was chaos. Roscommon were presented with the cup but subsequently had the game taken away in the smoky GAA corridors of power. Eventually the Rossies won the replay ordered by the Connacht Council.

## THE END GAME

Shane's intercounty career controversially ended not with a bang but with a whimper when John Maughan took charge of the Rossies in 2006. After two and a half seasons under Tommy Carr, Maughan was in the mood for change, much to Curran's chagrin:

'For some reason, people weren't happy with Tommy. I could never figure it out. I knew myself from the inside he was doing a brilliant job. He was removed as manager with two or three games to go in the League and I just felt we never recovered momentum after that. 2005 petered out with a defeat to Louth and that was the end of that season. We weren't to know it, but it was the end of numerous inter-county careers. I remember vividly Sharon [his wife] coming in with the *Roscommon Champion* as it was at the time [saying], "Famous five have been dropped by new Roscommon manager." What was put out to the general populous was basically that there were five troublemakers being let go. The county board never corrected the record which was wrong.'

# 47

## MONEY. MONEY. MONEY

*GPA Make Groundbreaking Deal with Marlborough*

I was brought up with a reverence for 'the prince of midfielders', Derry's Jim McKeever. One of the stories Jim told me lives in my memory:

'In 1965 I was selected as one of the fourteen hurlers and footballers to be guest players in the Cardinal Cushing Games in New York, Hartford and Boston. The games were important to our hosts and to Irish-American spectators and we played them seriously, but it was the off-field events which were memorable. The highlight of the New York part of our tour was being greeted individually in Gaelic Park by Bobby Kennedy, who was at that time electioneering in New York. His brother, the president, had been assassinated two years earlier, and it was impossible not to sense a vulnerability and an exceptionalism in the presence of this small man.

'As a postscript to the tour, I learned on my return that the Ministry of Education in Belfast had refused to allow me time off to travel and deducted fourteen days' salary which included two Saturdays and two Sundays. When many years later I retired, they further informed me that I had lost fourteen days pension contribution and for years I have been a little poorer each month. In "our day" we really were amateurs and I have no regrets. The genuine friendships, the integrity of not being a "bought" sportsman and the rich, irreplaceable memories are ample compensation.'

I thought of Jim when I heard a deal that brought the GAA where it never had gone before. Crossing this 'brave new world' would generate anxieties for many of its traditional supporters.

In 2009, the GAA celebrated its 125th anniversary. Fr Harry Bohan stated: 'All through its existence the GAA has been bound up with a sense of place, belonging and a sense of community. This has bonded people together and given people stability. Today we live in a cloud of instability and confusion. We have witnessed a loss of trust in institutions, spiralling unemployment, the continuing collapse of culture shaped by consumerism and borrowing. If we are to bring stability and security to our own lives, we will need to redicover a sense of place and take pride in who we are and the culture that shapes us. Without a vision people die.'

Mick O'Dwyer claims: 'When I played, we got a piece of orange at half-time, and, if you were very quick, you might get two.' Those days are long gone.

As manager of Roscomon in 1993, Dermot Earley saw a more mercenary attitude on the part of some players:

'Just before the Connacht final in 1993, our County Secretary, Paddy Francis Dwyer, God rest his soul, had purchased a new set of jerseys for the team. The first two jerseys he took out had no numbers on them. For a moment there was panic. What would we do with without numbered jerseys? Then we discovered the unnumbered jerseys were just spares. Things got back to normal. Shortly afterwards, I noticed that one of the players was trying to sneak an unnumbered jersey into his kitbag and that another player was trying to act as a screen for him. I found myself in a dilemma: should I intervene and risk the players going out to play a Connacht final in a state of disharmony, or do nothing? I opted for the latter. The loss of two jerseys was insignificant in itself but, looking back now, it speaks volumes about their focus and commitment less than half an hour before playing in a Connacht final.'

## NEW FRONTIERS

As major sponsorship deals filled the GAA's coffers, the question of pay for play would inevitably present itself with ever-increasing urgency. 2000 saw a defining moment in the history of the GAA. For years, there have been rumblings about moves to professionalism in Gaelic games. Then it seemed that the genie was out of the bottle, with the groundbreaking announcement that the Gaelic Players Association had secured a major sponsorship deal with the Marlborough Recruitment Group for ten prominent players, including Brian Whelahan, Brian Corcoran, Ja Fallon and Peter Canavan. They were to pocket £4,000 each for four commitments to the company each year with the remaining £10,000 going to the GPA directly.

Was this a seismic shift and the first step towards pay for play? Or was it, as its critics claimed, an elitist deal that would only benefit the privileged few and do nothing for the impoverished many?

Hell is a lesson learned too late. Although amateurism in rugby apparently ended abruptly, the reality was that the cracks had been there for years and widened every season. The two big questions which the Marlborough deal raised were: Would it invariably threaten the GAA's core philosophy? Could the amateur ethos be sustained? Gaelic games remained the last bastion of amateurism among the major sports in Ireland. It did not take a prophet to appreciate that, after the deal, the GAA's unique position would come under serious attack in the coming years.

One of the GPA's two most vocal and persistent critics (with Colm O'Rourke), Joe Brolly said of the deal: 'Elitism has replaced participation and a once healthy ethos has been corrupted.' Such elitism, he argued, created a focus on a minority and this created an 'unhealthy pressure' on players.

Brolly went on to bemoan the fact that the only time a top inter-county player makes themselves available for interviews today is when a commercial company hires them for promotional work – a practice he stated that was 'as tacky as the child in the beauty pageant'. That was just his polite warm-up for his criticism of the GPA which he described as 'a nasty, money-grabbing little cartel that has come to dominate the county game'.

In 2022, the GAA found itself again in dispute with its inter-county players' representatives over limits on centrally-funded training expenses, which the GPA claimed was leaving some players out of pocket.

# 48

## DONKEYS DON'T WIN DERBIES

*The 1990 Munster Final*

With typical reserve, Nicky English makes no mention of an incident in the 1991 All-Ireland semi-final against Galway when he was struck a little below the left eye, which might have caused him permanent eye injury, but which required nine stitches and caused a flow of blood with the intensity of the Niagara Falls. Despite repeated nudges, no comments on the incident are supplied:

'We won the All-Ireland again in '91 and it was important to us that we beat Kilkenny in the final because there were those who devalued our win in '89 because it was Antrim we beat and not one of the powers of the hurling. Of course, that's very unfair on Antrim but we had to show to the hurling world that we were worthy of a place at hurling's top table. My hamstring went in that year, and I came back too soon for the semi-final against Galway, and it went again. It went a third time because I didn't make it through the final. I think, although we won the All-Ireland, the injuries were starting to catch up and although we won the Munster title in '93 and a League in '94 we never could scale those heights again.'

Nicky is keen to defend Babs from one long-running criticism. Keating's comments that, 'You can't win derbies with donkeys', before Tipperary played Cork in the 1990 Munster final, was seen as a spectacular own goal when the Cork donkeys won:

'We did make mistakes in terms of selection for that match. I think after we won the All-Ireland in '89, our first in eighteen years, we coasted a bit and never had the same application as the previous year. We went to Toronto for a week in March to play the All-Stars and that was another distraction. When Cork beat us, Babs was blamed for his remarks. People said that because it suited them. It might have been used as a motivational tool in Cork, but it was not the reason we lost. Cork were hungrier than us and that was the crucial difference.'

Babs addressed his controversial comments for me head on: 'It was a stupid remark and no more that. It was used against us that year. We were decimated with injuries. It was a bluff game with us. We had no sub for the backline with injuries. We took a chance with Declan Ryan at full-forward, even though he was lifting bales with his father the day before and he just wasn't fit to hurl. Mark Foley got three goals that day and he never played liked that before or since.'

# 49

## THE DOCTOR'S DILEMMA

*Mick Loftus Opposes Guinness Sponsorship of GAA*

Sport has always been inextricably linked with the wider culture and has always had massive cultural implications in Ireland. Witness John Montague's incisive observation: 'The Protestant boys played cricket or kicked a queer-shaped ball like a pear. According to my Falls pal, Protestant balls bounced crooked as the Protestants themselves.'

In recent decades there has also been controversy in Ireland about the GAA's policy of accepting sponsorship from alcohol companies. The former President of the GAA, Dr Mick Loftus, has been a persistent critic of this position. Dr Loftus announced that he would not attend an All-Ireland hurling final again until the Guinness sponsorship of the hurling championship ended. Rugby too has been heavily sponsored by drink companies.

Sponsorship always raises potential ethical questions. Is it appropriate, for example, that crime programmes are sponsored by insurance companies who may have a vested interest in hyping people's fears about crime? However, there are particular ethical issues involved in sponsorship raised by alcohol companies. Alcohol abuse is one of the biggest social problems in the country. No drug has caused more damage to Irish families than alcohol. There is an ever-growing mountain of statistical evidence to show that alcohol consumption is widespread among teenagers and even pre-teens. Of course, the Guinness sponsorship of the hurling championship did not force young people to drink alcohol. Yet it would be naive in the extreme to think that executives of alcohol companies would fork out huge sums of money on sports sponsorship unless they were convinced that it would lead to a significant increase in their sales.

## THE DEMON DRINK

Pat Gilroy feels that sponsorship is not the only drink-related issue that the GAA needs to confront among its own members:

'Unfortunately, some of our stars of the past and indeed of the present have struggled with addictions like gambling, but the biggest problem has been with drink. Status can become like a drug and people are often not prepared for the end of their career. There are some terribly sad stories in the GAA. We are great at talking about some character and saying, "He was some man to drink", but then he is dead at fifty. This is not good enough and we must work much harder to try and change that culture, though I know the GPA is already doing some good work in this area.

'There is no question that if induction to drinking at a young age continues, harms in later life will be inevitable and I think ultimately the GAA will be the loser. I understand the financial imperatives for the Association but we also need to be mindful to our wider obligations to society.'

## OUT. OUT. OUT

As Clare manager, Ger Loughnane was aware of the potential for drink to be a corrosive influence on his squad:

'We never made a rule about drinking or eating. The players always knew that they could have a few drinks and that was it. One night going into training, coming up to a big Munster Championship match, we found out that one of the panelists had been out drinking the night before. Not alone was he drinking but he was drinking heavily. It was just not on. Every player knew the boundaries and that there were certain lines you did not cross. All the other players knew he'd been drinking and were keenly awaiting our reaction. I heard the news as I was going in the gate, and I decided immediately in my own mind he was going off the panel. I decided that before we would drop him, we were going to punish him.

'We went out on the field on a roasting, roasting evening and had a hard hurling session. After this, we decided we were going to do ten 200-metre sprints back-to-back. Up and down they went. The sweat was pouring out of the man who had been drinking and he was gasping. After the ninth sprint he couldn't run any more. I pulled him over and I said, "You were out drinking last night."

'He replied, "Oh I was but there was . . ."

'"I'm not talking about other people . . ."

'"Yeah, I was."

'"You're off the panel . . ."

'Cruel? Maybe, but that's the way it was. I wasn't happy just to let him go. I wanted him to see that this was a betrayal of his comrades and everyone else. A thing like this could not be tolerated. It also sent out a strong signal to everybody else.

'Fear had nothing to do with it. I would say a lot of players feared me. No doubt about it, but you don't motivate anybody through fear any more. A leader is someone who has willing followers not fearful followers. In an amateur game you wouldn't get fearful followers because they won't stay.

'At the same time, everybody knew they must produce the goods. Somehow the players found the contentment in that set-up. Any time we came across a huge obstacle or a big challenge there was always electricity between the players. It was like an electrical charge and you wanted to be in the middle of it. You felt totally energised by it. The players felt a confidence that they were indestructible. They'd face a firing squad and they wouldn't care, but they'd go out and do everything for Clare to win. I had to be prepared to do the same for Clare and take whatever tough decisions were necessary.'

# 50

## MICKO'S SNUB

*O'Dwyer Never Manages Ireland*

If at first you don't succeed, try again. Pat Spillane is a good illustration of that principle. It did not happen for him initially:

'We all make mistakes. After I qualified as a teacher and was established as a Kerry player, I wrote to RTÉ Sport, applying for a job. After weeks I was dismayed and bewildered that I did not receive a request for an interview. Finally, six months later I received a message from RTÉ that explained the reason I hadn't heard from them. It read: "Your CV was not attached as stated. I do, however, want to thank you for the Kerry match programme."'

Since his retirement as a player Spillane has become one of the best-known faces on Irish television as a pundit on *The Sunday Game*. Over the last thirty years there is one controversy he has consistently brought into the public domain:

'One constant is my perpetual bewilderment that Mick O'Dwyer has never been appointed manager of the Irish team for a Compromise Rules series against Australia. Why those in power constantly overlooked him is a bigger mystery than the third secret of Fatima.

'Could it be that there was GAA politics involved? I have heard people in Kerry wondering aloud: was there some horse-trading for votes in the GAA presidential election going on? I'm not making any accusations because these decisions are made in secret and, to quote Paul Brady: "The answer is nobody knows."

'Mind you, there are a lot of Kerry people who have their suspicions. When he was the chairman of the Kerry County Board, Seán Kelly was the most vocal critic when Micko was overlooked for the manager's job on previous occasions. When he became the first Kerry president of the GAA every one of us thought that at long last that oversight was going to be corrected. Not so. Seán, everyone in Kerry wants to know why O'Dwyer did not get the job? So, come out and give us an answer. Is it because he was not the best man for the job? If so, come out and say so. Tell us what more he needs to achieve before he is worthy of this honour.

'One of the biggest changes in the world of the GAA over the last thirty years has been the prominence of the manager. It began in the 1970s with Kevin Heffernan and Mick O'Dwyer. Without Heffernan and O'Dwyer, who knows what Gaelic football management might have been and, without the rivalry between their two counties that ignited the GAA in the '70s, it is doubtful if Gaelic games would enjoy the same profile as they do today.

'Micko was very, very disappointed when he was passed over as the manager of Ireland's first team for the Compromise Rules series against Australia. Instead, the job was given to Kevin Heffernan. O'Dwyer was also disappointed when the team captain for that series, "one of his own", Jack O'Shea, publicly praised Heffo. Kevin did an excellent job. I don't want to take that away from him. O'Dwyer, though, was very hurt when he did not get the job and he was repeatedly passed over many times since.'

# 51

## MATT-ER OF FACT

*Ruth's Controversial Goal*

The German philosopher Friedrich Nietzsche (1844–1900) said, 'Without music, life would be a mistake.' Had he known hurling intimately, he would surely have said the same about the beautiful game.

Matt Ruth's Kilkenny team of the '70s is considered one of the greatest of all time with players like Pat Delaney at centre-forward, Frank Cummins in midfield, Pat Henderson at centre half-back, Eddie Keher prowling with menace near the opposition posts and Noel Skehan in goal. However, Ruth carved a unique place in hurling folklore when he scored perhaps the most infamous goal in hurling history.

In the 1982 Leinster final there was nothing to choose between Kilkenny and the reigning All-Ireland champions, Offaly. Then comes one of the most controversial umpiring decisions in the annals of the GAA.

A long ball is sent in from the Kilkenny defence. The Offaly goalkeeper Damien Martin advances to shield the sliotar as it goes harmlessly wide. Martin is absolutely certain the sliotar is out over the line. Kilkenny's Liam Fennelly is advancing rapidly and swings his hurley – making a sweet contact and sending the sliotar across the goal where the ever-vigilant Matt Ruth has an empty net to aim at. He does not miss.

Martin cannot believe his eyes when he sees the umpire raising the green flag. His incredulity is genuine. It is in no sense an attempt to put the blame on somebody else for an error of judgement, but the indignation of a man who feels he has been the victim of a travesty of justice. He will go to his gave with 100 per cent certainty that the umpire made a terrible blunder.

It is the turning point of the game. Kilkenny win the match and go on to win the first of two back-to-back All-Ireland titles. But was their '82 Leinster title based on an error of judgement by an umpire? Inevitably, this was the main area of discussion when I spoke to Matt Ruth about the incident. As we talked during Wimbledon fortnight it was understandable that he should use a tennis analogy to explain the circumstances of the umpire's difficult decision:

'If you watch Wimbledon and see the speed at which the ball travels you will notice that both the umpire and the line-judge have all these fancy electronic gadgets to help them make the right decision, but still there are many times when the players think they have bad decisions made against them. The ball is hitting the line at such speed that it can be virtually impossible at times to say with absolute certainty if a ball is in or out. The same thing can happen in hurling.

'I know Damien Martin is totally sincere when he says the ball was out. I can't say for sure myself, it all happened so fast. All I can say is that Liam Fennelly doesn't think it was out. Nobody else but Liam could have pulled it off. He is left-handed and he hit the ball at an angle that virtually no other hurler would have done to get the ball across to me. I know that is very difficult to explain to someone who doesn't know Liam's style of hurling and his wrist action in particular. It probably sounds very technical, but I think that is probably the reason why he was able to get the ball across the line even though it seemed he had no chance of saving it. The use of video evidence in GAA matches came too late to resolve this controversy.'

# 52

## WHITEWASHED

*Kerry Undress for Bendix*

They were a team of stars.

Ger Canning tells a lovely story of how, at the height of their fame, which coincided with the peak of Maradona's popularity in the mid-1980s he watched some boys starting a game on a field in a housing estate. The first boy shouted: 'I'll be Maradona.' The second said: 'I'll be Jacko.' It was a small indication of the mass appeal Mick O'Dwyer's great Kerry team had. Not surprisingly, commercial companies wanted to surf on the wave of their popularity.

Pat Spillane has repeatedly said that you could write O'Dwyer's tactics on a postage stamp. In 1964, the great Joe Lennon published a book called *Coaching Gaelic Football for Champions*. Mick O'Dwyer made a point of not reading it. It didn't seem to do him any harm.

Spillane has also often professed his admiration for Micko's ability to recognise an opportunity to make a few quid. Hence the decision to accept £5,000 and the controversy about the Kerry team's infamous *Only Bendix Could Whitewash This Lot* advertisement. On the morning of the All-Ireland final in 1985, two Sunday newspapers carried full-page ads which showed several Kerry players in a state of undress as they posed around a washing machine.

Given the GAA's strict amateur ethos at the time, it was seen as a betrayal. One critic claimed that: 'It was the start of the slippery slope on the journey towards professionalism.' Another mused: 'Are the shades of Kerry to be polluted in this way?'

# 53

# SAM LOST IN THE LAND OF UNCLE SAM

*Sam Goes Missing*

It threatened to be a huge embarrassment for the GAA. Jimmy Deenihan has the inside story:

'In 1980, my club Feale Rangers won the Kerry County Championship. To celebrate we decided we would go on an American tour to Pittsburgh and New York. I was organising the trip and didn't want to bring the Sam Maguire Cup, but I was persuaded to do so. Pittsburgh Steelers had won the Super Bowl the previous year and another Pittsburgh side, the Pirates, won the World Series. Two of the most prestigious trophies in the world would be in the one city. Tom O'Donoghue felt it would be a good idea to have those two trophies photographed with the Sam Maguire Cup.

'We were staying in the Abbey-Victoria hotel next to Rosie O'Grady's pub in Manhattan initially. We had a function on the Saturday night before playing a game the next day in Gaelic Park. Everybody wanted to see The Sam so I reluctantly brought it along. We left the cup in the safe in Gaelic Park. It was a big strong one.

'The following morning, I got a phone call informing me that one of our travelling party had been involved in a serious accident. I went to see him in the hospital. I only got back to the ground in time for our match against the famous Ardboe club from Tyrone. I had to go back to the hospital after the match. I returned for the cup that night. The watchman told me that someone had come for the cup already, but no one knew who he was.

'We had to go to Pittsburgh for our match at Pittsburgh Steelers' ground. There were a lot of dignitaries there, all the leading politicians etc., and former Steelers' stars like Rocky Blair. Everybody was full of expectation. It was a total anticlimax when we arrived without the cup.

'I went back to New York on the Thursday to take up the matter with the local police. Initially they didn't take much notice but when they saw newspaper reports from Ireland, they realised its importance and carried out investigations. I was due home to play a National League semi-final against Galway. I stayed on to get the matter sorted out because obviously it would have been terribly embarrassing for me to have returned without the cup. It would have been a national scandal.

'Eventually I was told if I turned up in Gaelic Park on Monday, I would find it waiting for me. I did but never bothered to find out who had taken it. The cup was scratched and the words, "Up the IRA. Up Roscommon" were inscribed, though I suspect that the person involved was a sympathiser of neither. The irony was that six months later I received the cup when I captained Kerry to the All-Ireland final.'

# 54

## MAYO'S CRASH CURSE

*Mayo Bewitched*

Nothing lasts.

That is one of life's harsh truths.

Yet for over seventy years now, Mayo fans have reasons to question it.

Hope can be like hair – something a lot of men lose as they grow older. Not so Seán Flanagan. He captained Mayo to All-Ireland titles in both 1950 and '51.

Mayo's full-back on that team was Paddy Prendergast. His conversation drew you to him like a warm fire in a blizzard:

'I remember the joy was unconfined after the game. People don't realise how different Ireland was back then. We were on our knees in economic terms. The GAA made an awful difference to people at such a black time. The bonfires that blazed after we won were a sign that people could still have hope.'

Another All-Ireland came in 1951 but legend has it that it was then that the seeds of Mayo's woes were sown for decades to come, as Paddy Prendergast explained to me:

'People tell it slightly differently, but the core story is that when we returned with the Sam Maguire Cup in 1951, we interrupted either a Mass or a funeral and the priest was so enraged that he put a curse on the team that we would never win the All-Ireland again while any of that team were on earth.'

## THAT TAKES THE BISCUIT

Former star player David Brady confidently tweeted on the morning of the 2021 All-Ireland final that this was going to be their year as the green and red faced Tyrone. It was nothing but the same old story and Mayo's tale of woe continued. Afterwards a sarcastic Galway fan had a new riddle.

Q: What do you call the new biscuit they are making in Mayo?

A: Sammy Dodgers.

# 55

# CAVAN'S FAIRY TALE OF NEW YORK

*The Polo Grounds Final*

The 1947 All-Ireland final was held in New York as a gesture of goodwill by the GAA to the Irish people in America. Once it was announced it aroused great interest in every county. To get there was a great prize in itself. The teams left Cobh together for a six-day trip on the *SS Mauritania* to New York, after getting their vaccinations against smallpox, which were compulsory at the time. The fact that it was the first final played abroad gave it a much more exotic quality, so it really grabbed the public imagination.

However, the decision to play the final in the Big Apple was shrouded in controversy. There were all kinds of tricks going on behind the scenes to make this event possible. A breathtaking series of hair-raising machinations behind closed doors, involving moral blackmail, bribery of a kind, intimidation and blatant lie-telling, allowed this event to happen. Locating the 1947 All-Ireland final in the Polo Grounds was one of the great achievements of Canon Michael Hamilton's career. Initially, almost everyone seemed implacably opposed to the project.

Machiavelli himself would have admired the 'promptings' behind the scenes that finally persuaded a controversial Central Council meeting at Barry's Hotel that it was worth carrying through. Folklore abounds of how Milltown Mallbay's Bob Fitzpatrick's passionate speech to congress, complemented by the prop of a tear-stained handkerchief, swung the vote as he read from a bogus 'emigrant's letter'.

Pat Spillane has an insider's guide to the Kerry perspective:

'New York and the All-Ireland Championship hold special significance for my family. My late uncle Dinny Lyne captained Kerry in the famous 1947 All-Ireland final played in the Polo Grounds in New York. It was the only decider ever to be played outside Ireland. More than 34,000 thronged the Polo Grounds to watch Cavan beat Kerry by 2–11 to 2–7. It was probably the only time players had to endure temperatures over thirty degrees during an All-Ireland final.

'Preparation is the key to success in sport. In 1947, Cavan got it right – they travelled by plane from Ireland. The journey took thirty hours as they had to go via the Azores. Kerry opted to go by boat. It was a much longer, more arduous and tiring journey. This took its toll on match day. As with Tyrone in 2021, whoever said Kerry were cute hoors?

'Until the day he died, my uncle Dinny got angry when he talked about the game. He vehemently argued that refereeing decisions cost Kerry the match. He used to say to me: "If *The Sunday Game* was around in 1947, you would have had a field day highlighting the refereeing mistakes."'

### THE VOICE

The match itself almost provoked a controversy of its own. Micheál O'Hehir famously had the surreal experience of appealing over the airwaves to the New York telecommunications people not to cut off the commentary. This caused mild panic at home in Ireland as people listening on RTÉ radio thought they were going to miss the climax of the game.

# PART III
# Power to All Our Friends

*'Politics is the art of looking for trouble, finding it whether it exists or not, diagnosing it incorrectly, and applying the wrong remedies.'*

ERNEST BENN

We all walk with ghosts.

The first politician I ever had a serious conversation with was Jack Lynch. I asked him about how he became involved in politics:

'The Fianna Fáil approach prior to the 1946 by-election came from members of the Brothers Delaney Cumann in Blackpool. The brothers Delaney, who were from Dublin Hill, were killed during the Civil War. The Fianna Fáil members who approached me were Maurice Forde, Pat McNamara, Bill Barry and Garrett McAuliffe. They called to our small flat in Summerhill. However, a friend of mine, "Pa" McGrath, who had been a life-long member of Fianna Fáil was seeking the nomination and I wasn't going to stand against him. I told the delegation from the Brothers Delaney Cumann that I wouldn't seek a nomination on this occasion, but perhaps next time.

'My first overt political involvement was at a meeting during that by-election campaign in Blackpool Bridge, where I made my first political speech. I confined myself solely to extolling the virtues of "Pa" McGrath. He won the by-election easily. From 1946 to 1948, I had no active political involvement at all, but prior to the 1948 general election, members of the Brothers Delaney Cumann approached me again and I was also approached by Tom Crofts, the Chairman of the Comhairle Ceantar. This time I allowed my name to go forward. I didn't go to the convention as there was a law dinner on the same night. During the dinner in the Metropole Hotel, I was informed that I had been selected and was asked to go to the courthouse to accept the nomination, which I did, clad in dinner jacket. I hadn't formally joined Fianna Fáil at the time of being nominated, but I was one of four candidates selected.'

When I asked him what he thought of the politics of the GAA, he paused and puffed on his pipe before replying: 'A constant source of conflict.'

This section vindicates his judgement.

# 56

## WHINE OF DUTY

*Counties Breach Covid Rules*

They were like a bat out of lockdown.

We used to live in a world where being a close contact was a good thing; to give someone the elbow was akin to ignoring; Delta was an airline; we worried about who was in hospital and not how many and if you walked into a bank wearing a mask you put yourself in serious jeopardy. Covid-19 changed all that.

In March 2021, Dublin suspended senior football manager Dessie Farrell for twelve weeks after footage showed members of the All-Ireland winning panel involved in drills at Innisfails GAA in the north of the county. Dublin GAA said it was a 'serious error of judgement' and followed on from two other high-profile breaches of GAA guidelines earlier that year.

After the Dublin training session came to light, GAA President Larry McCarthy said any further breaches could affect the return to inter-county activity. However, a week later, Monaghan GAA admitted a breach of Covid-19 regulations after it was discovered some members of their senior inter-county team took part in a group training session. The Monaghan

County Board investigated the matter after it was reported that a dossier detailing the breach was sent to several different parties, including the Department of Justice. The video, as well as photographic evidence, seemed to show Monaghan footballers engaged in a training session.

A statement from Monaghan GAA said that manager Séamus McEnaney had admitted that this was a serious error of judgement and apologised unreservedly for the indiscretion. The county's management committee suspended McEnaney for twelve weeks with immediate effect and said they would fully cooperate and comply with any Croke Park investigation. An Garda Síochána confirmed it was making enquiries into the alleged breaches of Covid regulations while the GAA undertook to investigate the matter fully.

Previously, Down manager Paddy Tally was given an eight-week ban after members of the Down football panel were found training in Newry by the PSNI. The Down County Board did not appeal the decision, whereas Cork football manager Ronan McCarthy was handed a twelve-week ban, which he unsuccessfully appealed, after bringing his squad to a beach in Youghal for a team-building exercise.

GAA President Larry McCarthy said: 'I think it has done us reputational damage, which we're going to have to work to get back. There's no appetite for any breaches in society at the moment. So, undoubtedly it has. But we'll continue to work to get that confidence back from the public again.'

He confirmed that the GAA launched their own investigation into the Monaghan incident. The reaction to the Dublin breach, in particular, was generally negative. Seán Boylan, who himself suffered a major ordeal while battling Covid-19, said: 'I don't want to be tearing people down. But it baffles me what they did. Maybe I'm saying that as someone who suffered with Covid.

And it is such a thief. It really is. I lost ten kilos in six days and developed pneumonia so I'm very thankful and blessed to have made a great recovery but only after I suffered post-traumatic stress. I can understand the boredom and the feeling of wanting to get out, but this really shocked me.'

Former GAA President Seán Kelly said: 'I'm almost gobsmacked that such wonderful athletes and wonderful County Board would have engaged with this when there was no real need. To hear this happened is disappointing, and especially so soon after the GAA itself wrote to club and county secretaries outlining what was going to happen. They said it was more important now than ever to observe the rules because it could put the entire process of reopening for the GAA in jeopardy.'

Former All-Star footballer and Fine Gael T.D. for Mayo Alan Dillon added: 'I was really shocked when I saw it. In the GAA world Dublin are revered all over the country and they deserve all the plaudits, but the country has been through hell. This was a premeditated breach of rules that are there to protect people. The training session should have never taken place. I have some sympathy for the players themselves, they are athletes, they enjoy training. But if Dublin management are organising training, then players have been placed in a very difficult position given the ultra-competitive nature of the Dublin football. The guidelines are that no activities can take place on any GAA grounds. It's very, very disappointing.

'We're talking about the best GAA team that ever took to the field. We were at the highest level of restrictions and the reason is simple: to help people stay out of hospital and save lives. For a team of this calibre to blatantly disregard the guidelines is a kick in the stomach for a lot of our frontline workers who have sacrificed so much.'

Former Roscommon goalkeeper Shane Curran said: 'The Dubs are seen to be this "holier than thou" organisation and now they have been caught with their pants around their socks. But, really, I'd say everybody else is doing it.'

A month later, Dublin's Dean Rock would say: 'It was certainly a regrettable incident, and something that we deeply regret. We are obviously very apologetic about it. Look, we learned a lot of lessons from it. That's the thing, it was a mistake that we have acknowledged and accepted, taken our lessons from it, learned from it and moved on, and we look forward to the season ahead. But I think a big lesson for us is there are far more important things in life than sport and Gaelic football.'

## TWO KERRY VIEWS

Pat Spillane was dismayed:

'Ireland is a world leader in what the late, great, John Hume called "whataboutery". Discovering loopholes and bending the rules is part of our DNA. Rules are rules – and in this case, they look as if they have been broken. The previous year, when county Championship celebrations got out of hand and Covid rates spiked, the GAA acted swiftly and closed the club season. By doing so they saved the All-Ireland series.

'In relation to the Dublin incident, we don't know whether the training session was sanctioned by the team management. The Dublin training session included several of the All-Ireland-winning team. The regulations are full of loopholes. But, let's be clear: the "everybody is doing it" line is not a defence.

'The optics couldn't be worse. As a lifelong and passionate GAA man the incident has made me mad as hell. I'm very disappointed and feel I've been let down by those Dublin players. Fewer than twelve hours earlier a road map had been provided for the return of inter-county training. What the players did was against the rules of both the GAA and the government. Effectively, they were giving the two fingers to both organisations. This training session came on the same day as NPHET warned of the possibility of a fourth wave of Covid-19 and the need for extra vigilance over the next four weeks.

'We expect our role models to show us a good example. The Dublin footballers have been exemplary role models for a decade, but they let a lot of people down by their actions. Dessie Farrell was suspended for twelve weeks following the revelations. This was a massive blow to the GAA who were trying to get the new season up and running. It was a spectacular own goal as it provided canon fodder for the GAA's many critics on social media to lambast the Association. It's a bit like the brightest boy in the class suddenly being caught cheating, or you suddenly realise that the local parish priest has a wife and family in the next county.'

Tomás Ó Sé was more nuanced in his reaction: 'Five years from now, how will we remember these days? How will history frame the extremism of today, the appetite for sanctimony, the taste for demonising people. If I'm honest, I'm torn by a lot of what I'm witnessing. I can find myself questioning the stupidity of Dessie Farrell and Séamus "Banty" McEnaney, while, at the same time, feeling deeply uncomfortable with what feels like the virtual criminalisation of amateur athletes out training in a field.'

Later that year, Dublin GAA chief John Costello expressed his displeasure with the media commentary: 'The tone, at times, was one of "these lads should be arraigned for treason" and that they were guilty of burgling the bank of youth from the young citizens of the country.'

## BANNER BAN

Covid regulations spawned a new controversy in May 2021 after two Wexford hurlers tested positive. Then, to the surprise of many people in Clare and beyond, the HSE identified as close contacts two members of the Clare team who marked the Wexford players the previous weekend, obliging them to undertake tests (both were negative) and restrict their movements for two weeks. No Wexford players were considered close contacts, while both Clare players were stood down from the Banner's game against Laois as a precaution.

The Clare camp was puzzled by a number of elements. Of course, the critical question was: who named the two Clare players?

Clare manager Brian Lohan said: 'In one instance, in particular, where a substitute came on for Wexford, he named one of our players as a close contact so I find it very unusual that that would be the case. But, certainly, there was a whole lot of anger amongst our set-up as a result of what happened.'

The next day, Wexford chairman Micheál Martin branded Lohan's claim that two Wexford players who tested positive for Covid-19 identified members of his Clare squad as close contacts to the HSE as 'ill informed', 'outrageous' and 'hurtful'. He called on Lohan to retract his comments.

## CUTE HOORS

Later that year, a new controversy emerged when Tyrone were granted two postponements before fronting up to play Kerry in the All-Ireland semi-final. Before the game RTÉ pundits Pat Spillane and Seán Cavanagh engaged in a feisty clash over the Covid-19 cases in the Tyrone camp that resulted in the rescheduling of the All-Ireland semi-final. So intense were the fireworks that when Ciarán Whelan finally got to contribute he observed: 'If it's as tense out there as it is up here, it'll be brilliant!'

Spillane questioned Cavanagh about the reasons behind the postponement: 'You talk about anger and you talk about people not knowing facts, of course people don't know facts because no one has told us anything. When you have a vacuum of information as there was from the Tyrone camp. There was a vacuum of information. Into that vacuum comes misinformation, false narratives, innuendo, and that's what you got.

'Kerry have a reputation of being cute hoors, it is something we have earned over years – that tag of "cute hoor". But when you see another crowd acting the cute hoor and being even better at it than us, that was Tyrone. I'll tell you what Tyrone did. Tyrone played an absolute blinder. They called the GAA's bluff. They called Kerry's bluff. They played a game of poker. They hurled a grenade in and the GAA blinked. Kerry blinked.'

# 57

## STRIKING IT BIG

*The First Cork Hurlers Strike*

It is part of the GAA vernacular to say: 'This was a game of two halves.' The story of the Cork hurling strikes is to use a Tommy Tiernanism: a story of three halves.

In 2002, Cork hurling descended into chaos after all thirty members of the senior panel withdrew their services from the county, refusing to train or play again until their treatment from the county board improved.

Seven members of panel: Joe Deane, Mark Landers, Dónal Óg Cusack, Seán Óg Ó hAilpín, Alan Browne, Diarmuid O'Sullivan and Fergal Ryan gathered in Cork's Imperial Hotel to outline the reasons for their action on the same night as the All-Star banquet, the biggest night of the GAA calendar.

In a statement, signed by the entire panel, the reasons were explained as to why the players would not play or train again until the dispute was resolved:

'We the Cork senior hurling panel for 2002 wish to advise that we have concluded our discussion process with the executive of the county board. We regret to say that we cannot report any substantial progress has been made. Furthermore we cannot foresee any progress. We have decided as a result to withdraw our services immediately from the Cork senior hurling panel. It's been an enormous decision for each of us to make personally. And one we all regret having to make. The current difficulties have been there for many years, and the attitude of the board towards players has been far from satisfactory. However, because of a number of specific issues arising this year, the situation has deteriorated.'

They identified eight different areas that they wanted to see immediately improved if the dispute was to be resolved:

* Gear – Championship panel to be supplied with a jacket, a fleece top and two polo shirts as casual wear, along with shorts, socks, sweat tops, T-shirts, tracksuit and two Cork jerseys.
* Training facilities – membership of a gym within close proximity of the players' homes.
* Tickets – twenty complimentary stand tickets to be made available to each Championship panel member.
* Medical – team doctor and physio to be present for all League and Championship games. Insurance terms also to be clarified.
* Meals – standard of food to be improved in the canteen at Páirc Uí Chaoimh.
* Travel – bus travel only for short trips. Train or flights for longer distances.
* Mileage – to be paid at the premium rate.
* Holiday – a foreign holiday for at least one week for each Championship member and his partner.
* Daily allowance also to be included.
* Funding – increase needed in the players' fund.

The strike was resolved two weeks later when the Cork County Board conceded most of their requests. The Cork hurlers were seen to have answered their critics when they won consecutive All-Irelands in 2004 and '05.

## ME AND EUGENE MCGEE

One of my prize possessions is a picture hanging in my living room of a photo of when Eugene McGee visited me in Roscommon. At the time, I spoke to Eugene to get a sense of the mood of the GAA nation about the Cork hurlers. I have to confess that I was a little taken aback by how he saw right and wrong so clearly on one side:

'This will be seen as a landmark decision in the relationship between inter-county players and county boards. The Cork decision will force the GAA nationally to finally come to terms with the role of players in the Association. There has always been a pathological fear among GAA administrators that someday the players in some county would refuse to turn out for their county. But so strong is the cult of "the county player" in GAA folklore that these officials always consoled themselves with the belief that no matter how disgruntled players felt about their county board they would never go on strike.

'Officials were always confident that the fear of strong negative public reaction to such a move would be their greatest asset in any confrontation with players. In past times that was actually true. No player was prepared to take the abuse that would have been hurled at him from the supporters of the county team if he refused to wear the county jersey. But we live in a different climate in Ireland nowadays. Young people know their rights and they know these rights entitle them to fair treatment in all aspects of their lives.

'So, when the Cork hurlers took their drastic decision, after months of sham discussions with their county board, they knew they were perfectly within their rights, and they also knew that the vast majority of Irish people accepted that fact. GAA players are strictly amateur, at the GAA's insistence, therefore they are perfectly entitled to play or not to play for their team. For far too long GAA officials lived by the precept that the honour and glory of wearing the county jersey was so awesome for the players that it would override all problems associated with being a county player.

'Those days are gone. The former notion that young men are prepared to put the rest of their lives on hold for ten years or so in order to play for the county team is simply no longer true. That was fine when young men had little else in their lives to look forward to; poor jobs, no second or third level education and not much to do in their spare time except play football and hurling.

'The biggest change that has taken place in the GAA over the past twenty-five years has been the influx of money from commercial sponsorship which has transformed many aspects of the GAA. There are now hundreds of paid coaches and administrators, there are hundreds of GAA clubs whose assets are measured in millions of euros and the new Croke Park is the most obvious example of the GAA's new-found affluence. That is the background in which all matters relating to inter-county players must be considered. These smart, intelligent and ambitious young men, and their female partners, can see how prosperous the GAA now is by comparison with a generation ago.

'The reason the Cork players' decision is so critical at this moment is that it debunks the notion that the GPA and inter-county players in general want Gaelic inter-county games to become professional. What the Cork players are asking from their county board has nothing to do with professionalism but everything to do with the self-respect of the players. Cork GAA is the richest unit in the GAA by a mile yet they refused to fly the hurlers to Derry for a League game and insisted they take a day off work and travel 350 miles each way by bus. There was no compensation for the lost workday and no team doctor was available for that trip. Many people will find this hard to believe but Cork is not the only county where this sort of abuse of players is still going on.

'It is only a couple of years ago that the GAA at the highest level had to make a ruling regarding travelling expenses paid to players by county boards. Some counties were paying as little as thirteen pence a mile up to then. Civil Service mileage rates at the time were in excess of sixty pence a mile for the first 4,000 miles. The failure of GAA bodies to move with the times and reasonable demands of county players has led to undercover systems of rewards in many counties.

'Managers or sometimes the players themselves have resorted to raising finance privately to improve their players' lot. The most glaring example of this was the Kilkenny hurlers having to run around the local dog track a week after they won the All-Ireland in a fund-raising venture. This was disgraceful, and D.J. Carey was quite right to highlight it. I saw the same carry-on happening twenty years ago with the Offaly foot-ballers when I was managing them. But there are more subtle financing arrangements in other counties such as the secret "tapping" of business people and companies to come up with cash in return for accessibility to the players, particularly the more famous ones, for promotional or advertising activity. The Sam Maguire and McCarthy Cups turn up in unlikely places every winter as part of such operations.

'This sort of behaviour is demeaning for players and is the main source of unrest because it indicates a lack of respect for players and a complete misunderstanding of the role of players in the GAA. Too many GAA officials still regard players as some sort of hired help, to be flogged to death in terms of working for the GAA, but getting the absolute minimum in return. That day is over now, and the action of the Cork hurlers has announced that fact to the GAA. The Association will never be the same again thanks to the Cork hurlers.'

# 58

## A SAD, SAD DAY

*The Cork Strike 2*

Sometimes it's not the mountain that wears you out, it is the grain of sand in your shoe.

The second strike lasted ninety-six days and involved a row after the Cork County Board decided to return the choice of selectors from the county team manager in both hurling and football to the county board in October 2007. With the appointment of Teddy Holland as Cork football manager, the footballers refused to play under him since he accepted the job during their time of strike. The strike began on 10 December 2007 and ended on 18 February 2008.

On 9 January, the hurlers confirmed they would not play in the Waterford Crystal Cup and the county was forced to give a walkover to Limerick IT. Later in the month Teddy Holland issued a press statement announcing he would not resign. More than 100 club delegates voted unanimously in support of Holland at a county board meeting held on 30 January. In the week leading up to the National Football League game against Meath, the Cork County Board were unable to guarantee that a team would be available to play the game. As a result, on 30 January, the game was postponed.

On 7 February the players refused a solution offered by the county board and it was suggested that Cork would be removed from both the National Hurling League and National Football League and be relegated for the following season. It was claimed that under GAA rules, if a team was unable to take part in two league games they should be disqualified from the league. A second football match was to be played on 16 February while the second hurling game was due on 17 February. A poll showed that fifty-six per cent of fans supported the strike and seventy per cent believed the actions of the board damaged Cork's chance of winning All-Ireland Championships that year.

The then Taoiseach Bertie Ahern spoke in public about the situation and called on all sides to work through such a resolution. After a failure of arbitration to reach agreement initially, then President of the GAA, Nickey Brennan, described the impasse as 'a sad, sad day for the Association'. Ireland's top industrial relations mediator at the time, Kieran Mulvey, then chief executive of the Labour Relations Commission, brokered an agreement which involved the newly appointed manager of the football team, Teddy Holland, stepping aside.

The arbitration was intended to be a 'final solution' to the problems in the GAA in Cork. In fact, the outcome was the calm before the storm. Things would quickly escalate causing a whole new level of internal strife.

# 59

## STRIKING IT UNLUCKY?

*The Third Cork Hurlers Strike*

This one got ugly.

It only ended when Gerald McCarthy, a five-time All-Ireland winner as a player, resigned as Cork hurling manager in March 2009 after receiving death threats.

In late 2008, McCarthy was reappointed following the conclusion of his two-year deal and thus the unrest began as the Cork hurlers accused the county board of failing to implement the changes to appointment procedures agreed after the previous strike, which had only ended in February of that year. In January 2009, the panel from the previous year released a statement confirming their strike would go ahead. Thousands marched in the streets of Cork on their behalf.

The situation escalated as the months unfolded. The clubs were asked to put forward a motion of no confidence in McCarthy while Cork were forced to field weakened sides without their 2008 panel members in the early stages of the National League. The Rebels endured three defeats in a row. In that third match against Galway just 600 people attended.

The controversy eventually came to an end in March 2009 when McCarthy stepped down with immediate effect, stating that to continue would cause a safety risk to him and his family. The Cork hurling panel returned to play. McCarthy said: 'From my perspective they (the players) have dishonoured the Cork jersey and used it as a weapon and a threat.'

## WITH THE BENEFIT OF HINDSIGHT

In 2017, Dónal Óg Cusack said: 'Gerald was doing his best – he wanted to do his best. He was a great Cork player, but we felt there was better management propositions out there. When it was becoming pretty apparent what was ahead of us, myself and John (Gardiner) said we need to go and talk to Gerald face-to-face and tell him what was going on. So, we told him the story, told him that the players didn't have confidence in him. Gerald made it clear to us that night that he wasn't going anywhere. We went back to our players and said, "This is the choice that we have. What do you want to do?" I think it was unanimous that the players would go on strike.

'I regret anybody got hurt in it. I regret Gerald had to be in the position he had to be in, because the fight was between the players and the board, yet the board knew exactly what they were doing. But in terms of regretting what we did? The only regret I have is that we didn't give them half enough of it, that when we had our foot on their chests, we should have went all the ways.'

In a separate interview on *The Sunday Game*, Dónal Óg famously said that Frank Murphy (the then long-serving secretary) and the Cork County Board 'know as much about high level sport as I do about the sleeping habits of the Ayatollah'.

## REGRETS I'VE HAD A FEW

In 2020 Seán Óg Ó hAilpín struck a different tone. He said he regretted the 'filthy, callous, cold' fallout from the players' strikes on Leeside in the 2000s. The All-Ireland winning captain and the All-Star wing-back went on to express sympathy for some of those directly affected by the various disputes with the county board – in particular, former coach Gerald McCarthy who received death threats at the time. The Na Piarsaigh's man also referenced Bertie Óg Murphy's 2002 departure during the first strike:

'That's one thing I do regret, the casualties, that people did have to step down. The worst one was '09 and the one where there's still aftermath . . . the biggest casualty out of that was Gerald McCarthy. Probably one of – if not the greatest – Cork greats having to step down.

'That's twelve years on and not a day goes by when I think back to then, if things could have been done differently? There are certain actions, that would have been in hindsight . . . I can't speak for the other players per se but I know myself, I would have said some stuff that during that time, with proper reflection, I was probably best to just keep my mouth shut.

'At the end of the day, you had one part of the organisation which was the playing group, which were looking to go that way and you soon realise that you're not the biggest stakeholder or power broker – it's the county board that ultimately govern the Association in Cork. And obviously they didn't want to go that way with us, and they were going the other way. And we were going poles apart completely and when you have two camps going opposite ways it was only going to lead to ringside tickets in Las Vegas. There's a willingness now to just get Cork back to winning ways because you can talk about strikes or such a person, but the reality is Cork hasn't won an All-Ireland since 2005.'

# 60

# KANGAROO COURT

*Galway Players Oust Anthony Cunningham*

In June 1989, the late Seán Doherty sensationally lost his seat in Roscommon in the General Election. On live television, as he stood in the Roscommon count centre, Brian Farrell asked him: 'Seán Doherty, what went wrong?'

With a typical smile he replied: 'Not enough people voted for me, Brian.'

Despite the protestations of Joe Brolly, Gaelic games are now a results business. Many managers made the same discovery as Graeme Souness after he was sacked as Liverpool manager, which he blamed on the persistent hostility of much of the media against him. As Ronnie Whelan, himself a casualty of Souness at Anfield when he was sold permaturely, incisively observed: 'Souness is complaining the papers had him sacked. They did. They printed his results.'

In 2013, Roy Keane and Patrick Vieira made a television documentary about their turbulent relationship when they were players. Most of the media comment was, as usual, on

Keano, but Vieira made some interesting observations about his former boss. The conversation unfolded:

> Interviewer: 'What is Arsene Wenger's biggest strength?'
> Vieira: 'Trust – he believes in players and lets them get on with it.'
> Interviewer: 'And what is his biggest weakness?'
> Vieira: 'Trust. Sometimes players need a kick up the arse.'

The manager serves an interface between the old and the new, the fantastic and the real, the visionary and the practical, the playful and the serious, and the informal and the tactical. It is a difficult balance to strike. Just ask former Down great, Liam Austin. He was Martin McHugh's successor in 1997 after Cavan won a famous Ulster title. Austin was forced to resign as Cavan manager because of so-called 'player power'. Stephen King was the punters' favourite to take the job, but he declined to run for the post:

'I had just started up my own pub in Killashandra at the time so there was no way I could even consider taking the position.'

How does King feel about 'player power'?

'In general, I think it's a bad thing. The one thing I would say though is that players should be properly looked after by the GAA because it is the players that generate the big crowds and the revenue for the Association. Once that happens, I think players should concentrate on playing and not get involved in politics if that's what you want to call it.'

## MAYO MUTINY

Former Mayo joint managers Pat Holmes and Noel Connolly were also high-profile casualties of player-power. In 2015, their Mayo side looked like they were going to reach the

All-Ireland final when they led Dublin by four points in the semi-final replay. A few weeks later, the Mayo players passed a vote of no-confidence in the management team claiming: 'We, the players, have set very high standards . . . as they (the managers) have not met those standards and for this reason we do not believe that they can or should lead this team into 2016.' Connolly and Holmes walked the plank and were replaced by Stephen Rochford.

The manner of their appointment was itself the subject of controversy. Their former All-Star forward Kevin McStay had seemed in pole position having led St Brigid's to the All-Ireland in 2013. Gerry Bourke, a Mayo board executive, resigned over the manner of the appointment of Connelly and Holmes as joint managers for the senior football team. Chairman Paddy McNicholas was criticised for seemingly failing to adhere to the agreed procedure. Liam McHale, who was part of Kevin McStay's managerial ticket, was interviewed on *Off the Ball* and suggested that their proposal was deemed 'too radical' for the county board's liking. McStay would later speculate that he might have been 'too honest' in his interview for the position.

McHale added: 'I drove home from St Brigid's training at about 5 o'clock and Kevin rang me to say he had got a call from Paddy McNicholas again trying to arrange an interview with him for Tuesday. Kevin said, "Paddy, let me get this clear, you want me to go for an interview for a job that's already gone." Kevin felt that Paddy was trying to influence him into stating that he was going to pull out and obviously that would clear the way for Noel and Pat to come in.'

## MAROON MUTINY
The West was awake in 2015 because an even more high-profile revolt led to Anthony Cunningham's departure as Galway

manager following a mutiny by his own players. Cunningham took charge in 2011 and led them to an All-Ireland final the following year, though they lost to Kilkenny. Two disappointing seasons followed with a quarter-final Championship exit in 2013 before they were knocked out in the qualifiers the following year by Tipperary. In 2015, Cunningham brought the Tribesmen all the way to the final after a thrilling battle with Tipperary in the semi-final. However, they lost again to Kilkenny.

It was confirmed in September 2015 that the St Thomas' man would continue as manager having agreed to a two-year deal twelve months previously. This did not go down well with the players, and they passed a vote of no confidence in their manager. When efforts at mediation between the parties failed, Cunningham stepped down on 16 November, 2015, the victim of a player heave.

In his parting statement, Cunningham hit out at the players who had led the revolt against him:

'Despite extensive attempts at genuine dialogue including independent arbitration, there were no reasonable explanations offered or given as to the issues the players felt they had. They, through their actions, have shown scant respect for, and loyalty to, the goodwill shown to them by supporters, clubs and county GAA committees and management. I consider this a kangaroo court decision, led by a core group of players orchestrated with the help of others outside Galway, motivated by a desire to unjustly extend their lifespan as inter-county players, placing personal agendas above the greater good of Galway hurling.'

Later, Cunningham would reflect on the experience:

'It was unfortunate and soul-destroying, to be honest. I think there's a lot of different factors. Everyone sort of knew it was pushed by a few guys who wanted to extend their existence at inter-county level. That led to a few meagre souls being unhappy and wanting to stay there. There was huge work put in, it wasn't just one year, I was there since 2012 with back-room teams, improvements annually, trying to get to a professional level. You'd almost rear a number of these guys, a lot of guys needed help as well; nineteen, twenty, twenty-one-year-olds looking for guidance on work, life, hitting low spots and (needing) help with different aspects. Ultimately everyone wants to win, and we were in a leading position in the two All-Ireland finals and didn't go on to win. They were hard to take, bitter disappointments for everyone involved; players, management, county board. However, it was a bolt out of nowhere.

'Contrary to discussions, there was never any trouble in Galway. These guys played for years and never had a bad word out of them, or discontent. Behind the scenes, it's well documented what went on, an unfortunate aspect of the game that creeps into clubs and other counties as well. The associations of players and their bodies have got very strong. I don't think (county) boards, on the management side of it, have moved as professionally as the players' bodies.'

Cunningham went on to manage the Roscommon footballers and led the Rossies to the Connacht title in 2019.

# 61

## JUST-IN TIME

*Limerick Hurlers Revolt*

The late RTÉ GAA Correspondent Mick Dunne was a big admirer of Justin McCarthy:

'Justin was a wonderful hurler and had not injury intervened I am sure we would have heard even more about his talents as a player,' he told me. 'Even after the traffic accident he still had the "know-how", and he called the shots and dictated the flow of the game. It was an education just to see him in action. You sometimes hear a player described as "a class act". If there ever was a class act it would have to be Justin. I also found him to be one of the great characters in the game – though in a quieter way than a lot of players.

'He was very committed to everything he did and left nothing to chance. It was a very different time during his playing days. In 1966 he deservedly won the Texaco hurler of the year award.'

Not all counties are a natural hinterland for hurling. The great Paddy Downey, the distinguished former Gaelic games correspondent of the *Irish Times*, described hurling in Kerry as 'a lot like compulsory tillage'. After his retirement, Justin took up coaching and shocked the hurling world when he took on the job of coaching the Antrim team. As a coach, McCarthy's intelligence came into focus. In West of Ireland parlance: 'He wouldn't take a bite out of a stone.'

Stints coaching Clare and Cork soon followed and then McCarthy succeeded his old teammate Gerald McCarthy as manager of Waterford where he showed the complex web of talents that are necessary to be a successful manager. However, no trainer is an island. Ultimately, the boundaries of the success he can achieve are defined by the players at his disposal. McCarthy had a hugely successful spell with Waterford, winning three Munster titles and a National League, but he was unable to lead them to an All-Ireland final. In 2008, after the Waterford players made known their dissatisfaction with his regime, Justin controversially stepped down as the county's manager.

Later that year, he succeeded Richie Bennis as Limerick manager and steered the Shannonsiders to the All-Ireland semi-final in 2009, only for Tipperary to be easy winners, by twenty-four points, and, as a consequence, there was significant unrest over a protracted period about Justin's stewardship.

Following that capitulation, McCarthy understandably sought to make changes in the months that followed. However, trimming the squad was one thing – but the way he went about it caused ripples of discord. Most of the twelve players let go only discovered their fate through the local media. Moreover, the suggestion that the players were let go because of squad indiscipline and lack of commitment led to twelve more stepping away in subsequent months.

Huge names like Stephen Lucey, Niall Moran and Andrew O'Shaughnessy had been dropped while Ollie Moran, Séamus Hickey and Damien Reale were among those who went AWOL.

Unlike the Cork situation, where the county board was seen to cave in to the striking hurlers, in Limerick the powers that be were determined not to buckle in the face of 'player-power'. McCarthy won a board vote of confidence in December by 70–54. The closeness of the margin was an indication of the split in the county.

Sometimes silence is golden. Things escalated when Justin did a radio interview in January 2010. The twenty-four players responded in public for the first time with a lengthy statement and refuting many of the claims made by McCarthy and the Limerick County Board. In particular, while they conceded that they had not been happy with preparations under McCarthy through 2009 they refused to accept McCarthy's claim that some of the players were 'trying to get rid of us'.

When McCarthy won another vote of confidence in March it was evident that the Limerick County Board were sticking to their guns. Having lost all seven League games badly, Justin remained in charge when they lost to Cork by thirteen points in Munster before losing to Offaly in the qualifiers.

After that loss, Limerick established an independent three-man committee to appoint a manager for 2011. While McCarthy was nominated for another term, it was Dónal O'Grady who was appointed.

# 62

## THE SECOND COMING

*Babs' Era Ends in Tears*

While Kilkenny brought hurling to another level in the noughties, many managers perished in other counties as they failed to reach the same dizzy heights. Among the casualties was Babs Keating in his second incarnation as Tipperary manager:

'The first time I was Tipp manager I never heard of any player having any grievance. It was a huge culture shock for me when I went back the second time to see the lack of commitment I was getting from some of the players wearing the Tipperary jersey. I was also shocked that the advice I was giving to the Tipperary players who were supposed to be well educated went in one ear and out the other. I saw myself as a counsellor because these players were the same age as my own son and I wanted to treat them the way I would treat my own son. My basic job, as I saw it, was to serve the people who were paying their money to travel around the country to support the team because these are the people who make the GAA and fill Croke Park. I always recalled my father, a small farmer, taking us in his van to matches on a Sunday when there was very little money around.

'I couldn't get the message through to that Tipperary team. I know Brian Cody could get the message through to the Kilkenny team. In 2008 we saw that Justin McCarthy wasn't the problem in Waterford nor was John Meyler the problem in Wexford. Likewise, Gerald McCarthy was not the problem in Cork. The problems are more with the present generation who have an exaggerated opinion of their own importance. I think it would have been better if the likes of Dónal Óg Cusack, Seán Óg Ó hAilpín, Ronan Curran or Eoin Kelly had the approach of J.J. Delaney, Tommy Walsh and Henry Shefflin or Mick Harte's Tyrone because they were focused. I thought it was time many of our players stopped looking for what others could do for them and started asking what they could do for the game.

'The basic thing was that when I went in the first time to manage Tipperary a fella like Nicky (English) was an established top performer. I basically had very little advice for Nicky, but I had plenty of advice for the fellas around him so that I could make Nicky a better player. The discipline we had in the '60s was that nobody struck a ball without a reason for it. That message was driven into us in training. If a player ever came to me and asked me for advice about how to play the game and I couldn't give him an answer I would consider that I've failed him as a coach. My discipline was still the same when I went back a second time but there was too much carelessness and too much of an "it will be all right on the night" kind of attitude. It was a huge attitude problem and, unfortunately for us, we had too many with that attitude problem.'

Babs created two major controversies in 2007. The first was the failure to start star forward Eoin Kelly in big matches. The second controversy arose with the sensational decision to drop star goalkeeper Brendan Cummins:

'Looking back on my two years with Tipperary there's no decision I made which I wouldn't do again. I knew the knives were out. The county board took the easy option. They did what the Wexford and Waterford County Boards did in '08 and didn't stand up to the players.

'When I was interviewed for the Offaly job, ninety per cent of the interview was devoted to discipline. I had a similar interview for the Tipperary job. The people who interviewed me didn't stand behind me. If Tipperary are to be successful in the future, they've got to go back to the old values which are Brian Cody's values.

'I was having sleepless nights. I developed a rash all over my chest and stomach and had to get medical care for it. My whole nervous system was suffering. I am not sure I could have survived it for much longer and I've never given a county board the opportunity to sack me, so I stepped down. I was so disillusioned with what went on that I basically put hurling out of my head.'

## INTIMIDATION

In his second incarnation as Tipperary manager, Babs started off being warmed into new optimism although the problems nestled undetected in the corners and crevices. However, he experienced the pressures on managers today at first hand very quickly:

'The main hardship was the constant phone calls and text messages in the middle of the night. I gave the name of one of the main people involved to the guards, but they didn't take the final step with him. The calls and texts were from so-called fans – friends of the players. The most upsetting came at 2.28am from a guy high on drugs or drink. It was horrible, horrible stuff. I was staying with my daughter that night and one of her little girls was awakened by the call and could sense that it was nasty. That was very distressing for her and made it even harder for me to see her crying because of that. It was pure intimidation. I gave the guards the caller's name. I knew the house he lived in. The guards called on him and gave him a warning. Although my phone was off, the calls and texts would come during matches. Typical messages would be: "Do you know what you're doing?" Or: "You f**king idiot." And they are just the nice ones! The whole thing left a very bad taste.

'Everyone in Tipperary knows who was behind it. Those lads were well protected.

'The players have enough to do to go out and play rather than worrying about who is going to be manager. If you look back to the row in Cork in 2008, Gerald (McCarthy) has forgot more about hurling than those lads will ever learn. It certainly hurt me intensely when I heard there were twenty-seven players who came out against Gerald. When I was down to see Cork play Tipp that year there were only seven players I could see performing in the day, so I don't know where the twenty-seven came from. Would Waterford have been any worse in the All-Ireland final in '08 if Justin (McCarthy) was still in charge?

'The other thing that drove me from Tipperary was the dirt and sh*t some of the media wrote about me. These journalists were driven by the players who they were friendly with. One of the crazy stories that appeared in a paper was that there wasn't a place on the team bus to Croke Park for the Wexford match for all the players because my family and I were taking up too many places. In actual fact, owing to a family wedding, I wasn't even on the bus myself – not to mind any of my family.'

# 63

# IT'S A SIN

*Sin Bin Binned*

It came, it saw but it did not conquer.

The first few weeks of 2005 saw the GAA fraternity preoccupied by a single issue: the sin bin. It had been trialled in an effort to combat the cynical, deliberate fouling that was a blot on the face of Gaelic football.

The then President of the GAA, Seán Kelly, defended the new rule experiments, following criticism of the sin bin: 'Some people have questioned the timing of the experiments but when else could you do it? There is a very limited number of opportunities to experiment with rules, so the various warm-up competitions stood out as the obvious time. The only other competitions would have been the League or the Championship, and that's just not feasible.'

However, he conceded that the sin bin rule would have to be rethought, following criticism from high-profile managers like Mick O'Dwyer and Seán Boylan.

Paddy Collins, one of the best-known referees of his generation, was underwhelmed by the idea: 'I think a player being sin-binned for one yellow card is much too severe a punishment. I feel it would make sense if a player was sent to the sin bin after two yellow cards, and this would have a much better chance of being approved by Congress. The sin-binning after two yellow cards would, of course, be a less severe punishment than the situation where a player is sent off for the rest of the match after two yellow cards, and that would be a major attraction in its favour.

'If we decide to embrace the concept of a single yellow card meriting ten minutes in the sin bin, we're effectively saying that Gaelic football is a filthy, dirty game. But that's not the case at all. Under the existing arrangement, a player can be sent to the sin bin by running across the path of an opponent and without physically interfering with him in any way. Perhaps the rules could do with a little tweaking here and there, but I remain to be convinced that we need such draconian measures.'

Meath manager Seán Boylan was highly critical of the sin bin after three of his players were given ten-minute punishments during the last quarter of their O'Byrne Cup quarter-final loss to Kildare. However, referee assessor Tony Jordan hit back at Boylan's criticism by claiming that the new measure benefitted the Royals:

'The experimental rule certainly considerably helped an excellent footballer like Graham Geraghty, who wasn't nearly as often on the receiving end of negative tactics by opponents, because they were afraid of having to spend ten minutes off the field. As well, the sin bin helped the flow of the game, as there were only about thirty-five frees compared to the usual average of about fifty-five.'

Laois and Kildare both had four players sin-binned in their O'Byrne Cup semi-final clash. This led to a strong attack from the then Laois manager Mick O'Dwyer on the new rule and fuelled speculation that the measure would be scrapped. Given the furore generated by the controversy, the GAA shelved the sin bin for the National Leagues and the controversy melted away like snow in a thaw.

# 64

## THE KEANE EDGE

*Jack O'Connor Replaces Peter Keane*

They do things differently in the Kingdom.

In 2004, shortly after he won his first All-Ireland as Kerry manager, Jack O'Connor had an exchange with the outgoing Dublin manager Tommy Lyons. Tommy was explaining how he was being eviscerated by many of the Dublin supporters after failing to win the Sam Maguire. O'Connor replied: 'They're abusing you after you lost. Down here they're abusing me even though I won!'

Legend has it that in 2006, after O'Connor won his second All-Ireland as Kerry manager, he brought the Sam Maguire Cup back home to Cahersiveen in south Kerry. From the door of a pub, a diehard Kerry fan observed, 'There he goes now, and no talk of the All-Ireland he lost to Tyrone last year.'

In 2021, the Kerry County Board appointed O'Connor for his third stint as manager of the senior footballers. Shortly afterwards, outgoing manager Peter Keane released his own statement claiming he had the full support of the players to continue in the job.

At the end of August that year, O'Connor flagged his interest in the role on the *Irish Examiner* football podcast, stating: 'Of course, there is an allure there. Who doesn't want to coach Man United? There is that allure because of the tradition.'

At that juncture Peter Keane was still the Kerry manager, while O'Connor was still manager of Kildare.

Kevin McStay noted: 'Keane's statement said, "We were a united Kerry team with a great sense of purpose and ambition." That's past tense.' He mused, when reflecting on the change in management: 'Does that suggest it's going be a difficult transition? I don't know.'

He added, 'The manner in which it all came about was a little bit ugly, I'd have to say. There was a sense that the position was courted when there wasn't a vacancy – or a technical vacancy at the time.

'It was a disappointment that there was a kind of public grab. We all know this is a smashing Kerry team. They're going to win All-Irelands sooner rather than later, I'd have a great sense of that. There seemed to be a little bit of grabbing going on.'

Commenting on the remarks O'Connor made on the podcast, McStay added: 'To compare Kerry to Man United, Kildare to an easy life, pretty much all in the one podcast . . . when you're in a public position like that, the manager of Kildare of whom he had committed to as I understand, you have to be very careful with your utterances because, after all, you are the guardian of the county football team.

'There's a great responsibility and privilege involved in that. I just had the sense that it was messy, that it was an ugly crossover.'

# 65

## THE STRIFE OF BRIAN

*Mayo Revolt 1992*

This is not a story based loosely on the truth in the best tradition of Hollywood.

This is really a true story.

It happened in a Dunnes Stores car park.

A Mayo-born man was perhaps the first to threaten a players' strike. Contrary to public perception it was Roscommon's most iconic star Dermot Earley:

'Long before Cork made striking fashionable in the GAA, we were the first to threaten to use player-power. We were in New York to play Kerry in the Cardinal Cushing Games over two matches in 1981. We beat them initially in a thirteen-a-side in the first game. We had been promised money from John Kerry O'Donnell, who was "Mr GAA" in New York. We knew for a fact that Kerry had been paid but we got nothing, and we were running short of money. We held a council of war. As I was the army man it was appropriate that I chaired it! The word was sent back to John Kerry – no money no playing. As far as I know we were the first county to threaten to strike!

'Another memory I have of the trip is that we were invited to a formal reception hosted by the Lord Mayor. It was a real big deal for the county board. The problem was that the heat was almost unbearable. One of the lads brought down a keg of beer to keep himself distracted from the heat! Gerry Beirne went so far as to take off his shirt which was a major breach of protocol. The message quickly came down from the top table from the county chairman, Michael O'Callaghan, to get it back on quickly.'

## DRAMA IN DUNNES CAR PARK

However, eleven years later, there was a more dramatic example of a squad flexing their muscles. The promise of reaching the All-Ireland final in 1989 was not built on by Mayo, and their All-Star defender Dermot Flanagan looks back on the experience as a lost opportunity:

'The winter of '89 saw a form of euphoria because we had reached a final after such a long time and had played well which really took away from our focus. What should have happened is that we should have cleared off for a week and realised we had lost. People thought we were on the crest of winning an All-Ireland which created a lot of distractions and left us vulnerable in 1990.'

To this day, Flanagan finds it difficult to assess the way events unfolded after Mayo's defeat in the Connacht final replay to Roscommon in 1991:

'John O'Mahony departed in controversial circumstances. John has never spoken in public about all the details, and I suppose we should let him have his say on that. It is probably fair to say that part of the reason was that he was not allowed to choose his own selectors. Looking back, the circumstances of Mayo football were not right then.

'Brian McDonald came in as his replacement and a year later would find himself in a huge controversy. Were there any winners? Everybody was a loser to a greater or lesser extent. Brian had been a selector with Liam O'Neill in 1985. To be fair to Brian he had a lot of good ideas about the game but whether he was the man to get the best out of players was another question. The first thing he asked me when he took over as manager was if I was committed to Mayo football. I was totally committed. I was the first guy to do stretching before training and after training. Long before it was fashionable, I was doing acupuncture, watching my diet, reading sports injury books and doing power weightlifting – anything that would give me an edge or improve me as a player, so it came as a shock to be asked that.

'The issue that got into the media was about the players pushing cars as part of a training session. That was not the underlying problem. You needed to have a very strong skin to be able to handle Brian's comments in a training session. That was okay for the senior players but repeated exposure to this for the younger players could have undermined their confidence. We had a lot of younger players in the squad at the time.

'Again, in fairness to Brian, we did win a Connacht final in 1992 and could have beaten Donegal in the All-Ireland semi-final. We were not in the right frame of mind for an All-Ireland semi-final. There were a lot of problems with organisation. I was a man marker and I was on Tony Boyle for a short time in the game and did well on him but I wasn't left on him and he played havoc with us.

'Afterwards, the controversy broke in the media. The team was going nowhere. There were no winners in that situation. The tumultuous saga reflected very badly on the whole scene in Mayo. The county board had been deaf to any complaints. John

O'Mahony had left under a cloud. These situations don't come from nowhere. A lot of mistakes were made.'

The sins of the father were revisited on Flanagan:

'My dad wouldn't have been hugely popular with the county board in his playing days. One day he turned around and asked the County Chairman if he wouldn't mind leaving the dressing room. For that reason, some people believed that I was the most likely instigator of the "revolt" against Brian but I had nothing to do with it. I never had to push cars because I was training in Dublin and was too busy in my legal career to be "masterminding a coup".'

## GAA-ME ON?

The 1989 All-Ireland is yet another case of what might have been for Mayo's All-Star midfielder T.J. Kilgallon as he explained to me when we visited the infamous Dunnes Stores car park:

'After Anthony Finnerty got the goal, we were in the driving seat because having lost the previous two years they were starting to doubt themselves, but in the last ten minutes we went into disarray and let them off the hook. They finished strongly and got the final three points. It was over and done with – but not achieved.'

Mayo's next attempt at redemption would come in the All-Ireland semi-final in 1992: 'There was kind of a bad vibe all year and even though we won the Connacht final there was a sense in the camp that things were not going well. Probably the most memorable incident that happened in that game was that Enon Gavin broke the crossbar in Castlebar and the match had to be delayed.

'Things got ugly after that. It was more personal than it should have been. It was probably an early example of player-power. We said that if there wasn't a change of management a

245

lot of us would walk away. I was asked recently if we really did spend a training session pushing cars. We did! It was here in the Dunnes Stores car park in Castlebar and the cars were really big. There was not a great humour in the camp and the manager had to walk the plank. John O'Mahony had stepped down in 1991 because he was not let choose his own selectors and maybe that's when we should have acted.'

Pat Spillane has a different take on the controversy: 'I often think of what would have happened if Mayo went on to win the All-Ireland in 1992. They came within a whisker of beating the eventual All-Ireland champions, Donegal, in the All-Ireland semi-final. In a highly-publicised saga afterwards, the Mayo players signed a petition which called for the removal of their manager Brian McDonald and, in the process, released a list of training methods which they had used during the year which seemed to border on the farcical. Only one side of the story was told in public. Player power saw McDonald bowing out with Jack O'Shea taking his place, only for Mayo to be absolutely massacred by Cork the following year in the All-Ireland semi-final. With a bit of luck, though, Mayo could easily have beaten Donegal in 1992 and who knows what would have happened against Dublin in the All-Ireland final. McDonald, being very cute, improvised when there was no field available for training by getting fellas to push cars around the car park. If Mayo won that All-Ireland everyone would have said McDonald was a genius and car-pushing would have become part of training.'

# 66

# A VIGILANTE AMBUSH?

*Dom Corrigan Is Sacked as Sligo Boss*

It sounded like a scene from *The Sopranos*.

Many an inter-county managerial career has ended abruptly. Results were disappointing during Dermot Earley's two-year tenure and a significant amount of Roscommon fans were vociferous in their criticism of his performance. Things came to a head with the defeat to John O'Mahony's Leitrim by a point in the Connacht Championship in 1994. Although Leitrim went on to win only their second provincial title that year, the rumblings of discontent among Roscommon fans grew to a crescendo.

Jimmy Magee said to me:

'I couldn't get over the treatment he got in certain quarters. Some of it was vicious and they couldn't get rid of him fast enough. I remember thinking at the time: "My God, if they can do this to Dermot Earley, what will they do to somebody else?"'

Some weeks after the Leitrim game, Dermot met up with two senior officials on the Roscommon County Board to review his stewardship of the team. As attention to detail was his mantra,

Dermot had prepared a detailed plan for the coming year. When he was asked at the start of the meeting what he thought about things Dermot launched into his plan with his customary enthusiasm, but he quickly noticed that the two men did not seem to be really listening and were looking at each other rather than at him. He came to an abrupt halt and asked them bluntly: 'Do you want me to resign?'

One replied: 'Well, would you?'

Thus ended his managerial career with the county he loved so well.

Knowing about the meeting, I rang him the next morning. It was not like a Roy Keane and Alex Ferguson situation after United let Keano go. There was no bitterness or rancour. Almost thirty years on, his summary sentence, said not in anger but in a soft whisper of resignation, remains indelibly carved on my memory:

'They wanted my head on a plate, but they didn't want my blood on their hands.'

## DOM-INANT

However, one of the most colourful managerial terminations came in February 2006 when Sligo manager Dom Corrigan was dismissed by the county board.

Fermanagh native Corrigan was furious about the manner of his sacking which was relayed to him moments before county training was due to start. He accused them of 'shafting' him with 'ambush' tactics. He took to the local airwaves to give his version of events.

Corrigan contended that he first became suspicious when his players failed to show for a training session in Kevinsfort. He said that they were, in fact, in the dressing room of the nearby St Mary's GAA club, where he went to find them.

Before he could reach them, Mr Corrigan claimed he was confronted by two men, in the car park. He went on to claim that the men jumped from a van like 'vigilantes' before ushering him into a side room and formally sacking him.

It is thought that Sligo's defeat to an unfancied Waterford in Division 2B of the Allianz League the previous Sunday, following an opening-day loss to Tipperary, precipitated the change of management. Corrigan, however, believed that his sacking was the result of a premeditated decision, leading to his dismissal:

'I don't believe that the loss to Waterford was at the root of this. As far as I know, they're hoping to announce a new management team at training on Friday night. Now how could they know their new management team a matter of hours after I was sacked? I just felt that I was shown absolutely no respect or decency in the way I was let go. I thought the way they acted was sad and pathetic. All it required was a phone call to me during the afternoon to allow me to cancel training. Then I could have met them and outlined my position after a bit of thought. But they acted like vigilantes in the way they did it all. I didn't even get a chance to talk with the players because I was so shocked at it.'

## A DIFFERENT PERSPECTIVE

Eamonn O'Hara was the third Sligo player to win an All-Star award. His account of the events to me was more prosaic:

'Managers came and went, most controversially, Dom Corrigan. He was a very nice guy, but he was brought in to get results and they didn't come. Things were disjointed around then as well because some players decided to play in the Tommy Murphy Cup, some of us didn't, realising it was complete bullsh*t and people weren't on the same wavelength. But the way it ended was blown out of all proportion like it was from the Mafia or something. There was no white van, no players locked in the dressing room. He was normally there for training at seven, got delayed, rolled in the gate and the county board guys were waiting to have a quiet chat.'

# 67

## MAYO'S WALK-OUT

*Mass Exodus of Players in 'Player Welfare' Row*

Songs of praise are sung about her.

In 1959, the American activist Marian Wright Edelman famously said in Spelman College, 'You can't be what you can't see.' For a generation Cora Staunton has *been* the face young girls have seen. To some her genius is such that when she sparkled, she pointed, like a cathedral spire, to the heavens.

Her career with Mayo is punctuated by brilliance like the 4–13 she scored for Mayo against Leitrim in the 2009 Connacht semi-final and the 2–14 against Galway in the 2016 Connacht final. Then there were individual moments that were simply breath-taking like the League quarter-final against Meath in 2007 when she struck the ball over the bar with the outside of her foot from the sideline fifty yards out à la Ja Fallon in the 1998 All-Ireland final. In her twenty-third season, Cora Staunton led the way as Mayo reached the All-Ireland final again, only for Mick Bohan's Dublin to claim their first All-Ireland.

## THE SUMMER OF THE LONG KNIVES

There had been controversy in 2010 when Mayo's manager quit. The county board, unhappy at 'player power', refused to replace him, and Croke Park had to intervene. Improvements came slowly. It was not until 2016 that the Mayo squad got hot food after training and it was only thanks to the personal generosity of Andy Moran that they were given free membership of his gym.

But in 2018, Mayo's ladies' football was thrown into chaos by the sensational departure of ten players – including eleven-time All-Star Cora Staunton; captain Sarah Tierney and vicecaptain Fiona McHale – while Michael McHale (Fiona's father) withdrew his services from manager Peter Leahy's back-room team days ahead of a crucial All-Ireland qualifier clash with Cavan. They cited 'personal and sensitive player welfare issues'. The majority of those departing from Leahy's squad were from reigning All-Ireland ladies club champions Carnacon.

A storm of controversy ensued because words like 'unsafe' and 'unhealthy' were also used. Mayo LGFA attempted to expel Carnacon from that year's Championship over the walkout of their eight players, but the Connacht Council overturned the decision.

Peter Leahy made a statement some time later to address the issues: 'As far as I'm concerned, this is over. All sides have had their say and all that is happening now is we're giving the public the right to make insulting comments on social media which are hurting a lot of people. It's even going as far as affecting people's mental health, it appears, so I'm asking for people to lay off comments to players. Player welfare is a very open statement and can mean so many things. For example, the players who left have given reasons and examples of player welfare that the players who stayed, management, and county board think are not player welfare issues but management-player issues.

'As far as the players who have left the panel, I hold no grudges personally and I never asked anyone to leave the panel in the first place. I would be delighted to sit down with anyone who wanted to play for Mayo and discuss with an open and transparent view of them wanting to play for Mayo. This is about playing football and anyone wanting to play football for Mayo. I'm the appointed manager and they are welcome to come and play football under my management. The county board, the players and the general public have given me great support. But I mostly want to thank my wife and my three children who have gone through so much pain and suffering because of the speculation caused by words like "unsafe" and "sensitive nature".'

Despite the mass walkout, Mayo reached the All-Ireland semi-final in 2019, losing out to All-Ireland runners-up Galway with Sarah Rowe confirming her status as one of the stars of the game. In 2020, Peter Leahy stepped down as Mayo manager to join Meath's Under-20 football team's short-lived management set up under Bernard Flynn. Former All-Star Fiona McHale said she would be willing to line out for Mayo again in the wake of Peter Leahy's departure as manager.

# 68

# BYE, BYE BABS

*Babs Keating and the Sheep in the Heap*

There are decades when nothing happens and there are weeks when decades happen. The summer of 1998 was the GAA's example of this.

When he managed Celtic, Jock Stein said the essence of good management was 'keeping the six players who love me away from the five who hate me'. Babs Keating would have understood.

After Offaly lost the Leinster final in 1998 to Kilkenny, Babs controversially described the Offaly players he coached as 'sheep in a heap'. Babs met with the county board and decided to stay on as a team manager but the next morning he resigned. He was 'shocked' by an interview in a newspaper by Offaly's star midfielder Johnny Pilkington who had questioned Babs's record with the county, stated that Babs had abandoned Offaly's tradition of ground hurling and questioned the tactics against Kilkenny. Pilkington is not someone to hide his feelings:

'It really got to me. Babs was manager of Offaly. We had some very bad wides on the day and we had conceded two soft goals in the last fifteen minutes. It just seemed he was passing the buck. Maybe it was the players' fault but he was the manager and he could have come down on Tuesday night and said what he had to say in the dressing room. He always referred to Offaly as "them" – never as "us". It was a case of "they" were poor out there and "they" did things wrong.

'Babs's replacement Michael Bond came on the scene after about a week. He just said he liked Offaly hurling and off we went training. Nobody knew who he was. Nobody knew his hurling credentials or anything. We knew he was a teacher. Someone told us he was a principal. He spoke Irish and some of his instructions were in Irish. The training sessions upped significantly. We were a group of lads who were down at the bottom of the barrel. We were after speaking out against the manager. It wasn't anyone else's responsibility to pick it up – only the thirty lads who were there. After Bond came in there was a great buzz in training and we were thinking we were great lads again. We played Kilkenny in a challenge match, though, and they gave us an even bigger beating than they had in the Leinster final! So where did that leave us?

'Loughnane took his eye off the ball before we played Clare in the All-Ireland semi-final. If they had been playing Kilkenny or Galway it would have been a different story. He took Offaly for granted.'

Not surprisingly, Babs Keating's reading of the events of 1998 differs sharply from Pilkington's: 'Johnny Pilkington took great exception to my remark but one of my biggest battles at the time was to get Pilkington to train.'

Hubert Rigney, the Offaly captain, in his victory speech after Offaly beat Kilkenny in the All-Ireland final, said, 'We might have come in the back door, but we're going out the front door.'

Offaly came through the back door, having voted against it, and Offaly, true to form, voted against the back door the following year.

# 69

## WHIPPING BOYS

*Anthony Daly's Speech*

Hurling has produced few more charismatic characters or captivating captains than Anthony Daly. Only Joe Connolly has surpassed his 1995 All-Ireland winning speech. Two years later, though, a speech of Daly's was not as universally welcomed.

To understand his words that day it is important to get some context from him about his previous dealings with Tipperary:

'Any resentment I first formed against Tipp was framed from my experience in St Flannan's. Most of the Tipp borders were sound lads but you still always detected an underlying lack of respect they had for Clare. You could detect the same vibe from some of the clergy who taught, and coached, there. They were brilliant coaches, people who had huge influences on our lives, but even though they were very proud of their Flannan's heritage, you still got that sense off them: "We'll do the coaching because we're from Tipp, we know how it's done right, because ye're only from Clare."

'We didn't play Tipperary much in the early stages of my Clare senior career. But with Len Gaynor as our manager, and

Len having played alongside Babs Keating, we had a track beaten down to Tipp to play them in challenge games and pitch openings. We travelled to every corner of Tipp and it was pure torture. Tipp would regularly hammer us, and it was just a total show for Babs in the lead up to the Championship. He'd have the half-time team talk in the middle of the pitch and the whole Tipp crowd would circle in around him and the players to listen to what Babs had to say. Tipp would be trouncing us by ten or fifteen points and you'd look over and see Babs pointing at players, almost scolding them for not being ahead by twenty points. You could just imagine lads from all over north Tipp going back to the pubs around Nenagh and Toomevara and everywhere else that evening: "Did ye hear what Babs said to Fox and Nicky at half-time?"'

Dalo has one incident that he feels encapsulates the old attitude of Clare hurlers to Tipperary:

'We played Tipp somewhere. I wasn't playing but I was sitting on the bench. At one stage, right in front of us, a ball dropped between Mikey McNamara and Bobby Ryan and Mikey just let fly. Mikey's timing was off, and he met Bobby with full force across both shins. Bobby's shrieks followed that unmistakable sound of ash on bone. Subconsciously, Mikey apologised in full earshot of everyone. "Sorry Bobby." His nickname after that was "Sorry Bobby". It was just a reflex response from Mikey because we were just too deferential to Tipp. We never really believed we could beat them, and the 1993 Munster final annihilation just confirmed what we'd always feared.'

Dalo has one story that he feels illustrates the old Tipp attitude to the Banner:

'I was part of the 1993 Munster Railway Cup which lost to Ulster in the semi-final in Casement Park. Most of the lads were out on the town the night before and were in no fit state to play a match but Babs – who was the manager – was disgusted with the position we were in at half-time. At one stage, he referenced me and Davy Fitzgerald. "It's not young Daly or young Fitzgerald's fault we're in this position," he said, before rounding on the Tipp lads. His point was that Munster can't be relying on those lads to dig us out of this hole, that the digging would have to be done by Nicky (English) or (Johnny) Leahy or Declan Ryan or whoever else from Tipp on the team. He may not have meant it that way but that's the way it appeared to me. We all had to learn but we had to start standing up to Tipp too if we were to ever start beating them.'

It took time for Dalo to change his attitude:

'Before the 1993 Munster final started, Aidan Ryan stood in front of me. He just stared at me for about ten seconds before ambling off into his corner. I met him at the All-Stars later in the year and asked him what he was at. "There was all this talk about you before the game because you played well against Cork," he said. "I'd never heard of you, so I wanted to take a good look at you."

'It just confirmed how tuned out I was. I should have planted him. When we met Tipp in the Munster quarter-final the following year, I was ready. When Ryan stretched out his hand before the game, I caught it and pulled him out the field a few yards. The message was clear – you'll know all about me after today. Tipp never saw our victory coming. I was so overcome afterwards that I cried inside in the dressing room. It was one of the most special days of my career.

'It was a massive breakthrough for us, but Tipp struggled to accept we could beat them. After 1993, Babs came up to our dressing room and made a brilliant speech. When we beat them in 1994, Babs sent up Tommy Barrett to do the talking. That pi**ed us off no end. That day in 1994 was his last time managing that team. He was obviously deeply disappointed, but it was almost as if he was too ashamed to show his face after losing to Clare.

'It was that kind of stuff which prompted the unscripted line "We're no longer the whipping boys of Munster hurling" in my 1997 Munster final-winning speech. Beating them again in the All-Ireland final two months later was the ultimate for all of us in Clare.'

## THE BOYS OF SUMMER

Daly gives a revealing insight into his relationship with his manager:

'I was absolutely honoured to captain the Clare team for eight brilliant years. When the captaincy finally ended, the bould Ger Loughnane came to me one night before training and announced his intention.

'Is that ok,' he said to me, by the way, not really asking but more or less telling me it was happening.

'No problem, Ger, but can I ask who the new captain is?'

'Brian,' he said.

'Lohan?' (Nobody in Clare calls him Brian).

'Yeah.'

'Brilliant,' I said. I went straight over to Lohan and hugged him.

Given the massive respect he had for Daly, Loughnane was not going to stand idly by when it seemed that the hounds of hell were unleashed to hunt him down after his controversial speech:

'Following Clare's victory in the epic Munster final over Tipperary in 1997 Anthony Daly made a speech in which he articulated the feelings and motivations of all Clare players and supporters on that day. Daly had that uncanny knack of putting into words exactly what everybody was feeling, and his comment, "We're no longer the whipping boys of Munster" captured perfectly the mood of the day. A massive cheer went up from the Clare fans when he uttered these words.

'To the utter consternation of everyone in Clare, Liz Howard, the PRO of the Tipperary County Board, wrote in a newspaper article that the statement was "conduct unbecoming". Liz, or Libby as she was then known, spent most of her youth living in Feakle, where her father was the local sergeant, so her comments hit a nerve, especially in her former home village.

'However, when she repeated this "conduct unbecoming" theme two weeks later, the whole thing spiralled out of control. Other newspapers picked it up and it became the topic of conversation. Dalo said to me, "This whole thing has gone out of control." So, I said to Dalo to leave it to me. I wrote an open letter to Liz Howard and that's when the whole controversy really started.

'It finally came to a head when Dalo called me and said that a man came to the door of his shop in Ennis and said, "You shouldn't have said that."

'Dalo replied, "What did I say?"

'"Well, I don't know. But you shouldn't have said it."

'That is the perfect illustration of what people pick up from the paper. That's why I'm glad I always treated the press with the respect they deserved.'

**SELECTION BOX**

The philosopher G.W.F. Hegel (1770–1831) believed that history was ruled by what he called the 'master-slave dialectic'. Applied to our societal history, it tells us that, when left to ourselves, we often organise our lives according to the principle of domination. Loughnane believed in a hurling version of that. In the early part of his life, hurling was dominated by three super-powers: Kilkenny, Tipperary and Cork and they only gave crumbs from the table to everybody else. As Clare manager he wanted to challenge that power imbalance and he was going to take unorthodox measures to do so.

Loughnane annoyed the media by innovating a new technique. It has long been part of the culture of big GAA games as the spectators gather to watch a match to hear the famous 'fógra' and discover that a star player has recovered from an injury, in a miracle of Biblical proportions, and is to take the place of 'A.N. Other' despite all the media stories to the contrary. Ger Loughnane took the deception a step further by announcing dummy teams.

Loughnane's reading material stretched into dense business manuals. He was very taken by an idea in the *Sloan Management Review* which stated that, 'By breaking the rules of the game and thinking of new ways to compete, a company can strategically redefine its business and catch its bigger competitors off guard. The trick is not to play the game better than the competition but to develop and play an altogether different game.' From the time he took over as Clare manager he sought to put that philosophy into practice.

Clare's preparations for the 1998 Munster Championship appeared to get off to a bad start when Cork handed them out an eleven-point drubbing in the National League semi-final on 3 May in Thurles. Seven weeks later the two teams would meet again in the same venue in the Munster semi-final. Michael O'Halloran and Conor Clancy were both named in the original selection but, instead, Brian Quinn and Alan Markham took the field against Cork as Loughnane recalls:

'In '98, the Munster semi-final against Cork was always going to be a crunch game for us. We drove home the message to the players beforehand that we couldn't let Cork beat us. That was the game we played our first real dummy team. I can still see their management team, Tom Cashman and Jimmy Barry-Murphy, looking out at the field, looking at their programmes, looking at the numbers on the players' backs and trying to figure who exactly was playing and who wasn't. They were totally confused!

'We wore Cork down physically and in the last twenty minutes we completely outhurled them with speed and skill and everything you'd want to see in your team. At one stage Brian Corcoran got the ball. He turned to his right and P.J. O'Connell was there. He turned to his left and Jamesie (O'Connor) was there. Jamesie took it off him and put it over the bar. Corcoran looked out at Jimmy Barry-Murphy and threw his arms up in the air. It was like he was asking: what can we do?'

### REVENGE IS SWEET

Many within the GAA community and the media were perturbed by Loughnane's use of dummy teams. He was unfazed by the controversy:

'Nothing characterised the team spirit better than the switching of teams before games. There were articles written in papers about how their families felt and all this kind of rubbish. To me that was utter nonsense. The whole dynamic driving the squad and those of us on the sideline was that each of us would do everything possible for Clare to win. When we switched around teams before games everybody understood that. We used every tactic possible to outwit the opposition in order to win. Everyone on the panel understood that. It was the people outside the panel who didn't understand.

'The idea of the dummy teams came about from the temperament of certain players that if they knew they were expected to play they would get nervous and over-excited and not do themselves justice on the big day. We had a meeting before the 1997 All-Ireland final and someone said we can't start Niall Gilligan because he started against Cork in the Munster semi-final and he played poorly and was taken off. We decided that we'd get around that by not naming him on the original selection – so that he'd be on but wouldn't be on!

'It worked really well with Gilligan. He was going to be on Paul Shelly who had a big reputation, and everyone would be telling him what Shelly would do to him. He didn't know he was going to be till a few hours before the game which meant that he was so unfazed by the occasion that he'd scored two points before Shelly knew where he was. Niall was very young and inexperienced and maybe if he had known he was playing, he wouldn't have performed as well.

'Another thing is if you have a hot sunny day when the game is going to be very fast it will suit a certain type of player, so picking your team on the Tuesday night when you don't know the conditions is absolutely nonsensical to me.

'It worked so well from the start that we decided to use it for other players and after a while the players started to like it because once the team was named it meant nothing. They knew that it could be any combination of six forwards out of nine. This meant that everybody had hopes of playing until the day came. Often times, I didn't tell the players until we had the puck-out who was on and who was off. It worked extremely well and never caused dissension except one time with Colin Lynch. I always said that once they had a good game from the start you could let them go. After Gilligan played well in the '97 final we could pick him from the start.'

# 70

## ROCK STAR

### *Cork Take the Train*

Barney Rock was a darling of Hill 16.

The love affair started slowly in 1978 when he was a star of Dublin's minor team. Things moved up a gear the following year when he was key to the Dubs winning a minor All-Ireland. His senior career with the Dubs began in 1980 and he scored thirty goals (and 360 points in his ninety-nine competitive games) for the boys in blue. However, the Ballymun Kickhams sharpshooter will always be remembered for two goals – though his late goal against Cork in the 1983 All-Ireland semi-final to draw the game deserves a more hallowed place in the canon of important goals.

A few weeks later, he showed amazing skill to deftly lob Galway keeper Pádraig Coyne in the 11th minute from 40 metres in the most atrocious weather conditions in the All-Ireland Final. It was the rock Galway perished on as the 'Twelve Apostles' famously defied the odds against the Boys in Maroon and White.

Rock's second most famous goal had a pantomime quality. The 1987 League quarter-final clash between Dublin and Cork has its own unique place in the annals of the GAA.

After the regulation seventy minutes the scores were level. Both sides headed to the sanctuary of the dressing room to prepare for extra time. Or so we thought. Then like a bolt out of the blue Cork announced that they would not be playing extra time. As the Croke Park officials frantically sought to find a resolution to the shambles, the Cork mentors upped the ante by stating that they had not been told that extra time would be played. It later emerged that some had but they had not passed on that important detail to all concerned. Then, as chaos and confusion reigned supreme, Cork announced that they could not afford to stand around and debate the relative merits of extra time as they had a train to catch.

As the Cork team headed to the station, Dublin sauntered on to the field all by themselves. Not surprisingly they won an uncontested throw-in. The ball was pumped in to Barney Rock who calmly dispatched the ball into the net.

This tale of the unexpected was the most bizarre ending to a big game that Croke Park had ever seen.

# 71

## DOUBLE HUMILIATION

*Dermot Earley Embarrassed*

He was a big man who twice in a few weeks was made to feel like a speck of dust.

In 1975, Roscommon played in a League match. In the course of the game Dermot Earley was fouled and fell heavily as the sizable frame of Jimmy Keaveney came tumbling down on top of him. As Earley rose to his feet a scuffle broke out in which there were four minor altercations with Dublin's Bobby Doyle. After the fourth incident, Earley's patience snapped and he punched Doyle on the nose. Nothing electrifies the crowd like a good fight and there was a surge forward and backward that grew thicker and thicker as people got the news that finally, thank God, something interesting was about to happen. The referee had no option but to send him off. As he made the lonely journey to the dug-out, Earley's brain was spinning and his spirits were absolutely crushed:

'It was the most devastating thing that ever happened to me playing football – much worse than losing the All-Ireland. As I walked back to the line, the realisation of all the things that were going to happen came.

'I always tried to be as fair as I could. Even if I fouled, I always felt it was wrong afterwards. I would be concerned if I fouled in the course of the game on a number of occasions. To be warned by a referee is a blot on your copybook but to be sent off is incredible.'

Although he was just a young boy at the time, Paul Earley, Dermot's brother, remembers that day well:

'I have to confess I remember being delighted he did what he did that day. I always felt that he took much punishment on the pitch without taking any action. When the game was over our eyes met through the crowd. He came over to me with his head down in a state of total dejection. He was unable to look me in the eye as he said: "I'm sorry I let you down".'

The sending off was extensively reported the next day in the newspapers. The incident was the major talking point as his fellow army officers gathered for their coffee break in the morning. When Earley walked into the officers' mess there was a sudden silence:

'Someone asked me if I had anything to say and I replied: "I shouldn't have done it." After that everything went back to normal.'

The situation was complicated by the fact that Earley was due to travel with the All-Stars the following month to America. The rule at the time was that any player who was sent off was ineligible to be selected for the All-Stars that year. Would Earley make the touring party?

The situation was resolved shortly after when he received a telegram from the legendary John Kerry O'Donnell in New York who offered to pay his expenses for the trip because:

*Red-blooded men are welcome in Gaelic Park.*

## FROM ELATION TO DEFLATION

Although he did travel, Earley regretted it. He had been given to understand that he would be part of the touring side, the same as everybody else, but that was not the case. This was brought home to him almost immediately. A welcoming committee greeted the team at the airport. Each player was called forward individually and presented with an envelope which included details of accommodation, itinerary and the allowance provided for the tour. Although Earley was called forward there was no envelope to be found for him. He wished the ground would open and swallow him he was so embarrassed. Similar incidents were to occur three more times on the tour.

However, the most galling part came at the end of the tour when a non-GAA traveling official reminded him that John Kerry O'Donnell had paid his expenses on the tour and, accordingly, he should thank John Kerry before he left. Earley felt like the most junior pupil in school receiving a lecture from the headmaster. Such a reminder was totally unnecessary.

## STRANGE BUT TRUE

A sending off has ruined many players' chances of winning an All-Star down the years. The most bizarre case was that of Monaghan's Eamonn McEneaney. Throughout the 1985 Championship he showcased, particularly in his wonderful performance against Kerry in the All-Ireland semi-final, that he was the best centre half-forward in the country. However, he missed out on the All-Star he clearly deserved because he was involved in a minor skirmish in a seven-a-side tournament in Dublin. Consequently, he and an opponent were told by referee John Bailey to leave the field 'to cool off'. They were replaced and then permitted to play in the next match, which could not have happened if they had been sent off officially. McEneaney was notified a few weeks later that the episode was being treated as a dismissal, ending his chance of an All-Star that year.

# 72

# RING OF FIRE

*Christy Ring's Galway Clash*

In 2022, Madonna attributed her success to sushi. It sounds a bit fishy to me.

Carl Jung proposed the idea that there was not only a personal unconscious but also a collective unconscious from which certain universal symbols and patterns have arisen throughout history. This collective unconsciousness is linked with our ancestors. Jung would have understood perfectly why Christy Ring occupies such a hallowed place in the mythology of the GAA.

In the 1960s, Ring was being interviewed by Bob Hyland, a journalist then with *The Irish Press*. The previous week, Ring had read a piece that Hyland had written on the Tipperary All-Ireland-winning hurler Séamus Bannon who had contended that to strike the sliotar cleanly for a sideline cut he needed a soft tuft of grass. Ring took the journalist by surprise when he brought him out on the road. He placed the sliotar on the road and hit it with the sweetest cut of his hurley and drove it into the nearest field. Then he turned to Hyland and instructed him to write to Bannon and to tell him that, 'the grass never grew on the Mardyke Road'. A small fable of Ring's perfectionist streak and of his personality.

One of the many stories told about Ring is that as he was leading his team out of the tunnel, when they were halfway out, he turned them back to the dressing room. Then he took off his Cork jersey, held it up and asked his players to look at the colour and what it meant to them. After that the team went out with fire in their bellies and played out of their skins.

In his classic book *Over the Bar* Breandán Ó hEithir writes about how Ring could match his great skills with toughness. After one game a few young lads shouted at him that he was a dirty player. Ring took great umbrage at this suggestion and swore at them with such viciousness that they ran away terrified.

While he championed skill greatly, there was one quality Ring valued on the hurling pitch above all others: courage.

### CLASHING HEADS

Mick Dunne was a big fan of Ring but was aware that he was no angel:

'Without question the greatest player I ever saw was Christy Ring. He was probably the greatest player that ever laced a boot. He was the one I admired most, the man I was most happy to report upon and the man I was always pleased to talk with.

'He was involved in a few controversies in his time. In 1953, Galway hurlers, powered by the great Josie Gallagher, had beaten Kilkenny in the semi-final and qualified to play the Christy Ring led Cork side in the All-Ireland final. Galway had the game for the winning but failed to take off Mick Burke despite his obvious concussion. What made their inaction all the more inexplicable was that Burke was marking the great Christy Ring.

'The controversy which ensued stemmed from the fact that a large section of the Galway crowd had booed Ring throughout the game and that Galway appeared to have targeted the Cork legend for "special treatment".

'The post-match celebration was affected by events on the field. A blow had been struck on Burke during the game. So incensed were five or six of the Galway players by this that they had an altercation with Ring that evening at the official reception. They returned to the Cork hotel at breakfast the next morning to vent their displeasure again, albeit only using verbal means on that occasion.'

# PART IV
# The Hand of History

*Croke Park, Hill 16 hecklin' with the supporter's crew,*
*Screamin' for the boys wearin' the navy & blue.*
*Downin' pints of the black stuff after the game in Quinn's,*
*We're rarely disappointed as Dublin almost always wins!*

The terrifically talented young poet Emma Dennis captures the sheer joy of being a fan of Gaelic games in these lines. At its best, sport can bring people together. Who will ever forget the spirit in Ireland during the glory days of Italia '90? Think of the pride in Westmeath after their thrilling draw against Wexford in the 2022 Leinster Hurling Championship or, a few weeks earlier, the joy in Sligo when they won their first ever under-20 Connacht title.

Yet sport can also be an agent of division. In 1998 while Bertie Ahern and Tony Blair were negotiating the historic Good Friday Agreement the GAA continued its ban on members of the RUC or the British security forces playing Gaelic games.

Martin Luther King claimed that 'We are not makers of history, we are made by history'. The reality is that history casts a long shadow in Irish life generally and in the GAA in particular. Our nation's changing history has provided the soundtrack to controversies for the GAA and this section revisits some of them.

PART II

The Hand of History

# 73

# ARE YOU RIGHT THERE MICHAEL?

*Michael Cusack Ruffles Feathers*

James Joyce immortalised him as 'The Citizen' in *Ulysses*. 'Citizen' was a regular term by which he greeted people by.

Like so many Irish organisations since, almost the first thing the GAA did was to have a split. From the beginning the GAA has had a history of abrasive personalities, with the gift of rubbing people up the wrong way. Michael Cusack will always be remembered for his role in founding the GAA in 1884.

He was born in a tiny cottage in a small village called Carron on the fringe of the Burren, one of six children to a shepherd and his wife. He qualified as a national teacher, teaching in such prestigious schools as Blackrock College, St Colman's College, Newry, St John's, Kilkenny and Clongowes before founding a Civil Service academy in Dublin's Gardiner Street for students preparing for entrance exams into the British civil service.

Cusack won the national shot-put championship in Lansdowne Road. He was annoyed that sport in Ireland was run by and for the benefit of the Anglo-Irish ruling class. Although he played rugby, he criticised the elitist manner in which it was run and he argued that all sport in Ireland was being anglicised.

As a member of the Fenian Brotherhood he wrote in the *United Irishman*, 'In order to be a Fenian, I had to be a hurler.' The problem was that ince the famine hurling had gone into sharp decline. In an effort to revive the game, he set up the Dublin Hurling Club and began campaigning for a new association devoted to 'the preservation and cultivation of our national pastimes and for providing national amusements for the Irish people during their leisure hours'. As a result, he called a meeting of interested parties in the billiard room at Hayes Commercial Hotel, Thurles, on Saturday 1 November, 1884. The rest is history.

Cusack chose some allies wisely. He invited Archbishop Dr Croke to become the first patron. The powerful cleric's written response so succinctly captured the reasons why the GAA was being formed that the first edition of the rule book recommended Croke's letter be read aloud at every annual meeting thereafter, just to remind everybody what this was about. The letter remained in every Official Guide every year. Cusack played a vital conciliatory role in holding the fledgling body together after the Fenians hijacked the 1887 Convention.

Yet, having given birth to the Association, Cusack almost strangled it in its infancy, because of his abrasive personality. People often miss out on the historical significance of the 'Athletic' in the title of the GAA. In the early years it was envisaged that athletics would play a much greater role in the life of the GAA. One of the people trying to ensure this was John L. Dunbar. He wrote to Cusack in December 1885 suggesting that the GAA and the athletics organisation should meet 'with a view to a possible merger'. Cusack, an enthusiastic hurler, did not mince or waste his words in his response. The letter read as follows:

> *GAA*
> *4 Gardiners Place*
> *Dublin*
>
> *Dear Sir,*
> *I received your letter this morning and burned it.*
> *Yours faithfully,*
> *Michael Cusack*

Cusack also alienated Archbishop Croke who stated that he could not continue as patron 'if Mr Michael Cusack is allowed to play the dictator in the GAA's counsels, to run a reckless tilt with impunity and without rebuke'.

# 74

## DOWNHILL FROM HERE

*The Origins of Hill 16*

The founding of the GAA is part of the story of struggle, the spirit of a nation in chains trying to break free, of wanting something more and finding the courage to run away from the greatest empire the world had ever known.

The demand for independence would grow, culminating in the 1916 Rising. The GAA was affected by the Rising in a number of ways. To take one example, Roscommon started to wear green and black jerseys: green for Ireland and black as a sign of sympathy for those who lost their lives in the 1916 Rising.

However, the link between 1916 and the GAA was sometimes exaggerated. When I was in my early twenties I got involved in writing about sport and one of the first people I spoke with was the late Raymond Smith – who at the time was to the print media what Mícheál Ó Muircheartaigh is to broadcasting. He had built his reputation on the basis of some brilliant writing such as his description of the funeral of hurling's most iconic name:

'Christy Ring, the undisputed genius of three decades of competitive hurling, yesterday drew the crowds for the last time. But never did they return out in such spontaneous tribute as they did for the final, sad procession as the nation's superb hurler went back to the soil of his native Cloyne.'

Raymond told me the story of how Hill 16 got its name – how it was built with the rubble from the 1916 Rising – and he told me about the time he had a drink with a man who got five shillings for wheeling the rubble into Croke Park. This story and this belief was, I thought, universal largely because Raymond propagated it with such gusto.

The only problem was that I discovered that the hill was actually built in 1915.

# 75

## I CAN'T CLOSE MY EYES AND MAKE IT GO AWAY

*Bloody Sunday*

*'To the living we owe respect, but to the dead we owe only the truth.'*

VOLTAIRE

There was a battle outside and it was raging.

The promotional posters advertised it as a 'Great Challenge Match' between the footballers of Dublin and Tipperary. It was just minutes old when British soldiers began firing. There was a political context.

The British prime minister David Lloyd George on 9 November 1920 in a speech to the Guildhall in London about his armed forces' standing in Ireland at the time claimed that they had the Irish resistance all but crumbled. What he did not know was that Michael Collins had a plan.

Collins had been preparing detailed dossiers on suspected members of the so-called Cairo Gang (because of their fondness of socialising at Cafe Cairo in the city), an elite group of

British Intelligence Officers operating in Dublin. One of Collins' sources identified the members of the gang and suggested to Collins that the next Sunday morning was the most opportune time to move.

That Sunday was 21 November. The night before, men were selected to head the assassinations teams.

Harry Colley in an interview with the 1947 Bureau of Military History said: 'It is well to place on record that Seán Russell, the O/C, explained to them that the men to be shot were members of a new secret service which the enemy had brought into this country; that if any man had moral scruples about going on this operation he was at full liberty to withdraw and no one would think any the worse of him; that he wanted every man to be satisfied in his conscience that he could properly take part in this operation.'

At 9am on the morning of Sunday, 21 November, IRA units, under orders from Collins, shot nineteen men in their bedrooms, hallways and gardens. Fourteen were killed on the spot and a fifteenth died of wounds weeks later. All within fifteen minutes.

At 38 Upper Mount Street, Vinny Byrne asked to see Lieutenant Peter Ames and Lieutenant George and was allowed enter. Later he told the Bureau of Military History: 'As I opened the folding-doors, the officer, who was in bed, was in the act of going for his gun under his pillow. Doyle and myself dashed into the room, at the same time ordering him to put up his hands, which he did. I marched my officer down to the back room where the other officer was. He was standing up in the bed, facing the wall. I ordered mine to do likewise. When the two of them were together I thought to myself "The Lord have mercy on your souls!" I then opened fire. They both fell dead.'

Michael Collins, during the Anglo-Irish Treaty talks in 1921, defended the attacks: 'My one intention was the destruction of the undesirables who continued to make miserable the lives of ordinary decent citizens. I have proof enough to assure myself of the atrocities which this gang of spies and informers have committed. Perjury and torture are words too easily known to them. If I had a second motive it was no more than a feeling such as I would have for a dangerous reptile. By their destruction the very air is made sweeter. That should be the future's judgment on this particular event. For myself, my conscience is clear. There is no crime in detecting and destroying in war-time, the spy and the informer. They have destroyed without trial. I have paid them back in their own coin.'

### REVENGE MISSION

The British forces responded to their casualties by sending soldiers to Croke Park. Officers of the Dublin Brigade of the IRA came to Croke Park an hour before the match to recommend that the afternoon's big football match between Dublin and Tipperary should be postponed. They had heard rumours of a raid on Croke Park by British forces. However, GAA officials resolved to go ahead with the match fearing that a cancellation would lead to panic and a rush to the gates that would create a safety risk.

There were more than 5,000 people in Croke Park as the ball was thrown in at 3.15pm. Jack Shouldice, an IRA man who had previously won an All-Ireland Football Championship with Dublin, was central to the planning of the game. He described the events: 'The game had only started when trouble began. An aeroplane, rare at the time, flew over the grounds and returned, apparently to report or give some signal to the Black and Tans and Auxiliaries. We had not long to wait, for the game was not in progress more than fifteen minutes when lorries of the raiders swooped down on the grounds and without any warning burst their way to the railings surrounding the playing pitch, opened fire on the people on the far side and on the players.

'Hundreds were wounded or injured in the mad scramble that followed, trampled or torn with barbed wire on the walls. They were perched up on the old stand, on the railway walls and any position overlooking us. Rifles and machine guns were trained on us. The commands rung out: "Put up your hands and keep them up." The searching went on for an hour or more.'

After the shooting had ended, two Tipp players lay on the field. Despite the fact that he was covered in blood, Jim Egan got up and walked towards a priest in the crowd, asking him to perform the last rites for Michael Hogan. The full-back from Grangemockler was already gone to meet his God by the time the man of the cloth reached him. Thirteen others, some of them children, were gunned down that afternoon but, as the only player to be killed, Hogan's death cast a long shadow. The most celebrated stand in the whole GAA is named after him.

Some of the mourners were joined by Luke O'Toole, the general secretary of the GAA, as he meandered through the bloody grass of Croke Park, shadowed by a journalist. They heard a woman sobbing deeply, her attempts to stifle the sound spilled into stuttering gasps. A vigil of sorrow was praying at the spot where the light had faded from Hogan's eyes and it was as if he saw nothing but a trembling darkness.

To this day, Tipperary people carry the psychic wounds. Babs Keating is a case in point: 'My granduncle Tommy Ryan won two All-Irelands with Tipperary. He was playing in Croke Park on Bloody Sunday and helped remove Michael Hogan from the pitch after he had been shot by the Black and Tans.'

Eugene McGee believed that Michael Hogan's enduring legacy may have been that his murder reinforced the opposition to deleting Rules 21, 27 and 42 for decades after.

Having beaten Dublin in the 1920 All-Ireland final (played, confusingly, in 1922 because of the political turmoil), Tipperary would never win the competition again. Perhaps the most direct consequence was that General Frank Crozier, the man in nominal charge of the Croke Park operation, became a committed pacifist later in life.

A plaque in Croke Park carries the name of the Bloody Sunday victims and speaks to the whispering voices of faceless generations, the GAA's unique sacred scripture.

It is a voice for the dead, the names engraved eternally on the hidden chambers of the heart.

They are custodians of our troubled past.

They continue to speak to a requiem of voices.

Go ndéana Dia trócaire ar a n-anamacha dílse.

## LEGACY?

The real political ramifications of Bloody Sunday are difficult to assess. There was a legitimate outrage in Britain about the actions of Collins and his men. Internationally, though, there was massive condemnation about the actions of the British forces in Croke Park. Not for the first or last time was Collins proven to be prophetic when he said that the ultimate victory would come not to the side that afflicted the most but the side that endured the most. It would take months but the international mood music after Bloody Sunday was such that the British were moved to come to the table. Whisperings grew too loud to be safely ignored.

Was the bloodshed of the War of Independence worth it? That is a political judgement but what is striking is how quickly disillusionment set in. The sheer energy expended in removing British forces may be one reason. The Civil War is another. Both left people with very little energy with which to reimagine a society. Instead, exhausted revolutionaries lapsed back into the inherited English forms. The Civil War induced a profound caution, making many distrustful of innovation. Fancy theories about a republic had, after all, cost hundreds of Irish lives.

# 76

## STAIRWAY TO HEAVEN

*Ban on Priests Playing*

The late Brendan Behan once went into a bookshop and saw a copy of the *Catholic Standard* and remarked: 'Ah here is the news of the next world.' This is a revealing observation highlighting as it does the way in which many people think of the Christian life, to prepare our souls here in this world for the next world. This kind of dualism between heaven and earth or body and spirit dominated Catholic theology for centuries.

The long relationship between the GAA and the Catholic Church is rich and complex. Although culturally, and in many respects spiritually, they were very close and the Catholic Church was to the forefront in promoting the GAA, the Church banned its priests and seminarians from actually playing inter-county football for years. Seminarians and priests had to assume a name to allow their footballing careers to continue at the highest level despite the curious irony of men who so often preached the truth practising deception. Everybody knew who they were, including the bishop, and a blind eye was turned. It was a Jesuitical solution to a uniquely clerical problem.

## MUNDY

Kerry is the only county that has produced a bishop who was the holder of an All-Ireland medal. In 1924, Kerry faced Dublin in the All-Ireland final. Kerry's Mundy Prenderville was a student priest in All Hallows College in Dublin at the time and was spirited the short journey down the road just in time to play and helped Kerry to win. Christianity is all about forgiveness, but they took football seriously back then and Mundy was refused readmission to the college after that! He had to find a new seminary to continue his studies and subsequently became Archbishop of Perth.

In 1955, the late Michael Cleary was in line for a place on the Dublin team to play Kerry in the All-Ireland football final. The problem was that he was also attending the diocesan seminary in Clonliffe at the time. Under College regulations there was no way he would be freed to play the match. It was a straightforward choice: which was the more important to him; to play in the final or to become a priest? He chose to become a priest but as the final was being played he could practically see the ball down the road in the college. After his ordination he played for Dublin under the name of Mick Casey.

## NO CAPTAIN MARVEL

The late Seán Freyne captained the Mayo minors in 1953, but missed out on playing in the final because he had entered the seminary in Maynooth and the rules of the Catholic Church precluded him from playing. He navigated the choppy waters of deception and finally got the opportunity to play for Mayo seniors in 1956 against Galway under an assumed name. Before the match Tom Langan told him that he would send him in the perfect ball. Uncharacteristically he did not.

Ten years later Seán was walking into Croke Park and met Langan for the first time since that day: 'I got a very revealing

287

insight into Langan's perfectionism. Tom's immediate response was to say to me: "Jaysus that was an awful ball I sent you."'

Seán left the priesthood and went on to become Professor of Theology in Trinity College. He explained the Church's thinking to me in relation to the ban on priests playing Gaelic games:

'There were two aspects to it. The Catholic Church was and is always preoccupied by appearances. If a priest was spotted playing aggressively it was seen to reflect negatively on the Church.

'There was also a deeper issue. Playing sport was of this world. Priests were supposed to be of the next world. Salvation then was attained by rejecting and shunning the worldly dimension of our human existence. Modernism was condemned and thus Catholic theology was prevented from engaging with developments in human thought. Human existence itself was often seen as sinful and unworthy and the emphasis was on the salvation of one's soul which would be attained in the next life. This culture promoted a restrictive approach to human behaviour and reflected a highly paternalistic mindset. There was a risk that the ecclesiastical apparatus of the Church might overshadow the action of the Spirit and of grace in people's lives. The shadow of the temptation to a deep attachment to habitual forms of religious expression rather than to the spirit of life they aimed to express hovered ominously.

'"Rome has spoken: the issue is decided" summed up the strength of the institutional dimension. The people of God had not come of age; they were "the simple faithful" who obeyed out of unquestioning conviction or out of fear, or both. The term "flock" has been described as the saddest way to describe a group which has enough conviction to live out their religious beliefs in public.

'That all changed in the 1960s and the Second Vatican Council when the Church lost its controlling power: but that was arguably good. To have no power is better than to misuse it. In the New Testament those who wish to wield power must become servants of all. The Church always needs reform, and with Vatican II now upon it, at last this area of authority was seen as humble service. In the vision of Vatican II Catholics were to be active: peace-making and forgiveness were to be distinctive hallmarks of a renewed Christian people, who must never become self-absorbed but keep looking outward. What was left, then, after the Council was a church shorn of outmoded accretions, whose members were freed to live out the Good News in creative ways. The ban on priests playing Gaelic games was quietly and quickly shelved. This allowed someone like Iggy Clarke to become one of the biggest names in hurling, winning multiple All-Stars for Galway even though he was a priest at the time.'

Two-time All-Ireland-winning manager John O'Mahony was one of the last to be confronted with the rule. He attended Maynooth as a clerical student. His bother Dan did too and is a priest. John O'Mahony turned his back on the priesthood. 'I didn't last the pace and nearly didn't get to play in the 1971 minor final. I remember going up to Monsignor Newman, the college president, at the time, and there was no guarantee that I'd be allowed play. There was a retreat on the day and Dan and I had to break the rules to escape because you weren't meant to leave. We had got the press onside by asking them not to print our names in the report. We appeared in the papers as J and D Maloney!'

# 77

## BAN-ER HEADLINE

*The End of the Ban*

1971 marked a momentous event in the history of GAA which also made a powerful statement that Ireland was becoming more tolerant.

In 1887, Maurice Davin had called for a ban on rugby and soccer. The political leanings of the GAA had been clearly manifested in 1902 when Rule 27, 'The Ban', was introduced. It prohibited members of the GAA from playing, attending or promoting 'foreign games' like soccer, rugby, hockey and cricket. Ireland's first President, Douglas Hyde, was removed as a patron of the GAA within a few months of his inauguration in 1938. This was because Hyde had the temerity to attend a soccer game between Ireland and Poland at Dalymount Park and, in the process, he breached the GAA's ban on foreign games. In effect, the GAA had a vigilante committee whose brief was to attend 'foreign games' and report GAA members in attendance either in a playing or supporting capacity.

One of the most interesting illustrations of the ban was the story of Ireland rugby legend Moss Keane. Initially, Moss was a Gaelic footballer before switching to rugby in UCC. As his rugby career took off, he played under the assumed name of Moss Fenton. Then once the ban was lifted, he was able to play under his real name. Hence the report in the *Evening Echo*: 'Fenton was dropped for Moss Keane, the well-known GAA player.'

Thanks in large measure to an ongoing campaign of Dublin's Tom Woulfe, the GAA ban on GAA players playing or even watching Gaelic games was revoked by 1971.

The actual moment itself came during a congress vote on Saturday 10 April, 1971 in Queen's University Belfast when the Association ditched the prohibition and triggered a decades-long process of divesting itself of exclusionary rules.

The *Irish Times* GAA correspondent Paddy Downey observed: 'Today, the 86th annual assembly of GAA legislators opens and it is fair to say that this meeting, which continues tomorrow, will be the most momentous in the long and chequered history of the great organisation.'

Only Antrim and Sligo opposed it. The abolition of the Ban did not happen in a vacuum. Instead, it was a cumulative process throughout the 1960s even though its failure to achieve one third of the delegates' votes in 1962, '65 or '68 meant it could only be considered every three years.

The GAA and the country at large changed profoundly in the 1960s. In terms of sport an important catalyst for change was the 1966 World Cup, held in England, and which was seen widely on Irish television because RTÉ broadcast highlights.

A motion from Mayo in 1968 to commission a report into the reasons for holding on to the Ban culminated in another motion in 1970 tabled by Meath to the effect that ordinary members should be allowed vote on the matter before it came to congress the following year.

At the turn of 1970 and early '71, the message coming out of county conventions all around the country was clear. The end was nigh for Rule 27. Thirty counties and four British delegations voted for abolition.

That is not to say there were no dissenting voices. One delegate described it as 'Paisleyism in reverse'.

Pat Fanning, the then GAA President, continued to believe in Rule 27 and was concerned that the Association was in danger of losing its soul:

'In a short while now, you will acknowledge the expressed will of the Association and delete a rule, which for many of us was a rule of life and reflected and epitomised the very spirit of the Association. The rule deleted – what then? Do we then reject the past and with deletion, proclaim ourselves a mere sports organisation?'

Nonetheless when the motion was passed to end the ban, Fanning said: 'Let there be no sounding of trumpets as the rule disappears. Nor should there be talk of defeat. If victory there be, let it be a victory for the Association.'

Another proposal was the deletion of Rule 26 or the prohibition on members of the Northern security forces joining the GAA. As the storm clouds from the Troubles in the north were gathering, the motion was withdrawn and in his speech to Congress, Fanning described the very prospect of it succeeding as 'a rejection of the very basis of GAA national thinking'. The escalating violence and political tensions meant that abolition of that rule would take another thirty years.

Fanning and 'the traditionalists' did secure a victory with Rule 42, the prohibition on other sports being played in GAA grounds. It was the creation of a group set up by Fanning to alleviate the damage done by the dilution of the ban. He argued:

'Are our clubs, their roots deep in parish, town and city to cease to be GAA units as our fathers moulded them? Is it possible our Gaelic fields, purchased and developed with GAA money so that Irish boys should play Irish games, may be used for other purposes to weaken and perhaps ultimately destroy the Association?'

In the interest of fairness, it is important to also note that Fanning's address in 1971 was much more positive and outward looking. He spoke of exhibition matches between the All-Ireland champions Kerry and an 'all-star team drawn from several of our counties' that had taken place in 1970 and said that such events 'were capable of becoming a permanent feature of the GAA year'. In December, the first official All-Stars selections were announced.

In fact, Pat Fanning also set out a message of openness and positivity that indicated that great days were around the corner. Hopefully it continues to have a deep resonance for the GAA and for the wider society today: 'The future is ours to shape. Let's move towards it with confidence.'

# 78

## ALL ALONG THE WATCHTOWER

*The Occupation of Crossmaglen*

To paraphrase Bruce Springsteen, troubled times had come to their hometown.

At half-time during the 1981 Ulster final, the Clones playing field was filled with people carrying black flags, supporting prisoners who were on hunger strike for political status in Long Kesh prison. Ulster football could not escape the dark shadows cast by the Northern troubles. In July 1972, Frank Corr, one of the most prominent GAA personalities, was shot dead becoming one of the first of more than forty people to die in Northern Ireland because of their involvement with the GAA. In May 1972, during a match between Crossmaglen and Silverbridge, a young British soldier got out and shoved his rifle into the face of Silverbridge player Patrick Tennyson. Indeed, Crossmaglen was to have its ground occupied by the British army for thirty-seven years.

Margaret McConville, the club's officer, became a household name because of her media appearances and famously described her home place as 'the town the army took over'. The club's premises and playing pitches were requisitioned in 1971 and it stood for more than twenty-five years as a potent symbol of the GAA's importance in the community.

One of the most infamous images in the GAA's history is of British army helicopters landing on the Crossmaglen pitch. Star player Oisín McConville was shown a clip from a television programme made in 1980, during which soldiers serving in the town were interviewed. One helicopter pilot commented as he flew over the area:

'We're approaching Crossmaglen now; it's about a mile north of the border. It is without doubt the worst area in the whole of Northern Ireland and has been responsible for one in six of all the security forces killed in the present campaign in Northern Ireland. It just happens that everybody who lives in this particular area is violently pro the IRA and therefore it's always been a stronghold of republican feeling and I think has now identified itself more closely with the cause or the struggle or whatever – the terrorist campaign – than any other particular area.'

In response, Oisín noted, 'Some assumption to make for somebody flying in a helicopter above your town.'

In 1974, some of the club's land had been requisitioned for a helicopter pad. Two years after that, a right of way over the front of the club was also requisitioned. The popular view is that it was only the intervention of the then Minister for Foreign Affairs, the late Garret FitzGerald, that prevented the whole club premises being requisitioned. But the catalogue of harassment continued abated. In 1978, an under-14 match had to be moved to a different venue when the army refused access to the pitch.

A year after the Good Friday Agreement the then Northern Ireland Secretary Mo Mowlam ordered a complete withdrawal of British troops after twenty-eight years.

Springsteen would have said: Hello sunshine. Can you please stay?

# 79

# NO CHRISTMAS CHEER

*The RDS Affair*

It was clear that it was a big issue because John Bowman was talking about it at length on RTÉ's then flagship current affairs programme *Questions and Answers*.

It was a public relations debacle for the GAA.

Yet it all started innocently enough when Ringsend GAA club Clanna Gael Fontenoy had an idea for a fundraiser: to stage an inter-county match in Dublin 4 on 15 December 1991.

Their original choice for a venue, Shelbourne Park, was ruled out. The club then came upon the idea of a double bill at the RDS – including a League of Ireland soccer fixture between Bohemians and Shamrock Rovers (who at the time were tenants were based in the RDS). The glamour Gaelic football match was to feature League holders Dublin and All-Ireland champions Down. Dublin were riding the surf of a popularity wave at the time on foot of their epic four-game saga with Meath that summer which enthralled the nation. There was a suggestion that it might have to go 13-a-side because the soccer pitch would not be big enough.

Shamrock Rovers agreed to the double bill. Then Dublin and Down County Boards said yes. When he was approached, the relatively new GAA President Peter Quinn (he was only eight months in office) directed them to the Games Administration Committee. They said no because the RDS was not a ground vested in the GAA.

The GAA's Management Committee then entered the fray just days before the game was due to take place, with press advertisements for tickets already published, and ruled that the vested ground argument did not have to apply. However, there was disquiet in certain quarters of the GAA and its Central Council then stepped in and refused to sanction the game. In its statement the GAA outlined that because it was being billed as a joint venture with Shamrock Rovers 'the conditions relating to the collection and disbursement of monies was not being adhered to' and that all the relevant GAA bodies had not been 'informed or consulted in relation to these arrangements'.

The optics were terrible and were compounded by three separate changes of decision in the space of ten days. However, Peter Quinn claimed that if a decision was correct, PR considerations were irrelevant. Certainly, there was a media onslaught.

Jack Lynch, then a former Taoiseach, expressed 'bitter disappointment' over the RDS decision. His intervention highlighted some of the tensions between the northern and southern GAA families. There were mutterings that Lynch had stood idly by when clubhouses were burned down because of the Troubles in Down. A newspaper poll revealed that eighty-eight per cent of respondents in the Republic had blamed the GAA for the decision while eighty-four per cent in the North had supported it.

Having just returned from a four-year stint in New York as Military Advisor to the Secretary-General of the United Nations,

Roscommon legend Dermot Earley was bitterly disappointed with the unfolding events:

'The GAA has a great history but it should stand for something positive. Instead it looks like it stands for an anti-soccer crusade and the GAA looks like the Grinch who stole Christmas. This is a season when we remember those "for whom there is no room in the inn" but it looks like the GAA just don't want to share a room with two soccer teams.'

# 80

# NO ENTRY

*The Rule 42 Controversy*

In the GAA there are many rooms.

Some are less accessible than others.

In March 2004, news broke that there would be no debate on Rule 42, about opening up Croke Park, at Congress. The GAA's Motions Committee, which consists of ex-GAA presidents, decreed that none of the motions pertaining to Rule 42 should be debated as they were 'out of order' on technical grounds.

The then Chief Executive of the Gaelic Players' Association, Dessie Farrell, got to the nub of the issue: 'This is a blatant and dictatorial departure from anything resembling democracy and one would have to question the structures and procedures that have ultimately delivered the body blow to the GAA's member-ship. This issue warrants a full and democratic hearing at the top table. However, the question must now be asked just where the top actually resides. Is it within the supposedly hallowed, but arguably flawed, democracy of Congress, or amongst a gathering of former presidents under the innocuous banner of the Motions Committee? The average GAA person has never been as far removed from the decision-making process and we would urge all units and members of the Association to persevere with the difficult questions that need answering at this time.'

## SPAT SPILLANE

Even by his own standards Pat Spillane was very agitated by this decision:

'In my long association with the GAA this was the lowest point for me. That was the week that Brazilian World Cup star Gerson was so disgusted at being omitted from Pelé's list of top 125 footballers that he tore it up live on television. I felt like doing the same with my GAA membership card.

'Who were this unelected elite group to defy the wishes of the majority of the GAA members? How dare they deny their fellow members the chance to air their views on this important topic on the floor of Congress. How dare a group who were effectively has-beens, who were handed their P45s long ago, still have such a major say in the running of the organisation.

'Their decision smacked of the worst excesses of dictatorship. They behaved like an ageing politburo, determined to hold on to the strings of the power – and occasionally they manage to do just that. As an organisation, the GAA prides itself on its democracy. The reality couldn't be further from the truth. The GAA's version of democracy is a bit like the one George Orwell wrote about in *Animal Farm*: "All animals are equal but some animals are more equal than others."

'The decision was yet another nail in the coffin of the GAA's flawed version of democracy. The bottom line is that the motions to amend Rule 42, which I believe would have had the support of a majority of Association members, did not get an airing at Congress in Killarney in April. Why? Because these elder lemons found some technical flaws in the motions and opted not to correct those minor flaws, even though they were well within their rights to do so. The decision wouldn't have been out of place in Ceauşescu's Romania.

'In 2003, Eire Og delegate Pat Daly, at the GAA Convention in Cork, said, "It's about time the GAA woke up. The ban has been gone since 1973 – if Frank Sinatra can play in Croke Park, then why not the Irish international rugby team?" However, Munster Council Treasurer Dan Hoare went for an "out, out, out" approach: "I would not let anybody into the car park, not to mention into Croke Park." That is the kind of no surrender attitude that Ian Paisley would be proud of. The previous year a delegate at the Wicklow GAA County Convention said, "We are being asked to wake up some morning and see the English soccer team playing in Croke Park. Just eighty years ago the English came to Croke Park and shot Gaelic players."'

Spillane was taken by some of the contributors to the debate:

'The big hitters in the Association had been lining up behind the "No" campaign from early in the year. And boy did they come out firing on all cylinders. Ex-GAA President Jack Boothman was the first to join battle. He sent a letter to selected elected officers pleading with them not to change the rule.

'Then the usual suspects from Ulster came out of the woods. Of course, we should not have been in the least surprised that the Ulster counties were so trenchant in their support of Rule 42. One official suggested that unless there was a clear case for change then there were definite reasons not to change. Work out that logic if you can. If you do, you are way smarter than I am.

'The newly elected Ulster Council President weighed in with a real beauty. He said the GAA were not in the business of housing the homeless. So much for the age-old proverb, which we teach our children: sharing is caring. I suppose we should not be surprised at the degree of narrow-mindedness emanating from this source. After all, this was the same council which dug their heels in and insisted that a provincial semi-final between Donegal and Derry be played on the same afternoon as the Republic of Ireland played Spain in a World Cup soccer match in 2002. So long as units of the GAA make those kind of preposterous decisions, opponents of the Association are never short of ammunition to fire at Croke Park.

'To stress the small-mindedness of the Ulster Council, on the day of the Ireland-Spain match a journalist brought a portable television into the press box to keep an eye on the Ireland game. When he was spotted, he was promptly and pompously told by an official that it was not appropriate to have a TV there for that purpose and that he must turn it off.

'What I found difficult, though, is that the Ulster Council who espouse such lofty principles and are such great champions of tradition could then do a "Jerry Maguire" on it and say, "Show me the money", and have the Ulster final played in Croke Park. Lofty principles are great but it is one of the hypocrisies of the GAA world that when money comes into it, tradition and ideals go out the window.

'These former GAA bureaucrats had one great weapon which they used with consummate skill; the GAA rule book. They are greatly helped by the fact that the rule book, which is so badly constructed and written in such a way that those of us who didn't get a grind in GAA-speak would find it easier to read cave writings from the Stone Age. Of course, if, by some miracle, the rule is capable of producing a measure which will drag the organisation kicking and screaming into the twenty-first century, the old guard have yet another weapon in their arsenal – a technicality. What is even more galling for me is that in blocking progress in this way they will say in all earnestness that they are acting in "the best interests of the GAA".

'Surely as the foremost sporting organisation in Ireland our role is to provide youngsters with as many sporting opportunities as possible rather than having them messing up their lives with drugs or whatever. Opening up Croke Park would present new possibilities to fund much-needed coaching initiatives for the next generation of footballers and hurlers.'

The level of the arguments also distressed Spillane:

'Some of the rhetoric which poured forth from the anti-Rule 42 brigade in March 2004, when the controversy was at its height, made my blood boil. As a GAA member, I felt ashamed when I heard some of the arguments. In particular, the *Prime Time* debate on the subject was cringeworthy. The Cork representative who appeared on the programme was stuck in a time warp of outdated patriotism. He argued that the GAA should keep the ban in place as a result of what happened in Croke Park on Bloody Sunday.

'It is very sad to see people living in the past. If everybody was dwelling on what happened decades ago, we would never have had the Peace Process and we would be still waking up every morning as we used to in the 1970s and 1980s to hear headlines like, "A part-time member of the UDR has been murdered by the IRA in County Tyrone." Or we would be hearing about a poor Catholic who had been savagely murdered by a Loyalist organisation. The logic of those still living in the past is that Irish people shouldn't eat Danish bacon or drink Carlsberg because of what the Danes did to poor Brian Boru at Clontarf in 1014!

'What I also found revealing was that at a meeting of Central Council, rather than trying to learn the lessons from the debacle, delegates had expressed annoyance at the manner in which ex-presidents had been "pilloried" for their decision to declare the motions relating to Rule 42 out of order. Down's Dan McCartan said it was disturbing that men who had served the GAA so well were subjected to severe personal attacks: "It is deplorable that they should be treated so badly by our own members. Those who made the attacks brought shame on the Association."

'Yet again, I brought shame on the GAA.'

# 81

## CHARITY BEGINS AT HOME

*The Liam Miller Case*

Sometimes it boils down to just doing the right thing.

Pat Spillane famously described Larry Tompkins as the 'first professional Gaelic footballer'. He was speaking about Tompkins's dedication and discipline which drove him to push himself to the very limits to become the best version of himself as a player.

In the 1990 All-Ireland football final, Tompkins injured himself with fifteen minutes to go in a clash with Martin O'Connell. The Cork legend said nothing, continued to play on, and kicked two more points in that time.

The next day it emerged that he had torn his cartilage and his cruciate and medial ligaments. Such courage was the reason why he was so loved on Leeside.

Another star loved in Cork for his courage was Liam Miller. He won twenty-one caps for Ireland, played for Celtic until 2004, when he was signed by Sir Alex Ferguson for Manchester United. His bravery, though, was most shown in his gutsy battle against cancer. A tumour was found in his oesophagus and by the time the medics found it, it had spread to his kidneys, liver and lungs. In 2018, though, he died aged just thirty-six.

A year after he died, Liam Miller changed the GAA rule book forever. It started off innocently enough with a summer enquiry about the use of Páirc Uí Chaoimh for a charity soccer match. Understandably, there was a huge appetite in Cork and beyond to find a way to support Liam's widow and young family. The 45,000-capacity Páirc Uí Chaoimh was a better fit than Turners Cross which only held 7,000. The request was denied on the basis of the GAA rule book. There was a massive negative reaction within and without the GAA community. Things heated up another level when the government highlighted the €30m stadium redevelopment funding given by taxpayers from the state's purse.

The GAA hierarchy was initially deaf to the mood of public opinion, claiming that the Association, 'is prohibited in rule from hosting games other than those under the control of the Association in its stadia and grounds. The Cork County Committee and Central Council have no discretion in this matter. Only a change at Annual Congress can alter this situation. Congress takes place in February each year.'

To bolster their argument that legal advice was sought 'around funding received towards the redevelopment of Páirc Uí Chaoimh', the GAA claimed that it 'believes it is compliant with the terms and conditions laid down in September 2016.'

If their statement was intended to calm the troubled waters it only had the opposite effect. The public pressure intensified across a broad spectrum of society including those with no interest in sport who saw it largely as a humanitarian issue. In the face of overwhelming public opposition, the GAA and the event organisers reached a compromise after calling a Central Council meeting to give it the green light. A who's who of the great and the good of both Irish soccer and Manchester United played in the match including Roy Keane, Kevin Doyle and Gary Neville. The game was a great fundraising success.

Months later, when a more sedate atmosphere prevailed, the GAA's Director General Tom Ryan in his report to Congress highlighted in particular the intimations over a restriction of public funding:

'Any funding we receive is, and should continue to be, predicated solely on the intrinsic value of Gaelic games. I am not aware of any other sporting organisation being assessed on the degree to which it promotes rival sports. And nor should they be. I don't think any of us were enthusiastic about the outcome we reached. The overwhelming sentiment being that we felt we had been bullied into a course of action that we might well have taken anyway if given the chance.'

Nonetheless, a motion to allow for GAA grounds to be used for other sports in exceptional circumstances was passed with ease.

# 82

## GUESS WHO IS COMING TO DINNER?

*Gooch Cooper's Testimonial Dinner*

Joe Brolly was worried.

It was a new chapter for the GAA.

In 2017, it was announced that the first testimonial dinner of its kind to be held in honour of a GAA player, former Kerry great Colm 'the Gooch' Cooper, would take place on 27 October at the Intercontinental Hotel in Ballsbridge. Joe Brolly was highly critical of the news, describing it as 'cheap and self-serving' and that it went against the amateur ethos of the GAA.

In his column in the *Sunday Independent* he wrote: 'It is a great pity Colm has done this. The point of the GAA is supposed to be volunteerism and community activism. The question is supposed to be, "What can I do?", not "What can I get out of it?" As an icon of Irish sport, he could have set an example of altruism, but instead has chosen to enrich himself. What could and should have been a night the GAA could have taken great pride in, has instead become something cheap and self-serving.'

## LATE, LATE

Cooper, a five-time senior All-Ireland winner, went on *The Late Late Show* and defended his decision to host the testimonial dinner. He revealed that Kerry GAA and his club Dr Crokes would be given a portion of the proceeds from the night and that two charities, Our Lady's Children's Hospital, Crumlin and Kerry Cancer Support Group, set to benefit. It emerged that Cooper would pocket less than fifty per cent of the takings.

Asked on the programme how he responded to Brolly's criticism, Cooper replied:

'Sure, look, we all know that Joe Brolly's the greatest player ever so how can we challenge him on that . . . Joe actually sent me a text this week to say sorry about all the fuss . . . he wishes there wasn't the reaction that there was and that it's gone overboard. And he's apologising for it.

'So, he's obviously changed his tune since. And he fully respects that I'm entitled to have a testimonial night if I want. There's players doing dinner dances and speaking after events. There's brand ambassadors, there's players doing launches all the time. So, unfortunately for the GAA, there are players earning money. So, if that's the argument, I don't really get it.'

Brolly clarified his position on Twitter afterwards, however, saying that he never apologised and that he stands by 'every word'.

'I didn't apologise to Colm for anything I said. I stand by every word. I said I didn't intend him to be demonised as a result. This is a serious principled debate. I said face to face to Colm he was wrong in doing this. I stand by that absolutely.'

The GAA did not support Cooper's planned testimonial dinner. Then GAA Director General Páraic Duffy clarified that Cooper did not break any rules with the black tie €500-a-head gala event which took place in Dublin.

'The first thing I said to him was, "Colm, I've got a concern here about how this might impact on your status and our rules." I said, "I can't give you an answer, I've to look at it." I went away, we looked at our rules, got our legal advisors to look at them, and they came back and said he's not breaking any rules here. I went back to Colm and said, "Look Colm, you're not breaking any rules here. If you want to go ahead with it you won't be suspended, there can't be a charge levelled against you," which was my initial concern. But I did say, "Are you sure you're doing the right thing here?" and I did say to him that the GAA will not be supporting it, and we're not supporting it.'

Duffy drew a distinction between Gooch's testimonial, and other current and former players who earn money through media work:

"If you do an autobiography, or punditry, you're not taking funds that could go to the GAA in different ways. If you hold a major dinner, you're going to the same people to support the dinner, the testimonial, as you would to support a club event to raise funds. That's the big concern that I would have, plus the fact that it's against the ethos of the GAA to run a dinner that's for individual benefit. We don't do that. Can the GAA prevent it under our current rules? No. Do we need to look at it? Yes. It's tricky because our current rules don't allow us to deal with it, but I think we need to look at the rules.

'Our organisation doesn't want testimonials, and that's the message that I've got very clearly over the past few weeks. It's nothing to do with Colm Cooper whatsoever; it happens that he's the first one. The ethos of the Association is that we're an amateur association. We don't want to do that. You can say that in other cases maybe players benefit under the counter because we can't deal with it, but this is a public thing. It's there, we have to express a view, and our view is that we're not going to support it.'

# 83

# ROCK OF AGES

*The School of Dean Rock*

You cannot put the brakes on history.

2020 was a milestone year for Dean Rock. He overtook Jimmy Keaveney in the all-time list of Dublin scorers for League and Championship combined, in the ghostly and eerie environs of an empty Parnell Park (because of Covid restrictions). Keaveney's 30–402 (in 104 games) had lasted a generation. In that match against Meath, though, Rock scored 1–8 to move top of the list with 17–450. Later that year, Rock would be crucial to the team's six-in-a-row.

However, it was his off-field activities that got the GAA nation talking. His decision to launch the 'Dean Rock Free Taking Project' to 'inspire and educate current and aspiring free-takers in the game' generated huge criticism on social media platforms and much discussion in the national media. He was offering workshops, weekend academies, small group sessions and one-on-one training all aimed at improving the accuracy and reliability of attendees' free taking. A reported €350 for two one-on-one sessions was on offer.

The idea of a GAA player using their profile to make money was not new. Those of us of a certain age will have fond memories of sitting down to have our evening meal and watching Galway legend and farmer Joe Cooney channelling his inner Paul Mescal (himself a former underage star with Kildare who, before finding fame on *Normal People*, starred in an ad for Dennys sausages). As he held a feisty bullock in his arms and administered a dose, he plugged a product that would 'control roundworms, lungworms, mature and immature liver fluke in cattle and sheep'. Later, his fellow Galway hurling star Joe Rabbitte would do a uniquely Irish twist on the legend of Superman by juxtaposing the taking off on an electrifying solo run with giving a sickly sheep the requisite respite from worrisome worms.

Tipp hurling ace Bobby Ryan sang (not literally) the praises of Zerofen when it came to picking the right cow wormer. The Cork legend John Fenton's famous sixty-yard groundstroke against Limerick, apart from being one of the greatest goals, was somehow used in an ad to claim that he was 'smashing through mastitis'.

My favourite, though, was the great Kilkenny hurler (he's too nice a man to name and shame) who advertised the farmer's favourite Cheno Unction (for those of you who have never rubbed a cow's udder it is a cream to prevent mastitis or as Ray D'Arcy described it 'Sudocrem for cows') with the immortal line: 'It's a quare name, but great stuff.' Both Mike Murphy and Maureen Potter would use the phrase regularly in tribute to the brilliance of the ad and the phrase quickly entered the common vernacular.

However, there has always been an unease in the GAA about players using their fame to earn a little extra money. Such though was the level of online criticism over the reported prices Rock was charging that Kerry great Kieran Donaghy felt the need to intervene: 'This Dean Rock thing is p***ing me off. Shows the level of begrudgery we have bred into us. How dare a GAA lad start a business inspiring, teaching kids and adults on how to be better at a vital component of the game. Try and get the best.'

# 84

# NOT COLOUR BLIND

*Players Racially Abused*

The hardest part to change is worrying about what other people think of you.

Sadly, the GAA has not been immune from the monstrous barbarism of racism as players like Lee Chin have discovered to their cost.

In 1995, Jason Sherlock became the GAA's first pin-up boy when at just nineteen years of age he helped Dublin to win their first All-Ireland footall final in twelve years. His was fame of pop-star proportions after his bootless goal against Laois, his decisive goal against Cork in the All-Ireland semi-final and his pass to Charlie Redmond for the winning goal against Tyrone in the All-Ireland final. Nobody had ever seen any thing like it. The Dubs even had their own song about him.

Jayo's high profile over his fifteen years playing for the Dubs, though, came with a price, particularly when Dublin's form began to dip. 'I came from Finglas. I had a mother and I had no father in the household. My father was from Hong Kong, so I looked different, and Dublin or Ireland were in a place where we didn't understand other cultures in our society,' he says. 'Growing up had its challenges. I would have felt sport was a great outlet, because I was invisible. If you were good at sport, people didn't really care what size or shape you were.

'I grew up wanting to be accepted, and winning an All-Ireland at that stage probably was the start of being accepted, and when that happened my focus in what I wanted to achieve probably wavered. But as things changed in the Dublin context and we started to lose games, I was singled out and things went back to the old days and I did get racially abused.'

By his own admission it took Jason a couple of years for him to come to terms with the situation he was in at the time. 'Looking back now, I was never the biggest, I was never the strongest, but I like to think I had an aptitude and I wanted to commit. I did commit everything I had to play for fifteen years. I probably didn't get the trophies I wanted but in saying that I gave everything to be the best footballer I could be and also to try and encourage and bring my teammates on as well.'

## BIRTH OF A CAMPAIGNER

Since his retirement, Jason first became involved in the area of mental health through Cycle Against Suicide, a charity event where people cycle around the country stopping at schools to talk to transition years:

'I stood up with a microphone in front of 400 transition year girls out in Bray who wouldn't have a clue who I am, and just talked about growing up and how hard it was to feel accepted and how it made me feel. I talked about how I dealt with it or didn't deal with it, because it is important to share and ask for help,' he says.

'I wasn't sure how it would be received, but afterwards a fourteen-year-old girl came up to me in tears and said, "I know exactly what you mean, and you have really made me feel better," and she gave me a hug. That was very powerful for me, because I'm sure for any sportsperson at the end of their career, it is hard to comprehend what value you have outside the sport, and that was something I had to come to terms with. To get a message like that back was a very powerful thing and I was delighted. From there I moved into talking about racism and what I have encountered.'

When Jason first began speaking out about racism, he talked to his family about what it was like for them when he was growing up. 'My uncle said we didn't see you as different, we saw you as a Dub. That's the way we treated you and that's the way we wanted you to see yourself.

'Now, that was noble and what they thought was right, but what it did was force me into a situation where I couldn't understand why people saw me as different, because I just see myself as a Dub. If I had it around again, I would have liked [my family] to say, "Yeah you are different, and it's okay to be different, and we celebrate that." Then I might have been able to rationalise the negativity and abuse that I got a bit better.'

Over the years, Jason experienced racism on a verbal and physical level and did not know how to deal with it. He believes this affected his self-esteem and made him paranoid. In 2013, he was the victim of racial abuse online on the eve of the All-Ireland final between Dublin and Mayo, after his appearance on RTÉ's *Up for The Match* programme. A message posted on Twitter said: 'Sherlock you na Fianna reject . . . Back to Asia with you, you don't belong here.'

'There was a time when I would have been a victim of that, but I retweeted it because I don't want to be a victim any more,' Jason states. 'It was great to get the support that I got. The club he played for contacted me and he was suspended. Him and his parents wanted to apologise, which was noble of him. So I met him and one thing I said was when he woke up on Sunday morning and saw the abuse he was getting, I asked how did you feel, and he said he felt pretty bad. I said you did something to warrant that. Imagine you didn't do anything and you woke up to that every day, and that you felt like that. But times that by years, can you imagine what effect that has on you as a person?'

Jason believes the solution to racism is education: 'As a society we are changing. I always feel now when you look at a local GAA club and see one child who looks different, it's not just about how he is treated but also his parents – how they are received or welcomed. Every member of society, not only in sport, has a responsibility or a part to play in that.'

# PART V
# The Pundit's Corner

*'Whoever controls the media, controls the mind.'*

JIM MORRISON

One of the most influential people in the GAA's history was Clare's Monsignor Michael Hamilton, who was hugely influential in the decision to play the 1947 All-Ireland final in the Polo Grounds in 1947. Such was his grip on the Association that one year Congress was delayed until four o'clock so that he could attend after saying a Mass back in Clare. In 1937, he was the last man to commentate on an All-Ireland final before Micheál O'Hehir took on the mantle. Unfortunately, he made the error of informing the country that Cavan had won when it had actually been a draw. As a result, hundreds of Cavan fans on the journey home were baffled by all the bonfires which greeted them home.

In the wake of the county's Championship exit in 2020, a WhatsApp message suggesting Kerry players were on the brink of a heave against manager Peter Keane was widely circulated and this became a huge social media story even though it was not true. Sometimes we see molehills and turn them into mountains.

Pundits have created a number of controversies and have been the subject of others. This section recalls some of them.

# 85

## SO LONG JOE

*Brolly Sacked*

Sometimes the love we want the most is the love we lose.

In February 2020, as the world tumbled into horrors of a global pandemic, Clare County Council discussed the issue that had gripped the nation, divided families and shattered old friendships.

A group of Clare Councillors called for the national broadcaster to reinstate Joe Brolly to its coverage of Gaelic football. Independent Councillors Gerry Flynn, Ann Norton and P.J. Ryan submitted a motion for a meeting of the local authority to debate the matter. Their motion called on the Minister for Communications or Finance to request RTÉ reinstate Joe 'ASAP' as his dismissal from the panel had 'taken away from the enjoyment of the game for many people'.

Brolly's last game with RTÉ was the previous year's drawn All-Ireland Final between Dublin and Kerry, during which Brolly stated that the match official David Gough had been 'clearly influenced by propaganda coming from Kerry' in his decision to send off Jonny Cooper before half-time. He was dropped from the studio panel for the replay and replaced by former Mayo manager Stephen Rochford. Brolly took to Twitter to joke: 'If anyone has a spare ticket for the replay, I've just been let down.' Brolly subsequently contacted Gough to apologise for his comments.

RTÉ Head of Sport Declan McBennett rejected Brolly's assertion that his contract at the station was not renewed because of comments he made at half-time in the drawn 2019 All-Ireland final. 'The decision with regard to Joe's contract was taken before the first drawn game. It wasn't down to one thing in isolation but a combination of examples. One of the statements Joe made was that the manipulation of public opinion is great fun when you pit X against Y and throw in a few grenades. That's where I have the divergence with regard to pundits. I don't believe in the manipulation of public opinion. I believe in standards that are informed, that are based in some sort of fact, not statistical data that has to be churned out but based in fact. There are two reasons why people leave RTÉ. Number one is the passage of time means that things roll on. The other is if you have your contract cancelled and if your contract is not renewed you have to ask why was it not renewed.'

Eamon Dunphy launched a scathing attack on RTÉ after their dismissal of Brolly. Dunphy leaped to Brolly's defence, accusing the broadcaster of 'softening up' analysis and claimed he left RTÉ for that reason. For his part, Brolly said there was a 'culture of fear' within RTÉ, where the 'blander the better' was fostered: 'We got a memo to say we want to be more like Sky, which I put in the bin.' Brolly suggested RTÉ's coverage was getting increasingly 'script-based where really what they need are newsreaders, not people who are expressing an opinion' which was making the national broadcaster becoming like the civil service.

Brolly later revealed that his only regret from his time on RTÉ was his put-down of Marty Morrissey, of whom he described as being 'as ugly as Cavan football'. He said, 'It was a very insulting and a very personal thing. It was uncaring and cruel.'

## JOE 2

In 2021, Brolly was embroiled in another RTÉ controversy. He was invited to participate in a special edition of the *Claire Byrne Live* which was debating the issue of the need or otherwise for a poll on a United Ireland. Joe appeared in a segment which began with former Ireland rugby international Andrew Trimble discussing his experiences of being Irish and British. When Claire Byrne brought Joe, appearing via video link, into the debate he spoke about how his children had similar experiences to Trimble.

He then turned his ire on the DUP. One of their MPs Gregory Campbell had appeared earlier and laughed at Tánaiste Leo Varadkar, who had been speaking about the potential ability to identify as British and Irish in a United Ireland. Brolly levelled allegations against the DUP: 'You know, chuckling and guffawing at people when they're trying to have serious discussions, just like we saw Gregory tonight. Laughing at the Irish language, laughing at Gaelic sports, the homophobia, the racism, all those things.'

Ms Byrne responded: 'He might deny some of those charges.'

Brolly asked, 'Sorry, which ones would he deny?', to which Claire replied: 'Look, Joe, the man is not here to defend himself, and I'm not going to do it for him. I'm not going to have anybody called names on this programme who are not here to defend themselves and that's final okay.'

After that, Brolly was not brought back into the debate, which he has subsequently addressed on Twitter as he also shared screenshots from a number of news articles to back up the point he made on the show. He wrote: 'I was taken off air and told it was because RTÉ could not risk me saying the DUP were homophobic, racist or sectarian. I must apologise to the DUP at once.'

# 86

## ATONEMENT?

*Joe Brolly Revisits His Past*

Joe Duffy has a ritual before he goes on air to present *Liveline* every day. He goes to the bathroom splashes water on to his face and says two words: Libel (to remind himself to let no listener make slanderous remarks) and entertainment. He knows that his job is to grab and hold people's attention. Joe Brolly has a keen appreciation of that fact.

The one time of the year that the GAA is normally spared a controversy is Christmas week. The festive season in 2021 proved to be the exception. We should not have been surprised when we saw that Joe Brolly was the subject of two one-hour television specials.

To a generation, Brolly was part of a 'Holy (unholy?) Trinity' with Pat Spillane and Colm O'Rourke that were the faces of RTÉ's Gaelic football coverage. He delighted and infuriated viewers in equal measure but added to the entertainment of the nation. He inspired many after he donated a kidney to Shane Finnegan in 2012, and then set up the Opt For Life Foundation, which campaigned on both sides of the border for an opt-out donation policy.

However, in his 2021 interview, Brolly shed new light on his motivation for donating his kidney. He began by giving the context from his childhood.

'It was exhilarating – scary, I suppose. Very quickly it was clear that my father was a person of interest to the State. We were raided, turfed out of bed. Night-time was scary and there were a lot of very serious things going on.

'My father was interned; one morning they came and took him. He was taken away for three years. We saw him a few times during that period. A knock came on our door one day and it was the shopkeeper next door saying you have to go and pick him up. He came home in triumph and it was never mentioned again.'

Brolly also recalled how prominent IRA figures like the late Martin McGuinness would use his house to hide out in when on the run: 'Boys used to hide in our house, they'd come in and stay for a night or two. I remember a young Martin McGuinness in our house and my mother putting a fake moustache and beard on him.'

Joe described feeling 'ecstatic' after donating a kidney to a stranger:

'Then I hit the wall shortly after that. I think for years I had blocked out childhood – I couldn't even remember childhood properly. I realised soon afterwards that the reason I'd given the kidney was to, I think, atone for the taking of human life by people close to me, and to sort of somehow make amends for that.'

Almost immediately, the brother of a teenager killed in the 1972 IRA Claudy bombing urged Brolly 'to reveal what he knows'. David Temple, whose sixteen-year-old brother William was killed in the Claudy bombing along with eight other innocent civilians, wanted further clarification.

Brolly had not specified what he was referring to and whether his comments were in any way referring to the Claudy bombing.

## ATONEMENT?

Following calls for an inquiry into the atrocity, the PSNI detained four people in connection with the bombing in 2005 – including Joe's father, the late Francie Brolly who was a Sinn Féin MLA at the time. However, they were released without charge the next day and denied involvement.

The PSNI said: 'We are aware of comments made in the interview, and of subsequent press reporting in relation to those comments and will review the content of the interview.' Kenny Donaldson, of Innocent Victims United, urged the police to examine the video in order to 'establish if there are grounds for Mr Brolly to be spoken to on these matters'.

# 87

## BOYCOTT

### *Jim Gavin Lashes Out at Pat Spillane*

Television was blamed for all manner of new social ills –
typified in the late politician Oliver J. Flanagan's comment:
'There was no sex in Ireland before television.' Irish people
became aware that they had a lot of catching up to do in many
areas. Television would have a profound impact on the GAA on
a number of levels, but nobody could have foreseen in 1962 that
GAA TV pundits would become among the best-known faces
in Irish life.

Eugene McGee was a champion of high standards on and
off the field. As a journalist his concern for standards extended
also to sports journalism and he was particularly critical of the
tendency to get former star players to write newspaper columns
or to have them ghostwritten for. 'Their level of objectivity
and impartiality is often far removed from what should be
demanded by professional, properly trained journalists.'

Eugene was not a big fan either of aspects of television
punditry on Gaelic games but, nonetheless, I saw at first hand
the warmth of his engagement with Pat Spillane. McGee was

very diverted when the normally mild-mannered Jim Gavin had a pop at Spillane.

In the early 1980s, Liverpool ruled supreme in both England and Europe. Once they had a rare off day and got a bad beating in the League. After the match, the Liverpool players in the dressing room braced themselves for the hairdryer treatment. Joe Fagan stood up to speak to them. He spoke softly and said just one sentence, 'Let's make sure this never happens again.'

It never did.

A parable of good management. Jim Gavin was in that mode.

However, in 2017, Gavin refused to speak to the broadcast media after his side's victory over Westmeath in the Leinster Championship. In his post-match press conference he singled out Pat Spillane for comments made on *The Sunday Game* about Diarmuid Connolly's altercation with linesman Ciaran Branagan that led to a twelve-week ban:

'What concerned me was the way (Connolly's) good name was attacked before we even saw the referee's report. We had the national broadcaster in their post-match review. Both Pat Spillane and Colm O'Rourke, particularly Pat, they had a predetermined statement.'

On *The Sunday Game* later, fellow pundits Dessie Dolan and Joe Brolly chose to defend Gavin rather than their colleague. Dolan stated that the comments on the incident 'look a little bit pointed' and speculated that Spillane's comments might have been made because it would be advantageous for Kerry.

Brolly upped the ante, saying: 'You have to say, it was like watching counsel for the prosecution. Pat had everything on but his Kerry blazer and his Kerry tie. I thought to myself after, "the CCCC are going to act here!"'

As is his wont, Spillane did not take the comments lying down. Responding to the then Dublin manager, Spillane stated:

'As regards Gavin's comments about freedom of expression and the Irish constitution, all I can say is, "Jim, you must be having a laugh". Furthermore, I'm at a total loss to figure out how my former profession as a teacher had, as Gavin suggested, anything to do with my remarks.

'According to Gavin we should have waited for "due process" before making our comments. So, does he expect every media outlet to wait until the Central Hearings Committee hand down their verdict in every case before they comment on it? The logic of his argument is so flawed that it reinforces my view he was working to a different agenda than just defending Connolly.'

Spillane then went on to defend himself from the comments of his fellow *The Sunday Game* pundits who he claimed sought to throw him 'under a bus':

'According to them, not alone was I responsible for getting Connolly suspended, but I had deliberately set out as a Kerry man to achieve that goal. *The Sunday Game* has always operated on a very simple premise: the panellists offer their views based on what they have seen in front of them. Brolly and Dolan broke that golden rule by offering opinions which had absolutely no basis in fact.'

## SUSPENSION SEQUENCE

Two years earlier, Diarmuid Connolly had been involved in a previous suspension controversy. The GAA's Central Appeals Committee found he should be suspended for the 2015 All-Ireland semi-final replay against Mayo after he was sent off in the drawn game. Two of the Disputes Resolution Authority panel quashed it on the basis that fair procedures had not applied to him. However, the other DRA panellist, Brian Rennick's, dissenting opinion claimed that the decision of his two colleagues, former Supreme Court Judge Hugh O'Flaherty and solicitor David Nohilly, to absolve Connolly was 'fundamentally wrong'.

# 88

# WHATEVER YOU SAY, SAY NOTHING

*Armagh's Media Ban*

Contrary to popular perception, media bans are not a new phenomenon in the GAA. In 1968, the late, lamented *Irish Press* newspaper carried the headline 'Is This Sport?' over a photograph of a row in the League final between Tipperary and Kilkenny. Tipperary took great umbrage and banned journalists from their training session – the first known media ban. To reciprocate, journalists did not mention Tipp players by name in match reports.

Down the years there have often been fractious relationships between media outlets and county teams. One of the most notable controversies came in 2014 when Armagh manager Paul Grimley took exception to the 'disrespectful manner' by which his team were treated. He imposed a media ban upon the senior county panel. Grimley was aggrieved in the wake of their Ulster SFC win over Cavan, where a pre-match brawl dominated the coverage. 'I wasn't happy with the way the Cavan game was reported. I felt our team lined out in an orderly fashion and did nothing wrong. In fact, they defended themselves. We were in the parade a good fifty seconds before Cavan took their place and there are all sorts of arguments, but it wouldn't have been hard to swap the flags over. It is an unwritten code that the home team march on the inside.

'Some of the reports afterwards were saying children had to run for cover and that we targeted players on the Cavan team, and that people were verbally abused and this sort of thing. It got very out of hand. The media took on a different side to it and I thought it was a nastier side, camouflaging insults, and the reason was because we weren't playing their game. They were calling us childish, ignorant; they called our county board spineless.

'We are amateurs and really there is no particular professional training in the media for us. It probably was a lot of stubbornness on my part but there was a lot that I didn't like. They (the media) were a bit cheeky at times and I thought, "we'll teach them a bit of manners here".'

There was a second reason why Grimley was annoyed: 'They were also trying, in the way they reported things, to cause a wee bit of a problem within the camp between me and Kieran (McGeeney) or vice versa.'

Grimley also felt disrespected when his colleague was not interviewed at a media event: 'We sent Peter McDonnell; he was there for two-and-a-half hours and no one thought it was worth their while interviewing him. So, he was rightly upset about it, and he came back and said: "Look, if no one cares about what we have to say then we won't be saying anything to anybody."

'I was taken aback. I didn't obviously intend for it. But I think some sections of the media were saying we don't give a damn what Armagh think, but clearly they did as they kept writing about us.'

Consequently, Grimley imposed a media ban upon the senior county panel.

### THERE'S NO SHOW LIKE A JOE SHOW

Joe Brolly was less bothered by the media ban than Armagh's failures on the pitch and claimed that Grimley was 'out of his depth'. The Armagh manager was upset for his family:

'It was a personal attack, a certain amount of it was true but you know yourself with Joe – hopefully I made him eat his words. It is disappointing that Joe has to go down that road, but that's good television. It was tough on my family; my son and wife weren't too happy about it, and I had to rush home so my mother didn't see it on the TV.

'Maybe people do like to hear other people discredited on live TV and that's the society we live in. But I think it reflects poorly on the people who do it. I would have regarded that as below Joe and I would have thought he was far too intelligent to be involved in that. He should use the skills he has in a different way. He is a very articulate and intelligent guy, but he should use his skills for the GAA, arguing points outside the football remit. I think he belittles himself the way he goes on.'

# 89

## MAN UP

*Joe Brolly's Criticism of Seán Cavanagh*

Hell hath no fury like Joe forlorned.

Most of us live with our doubts and, worse still, the fear that they will come true.

Joe Brolly is cut from a different cloth.

As a pundit, Brolly was not one for holding back. Joe has had many a rant in the RTÉ studio in the past but few watching will ever forget his comments about Seán Cavanagh in the wake of the Red Hands' win over Monaghan in 2014.

Mickey Harte's side advanced to the All-Ireland semi-final with a two-point win over Monaghan at Croke Park but Brolly was fuming when Seán Cavanagh made a rugby tackle on Conor McManus when he was through on goal. Cavanagh's tackle earned the midfielder a yellow card. Notwithstanding the incident, he was selected as RTÉ's man of the match.

Despite meaningful attempts from Michael Lyster, Colm O'Rourke and Pat Spillane to intervene, Brolly could not be halted, accusing Cavanagh and his Tyrone team of cheating:

'I want nothing to do with that. It's an absolute disgrace. I see

Mickey Harte smiling and jumping up and down at the end like they achieved. I'll tell you what, they achieved something absolutely rotten. I can't believe somebody gave Seán Cavanagh a man-of-the-match award . . . it's not within the rules, you're not allowed to rugby tackle a player to the ground.'

However, what lives long in the memory is his comment: 'He's a brilliant footballer but you can forget about Seán Cavanagh as a man.'

### RIGHT OF REPLY

In 2021, Cavanagh was the subject of an episode of *Laochra Gael*. Inevitably, the Brolly incident was discussed. Cavanagh said: 'Joe has a great way of making things about him almost. Unfortunately, within the rules at that point in time, you could drag a player down and accept the yellow card. And it was difficult how Joe failed to see that. Anyone I spoke with around that time, including Conor McManus just moments after that game, had said to me, "I would have done exactly the same thing as you if it had been the other way around."'

Cavanagh also revealed that the controversy had implications for his professional life: 'I remember getting a phone call from a business that I work with and they wouldn't have followed Gaelic football. I remember the guy saying to me, "Seán, what have you done? There's all this stuff I am reading here about you cheating. Did you really hurt somebody? What did you do?"'

# 90

# TWO TRICK PONY

*McHugh v Gooch*

In the past, in a more judgmental Ireland, people were often called out at Mass for various forms of 'sexual immorality'. Pat Spillane is no stranger to controversy but not even he was expecting to be called out by a priest during a homily at Mass in the west Kerry Gaeltacht. His offence? His comments about Kerry in the 1995 Munster final defeat to Cork. The priest said: 'What he said on RTÉ television disappointed many people. I don't know why he did it and it wasn't good enough.'

## THE PONY EXPRESS

In 2012, Joe Canning made a mild criticism of Henry Shefflin which was actually a backhanded compliment to the 'cuteness' of Kilkenny in 'playing' referees. Sections of the hurling media appeared to think the sky had fallen in. The media have generated stories in the GAA as well as reported on them.

*The Sunday Game* created many controversies. One of the most bizarre involved Gooch Cooper. Eyebrows were raised throughout the football word when former Donegal footballer Martin McHugh described Cooper as a 'two-trick pony'.

On *The Sunday Game* both Kevin McStay and Dermot Earley were praising James O'Donoghue when McHugh suggested that the Killarney Legion forward was a far better footballer than Cooper.

It was the use of the words 'two-trick pony' that created a feeding frenzy on social media. McHugh was forced to concede that he overreached. In his newspaper column he wrote: 'I brought up Cooper but made a mistake by using the phrase "two-trick pony" to describe the Dr Crokes man. It's a clumsy phrase, no doubt about it, and one that doesn't stand up. But live television is unforgiving. You say something and it's out there.'

# 91

# SLIGO'S SPLIT

*Eamonn O'Hara v Kevin Walsh*

It was one of *The Sunday Game*'s standout moments.

In 2013, Sligo crashed out of the Connacht Championship to London in one of the shocks of the year; London's first Connacht Championship victory for thirty-six years. Having recently retired after a glittering playing career with Sligo, Eamonn O'Hara was settling into his new role as a pundit. He did so in a way that anyone watching will remember for a long time, particularly those in the Yeats County.

The former All-Star pulled no punches and offered a withering assessment of his former manager:

'I think he will (resign) and I think he should do the county board a favour. Kevin Walsh made big calls this year and last year. Every one of them has come back to backfire against him. For me I think he lost the players throughout the year. I think, going forward, Kevin should make the right decision for the sake of Sligo football and not anybody else.'

O'Hara then went on to explain the circumstances of his own retirement:

'Kevin Walsh came at the start of the year and he decided that he wanted full commitment from everybody from 1 November. He was asking players for commitment and a big commitment at that stage, but he hadn't accepted the Sligo manager role at that stage.

'There were reports he had shown interest in the Roscommon job and he was waiting for that to come through, in terms of would he get it, or would he get an interview.

'For me, he was asking me at thirty-seven years of age to commit to a training regime of four nights a week collective sessions on 1 November. It was crazy as far as I was concerned. Unfortunately work and everything else conspired against me committing to that and I said I would be available from 1 January.

'Kevin made it quite clear throughout the year he was going to stick with the panel of players that trained from 1 November, and you have no problem with that. But he opened the door to James Kilcullen, a Mayo man, and rightly so. James is a fantastic footballer and contributed a lot to the League. But, unfortunately, James was playing club football for his club Ballaghaderreen yesterday. So, he wasn't first-choice midfielder as he was throughout the year.'

Next up, O'Hara took aim at Walsh's training methods:

'These players deserve an awful lot more, to be honest with you. They have worked very, very hard and they have trained extremely hard. I know that first hand. But they deserve better training sessions. They deserve better quality in terms of tactical awareness and stuff like that and that hasn't come. Kevin Walsh has a lot to answer for.'

Finally, O'Hara pointed his pistol at the county board:

'There are a lot of problems within the county board from the top down. There is a lot of infighting and a lot of resignations at county board level. We have a centre of excellence that is at a standstill. The keys should be handed over on 1 June and that is not going to happen. There are a lot of problems there and Kevin Walsh's results over the last two years have gone unnoticed because of this infighting. He hasn't been held accountable to this. We got to a Connacht final last year but we're papering over the cracks.'

Former Laois star Colm Parkinson tweeted: 'So @eamonnohara8 what is it, are you a bitter man out for revenge, were you just telling the truth or are u trying to b like @JoeBrolly1993?'

Former Armagh footballer Oisín McConville wondered if the remarks were because of a 'personal axe to grind'.

Perhaps with the benefit of hindsight O'Hara might have been more accurate to suggest that there were 'rumours' about Walsh's future rather than 'reports'?

## SO CLOSE

Walsh's time with Sligo had achieved some high points and near misses – notably against Kerry in Tralee in a 2009 qualifier, when only a penalty save by Diarmuid Murphy from David Kelly prevented a Sligo victory. Kerry would go on to win the All-Ireland that year. In 2010, having won Division 3 by beating Antrim in the final, he led them to a Connacht final, after they beat Mayo before drawing with Galway and beating them in a replay. Sligo went to the Connacht final against Roscommon in the unusual position of being hot favourites. A stunning individual performance from Donie Shine gave the Rossies a narrow victory. In 2012, Sligo overturned a five-point deficit to beat a fancied Galway side only to lose to Mayo in the Connacht final.

A few days after O'Hara's criticism, RTÉ gave Walsh the opportunity of the right of reply to O'Hara's comments. He said: 'I felt it was very unbalanced in its presentation of the issues that did arise from Sligo in the London game. I felt *The Sunday Game* itself failed to comply with the obligations that are on RTÉ as a public service broadcasting company to adhere to the highest standards of balance in broadcasting. On top of that, there were certain allegations made that have no basis in fact. In fact, they were allowed to be made without challenge or debate.'

# 92

# NO ORDINARY JOE

*Joe Brolly v Jack O'Connor*

Páidí Ó Sé's successor as Kerry manager was the more low-key and low-profile Jack O'Connor. He led Kerry to what were seen by some as two soft All-Irelands over Mayo in 2004 and '06. Pat O'Shea led them to another All-Ireland in 2007 but against a Cork side that never got out of the starting blocks. The Kingdom, though, were plundered by Tyrone in 2003, '05 and '08. After the defeat in '08, O'Shea stepped down and O'Connor stepped back in as Kerry manager.

### DERRY WELL DONE

There was the odd controversy on the way. Joe Brolly found himself embroiled in one of them:

'On television you make a casual remark and people become suffused with rage. The odd time, people will berate you for that. I recall travelling on a train to Dublin when a fella in a Meath jersey got up and said to me: "You f\*\*king bollix." During an ad break in the Wexford-Armagh quarter-final in 2008, a man in his seventies burst into the studios and said to me: "You're a f\*\*king joke, yourself and O'Rourke. You're Dumb and Dumber." They almost had to push him out because the ad break was nearly over. I'm not sure if punditry has any point at all but if it has you've got say what you believe.

'On *The Sunday Game* I just walked in a bit before the game and talked about football because I enjoyed it. The odd time, people will cross the road when they see me coming because they've been told: "Don't talk to that f**ker."

'I could say something relatively trivial and RTÉ would get a thousand emails. I once compared Ciarán McDonald's braids to those of a "Swedish maid". The phones were hopping. A furious priest wrote a long complaint to the local newspaper. (Karma has come back to haunt Brolly in recent years. He has coached under-age teams that have lost a number of county finals. Much to Joe's chagrin as a result he has acquired the nickname 'James Horan'!)

'I said something about Paul Galvin after "an incident" against Armagh in '06. I said: "That's unbelievable and he's a teacher. That's real corner-boy stuff." Jesus Christ. All hell broke loose.'

Brolly was unfazed by the controversy:

'The Kerry manager Jack O'Connor was supposed to be furious. I am told that in his book he has a go at me for "crossing the line" but I never read it. I'm like Alan Partridge. He was interviewing a woman and asks her: "Is it true that you . . . ?" She answers: "Of course I did. Did you not read my book?" Alan replies: "No, I never read the books." In my review I said O'Connor's book was unlikely to trouble the Pulitzer Committee!'

Pat Spillane also had a view on the book: 'Jack O'Connor probably has learned the danger of rushing into print. He wrote a book with Tom Humphries in between his two stints as Kerry senior manager. Having written a book before

he was finished in the Kerry dressing room was not appreciated by all the Kerry players at the time. Jack's main gripe
in the book was that he did not get enough credit from the
great Kerry team that I played on. It was nice to know that we
still mattered.'

# 93

## PUKE FOOTBALL

*Pat Spillane Is Frustrated*

It is the most famous phrase in the history of GAA punditry.

The 2003 edition of *Reeling in the Years* chose the moment as one of their highlights (lowlights?) of the year.

With the benefit of hindsight, Spillane recalls his 'puke football' comments to describe Tyrone's ultra-defensive performance that day live on national television with a more temperate tone:

'I am not going to use the "P" word but, at its worst, Gaelic football is like watching Tyrone beat Kerry in the 2003 All-Ireland semi-final. A perversion of the beautiful game like that is like measles; it is something you should get over young, not at my stage of life. Football should leave you looking frenzied, looking mad with joy. Much Ulster football in those years simply left me looking mad. It was watching muck like this that caused me to grow old disgracefully.'

However, the evolution of that Tyrone team caused Spillane to re-evaluate his previous assessment:

'While I would not always agree with his methods, Mickey Harte earned my respect. He raised the bar, which forced teams like my beloved Kerry to follow them and ensured that they raised their standards of preparation and professionalism.'

## THE BITTER WORD

Spillane's 'puke football' comments made him the *bête noire* not just of Tyrone fans but of Ulster football fans generally. All his subsequent kind comments about Tyrone football have not been reciprocated. As a result of his 'puke football' remark Tyrone fans have favoured him some choice insults. The constraints of good taste and polite language limit me to two: 'Spillane's comment about puke football should be interpreted as Pure Unadulterated Kerry Embarrassment.'

The *pièce de resistance*, though, has got to be: 'Pat Spillane, what can you expect from a sickening dose but "puke"?'

# 94

## RADIO GAGA

*Loughnane on Clare FM*

I once asked Ger Loughnane why it was that in mixed company I only ever saw him in the presence of attractive women. He replied with a characteristic undercurrent of mischievousness, 'I've always had the capacity to look beyond personality!'

In 1998, the whole Irish sporting world seemed to be swept up in the myth of Loughnane. Having travelled the stoniest road to stardom, it seemed that the outrageous vicissitudes of his career came to a climax that summer. Loughnane's role in helping to lift hurling to unprecedented heights was seldom mentioned. Such was the media frenzy that when Clare faced Offaly in the All-Ireland semi-final the fact that his team were just seventy minutes shy of a third All-Ireland final appearance in four years seemed almost secondary. Hurling's capacity to outreach the wildest imaginings of fiction was shown that year.

Loughnane's notorious interview on Clare FM that summer raised things to a whole new feeding frenzy. He raised eyebrows by invoking the name of Don Corleone in describing an official from the Munster Council.

Then he escalated the drama still further when he described how the chairman of the Clare County Board, Robert Frost, attended the Waterford versus Galway All-Ireland quarter-final at Croke Park. He was in the V.I.P. section of the Hogan Stand. There were three clergymen seated immediately behind him. He overheard their conversation. It was impossible not to hear it. The Munster final replay of the previous Sunday was the main topic of conversation between them. The immediate response to this conversation was to the depiction of Loughnane and his players, the famous line that, 'the Clare team were tinkers, Loughnane was a tramp and the Clare team must be on drugs.'

When we walked on the fields of Loughnane's family farm in Feakle, smelling the sweet scent of summer, the lane was white with hawthorn blossom in the hedgerows, white like wedding cake:

'The really significant part of the discussion on Sunday, 26 July, was that it took place two days before the meeting (scheduled for Tuesday, 28 July) of the Munster Council to make a decision on the referee's report. One of the priests stated: "Seamus Gardiner (a reference to Fr Seamus Gardiner PRO of the Munster Council) has told me that he had been speaking with Donie Nealon (Secretary to the Munster Council) and that the Munster Council were going to get Ger Loughnane up on the Stand and suspend Colin Lynch for three months."

'On hearing this, Robert Frost stood up and challenged the three priests about what they had been saying and what they had said and, being embarrassed about having to do so in public, he then left. Of course, questions were immediately raised: how could three outsiders know Lynch's fate two days before the meeting to adjudicate on his "crime"? How could this possibly reflect proper procedures? Could justice be served in this way?'

## BEHIND ENEMY LINES

Robert Greene and Joost Elffers in their book *The 48 Laws of Power* articulate ingenious guidelines for dealing with your superiors, your colleagues and, most critically of all, your enemies. Enemies are unexpectedly vital stepping stones on your route to success and, the authors go so far as to exhort, 'if you have no enemies, find a way to make them'. Friends betray you more quickly and they are easily made envious but employ a former enemy and he will be more loyal than a friend. They quote the seventeenth century political philosopher Baltasar Gracián: 'You must learn to grab a sword not by a blade, which would cut you, but by the handle, which allows you to defend yourself. The wise man profits more from his enemies, than a fool from his friends.' Friendship blinds you to your best interests, while 'an enemy sharpens your wits'. Loughnane courted enemies with a passion. Of course, many people believed his rhetoric in 1998 was ultimately counterproductive:

'If something wrong happens, you have to speak out about it, whether it costs you an All-Ireland or not. As Anthony Daly said to me afterwards, in October of that year, we wouldn't change a thing about it, and we'd make no apologies for anything we did or said.'

Loughnane's primary purpose, to which he returned again and again, during his infamous Clare FM interview with Colm O'Connor, was to encourage the Clare fans to lift the team, especially the new players that would have to come on the team on Sunday. The interview achieved its objective:

'There was so much unfavourable comment in the media that the Clare players were starting to wonder when I was going to reply to it. I wanted to leave it as close as possible to the Offaly match to lance the boil. When I came into training that night all the players were looking at me! Although they said nothing, I knew they were relieved I had taken on the criticism. In all of the controversy, I never spoke to any of them about anything that was going on off the field. I wanted them to concentrate just on the hurling.

'In my experience of Gaelic games, I've never seen a team as united with its supporters as that first day against Offaly. When we came on to the pitch there was just an electric feeling and a great ovation. It was an incredible feeling of oneness with the crowd and, considering at that stage we had already won two All-Irelands, it was just incredible.'

Star forward on that team, Jamesie O'Connor, looks at it differently:

'I would say that even going back to '98, Loughnane making the state of the nation address, it didn't help. It seemed to just sap a bit of nervous energy from you. The players have enough on their hands to get themselves ready for the challenge that they face on a week-to-week basis and trying to work and to prepare in that environment as well was not easy.'

## LOUGHNANE UNDER ATTACK

Joe Brolly tells a story about the late John Morrison who was at the helm with Mickey Moran when Mayo reached the All-Ireland final in 2006 after a never-to-be-forgotten semi-final win over Dublin:

'When John was the manager of Antrim, he brought in a performance hypnotist to change the players' losing mindset. Before the quarter-final against Cavan in 1996, the hypnotist spent time with the group. As they sat in the changing room in Casement Park before taking the field for the big match, John placed a boom box in the centre of the room and played a recorded message from the hypnotist. The voice exhorted the players to hold an imaginary balloon in their hands and allow it to inflate, then deflate. The players sat there in silence, holding their balloons on their laps as the soothing voice intoned, "You will be calm on the pitch. You have visualised performing at your best today and this will happen. On the pitch you will be focused and composed."

'Their arms rose and then fell as the air went in and out of the imaginary balloons. Finally, the countdown. "Ten ... you are feeling totally relaxed, nine, eight, seven, six, five, four, three ... you are ready to perform at your best, two ... all you are aware of is your breathing, one ... You are ready for Cavan." At which point they described how the changing room exploded. Led by their captain, they jumped to their feet, shouldering each other, punching the door, and roaring. After ten minutes the score was 1–4 to 0–0 to Cavan and the game was already over. If Antrim had won the game, the players – in their minds – would have attributed it at least partly to the absent guru. Morrison would have been hailed as a genius.'

During his tenure as Clare manager, Ger Loughnane generated controversy about his frequent tactic of substituting his own substitutes often after they had only had a short time on the pitch. The argument was that it was humiliating and could break their spirit. Loughnane was not for turning:

'All egos had to be satisfied for the good of the team. For Clare to win was the only thing that was important. When the game was over, all the paraphernalia had no appeal whatsoever for me. All that mattered was what happened on the field.'

However, Lougnhane's judgement was vindicated in his biggest call of all:

'Before the All-Ireland semi-final in 1995 we went up to Croke Park for a training session to familiarise the players with the place and Éamonn Taaffe pulled his hamstring. He had pulled one of his hamstrings earlier on. That ruled him out of the semi-final. He was back training a few weeks before the final. He was off the pace. He wasn't even listed among the subs but we said we'd bring him along because if we needed a goal there was no better man to get it.

'We needed a goal! We brought on Taaffe and he was playing terribly. Worst of all, he was marking Kevin Martin. At one stage, Éamonn was coming out for a ball that he should have won but Martin cut in ahead of him, grabbed the ball, went on a solo run, and opened up a massive gap. He took a shot, but thanks be to God it went wide. I turned to Pat Fitzgerald and said, "Éamonn Taaffe is going off and Alan Neville is coming on." The slip was written out. I had it in my hand as Frank Lohan was fouled coming out of the defense. Dickie Murphy awarded a free to Clare and Anthony Daly took it. Dalo aimed for a point but the ball hit the post and came down. I was looking out on the field to see where the referee was to see if I could come on to make the switch. The next thing, I saw the Clare flags hitting the sky at the canal end. The ball was in the net.

'I thought it was Fergal Hegarty who had scored the goal but my mind immediately switched to other things. My first concern was to stop the game, no matter what, to give our lads time to settle. The most dangerous time for a lapse in concentration is after you score a goal. This is when defenses who had previously been so organised can lose concentration. So, I wanted to stop the game. I ran out to the referee, Dickie Murphy, and was about to hand him back the slip of paper – but at that precise moment I pulled back my hand. Dickie said, "Don't pull that one on me Ger." He knew what I was up to straight away. He grabbed the piece of paper and ran away.

'The one thing I didn't want to happen, happened straight away. The puck-out was taken quickly. An Offaly player was fouled. A free. Johnny Dooley pointed. Offaly were level and right back in the game.

'That's why Éamonn Taaffe came off when the goal was scored. Eamonn would not have been taken off only that I wanted the game stopped to give everyone on our side a chance to regain the composure, but Dickie outwitted me. Fair play to him. When Éamonn was taken off it became a joke and I let it go. That's the real reason though he came off so quickly. If it is to be, it will be.'

# 95

## ANIMAL KINGDOM

*Páidí Ó Sé Talks Himself into Trouble*

I loved Con Houlihan: the man, the myth and the journalist. I loved his flair for words. In his later years on the Kerry team Mick O'Dwyer transformed Páidí Ó Sé from a pillaging right half-back into a tenacious corner-back. Con compared the restriction of his attacking talents to 'tying a spaniel to a concrete block'.

I especially loved Con's powers of observation on the way Irish public opinion moves like a flock of starlings: all veering one way in a great cloud before suddenly turning and going together in the opposite direction. Páidí Ó Sé would learn that lesson the hard way.

As the late Enoch Powell famously observed of politicians, so one might say of football managers that every career is bound to end in failure; or, if not failure, at least not complete satisfaction. Páidí did not savour complete satisfaction as a manager.

As a player Páidí, though, was as tough as teak. When Dublin played Cork in the 1978 Cardinal Cushing Games the match was the most physically violent in living memory. A lot of old

354

scores had to be settled and markers were put down for the Championship later that year. Pat O'Neill broke Jimmy Deenihan's nose. Afterwards O'Neill was very contrite. He sent an apology later that night to Deenihan in the Kerry hotel. He told him he was very sorry and never intended to hurt him because he thought he was striking Páidí Ó Sé!

## CARR CRASH

In the 2001 All-Ireland quarter-final in Thurles, Maurice Fitzgerald produced a moment of genius from the sideline to save All-Ireland champions Kerry's blushes against Dublin, despite their manager Tommy Carr's best efforts to put him off. Carr's actions were widely condemned as unsporting. He has since apologised for it on a number of occasions. Fitzgerald's sideline point earned Kerry a draw.

After the match the Kerry manager Páidí Ó Sé was fuming because of his side's poor performance in his eyes. He drove home in his Renault Vel Satis in such a rage that he was stopped by a garda for speeding. The man in blue just said, 'Go on away, that's your second let-off today.'

Tommy Carr was restricted to the stand for the replay the following weekend but in the replay it was Ó Sé's turn to row with match official Pat McEnaney after he sent off his nephew Tomás for what would be described euphemistically as a 'robust' challenge. So furious was Páidí with the decision, he had to be held back by linesmen Gerry Kinneavy and Seamus Prior. Asked about the controversy afterwards, Páidí turned defence into attack and criticised the media about how pundits were influencing the way the game was being refereed.

Pat Spillane was a close friend. 'Páidí, like myself, was a rogue and, like myself, was a media animal. He was a good friend of mine and was probably one of the people I was closest to from the great Kerry team. He wore his heart on his sleeve but he was a lot cuter than most people give him credit for. People made him out to be blood, guts, shouting and roaring, and passion, and he was all that but he was much more.

'Having said that, I was watching him interviewed on the sideline after Westmeath's victory over Dublin in 2004. He was so passionate – and that's great – but he had a jugular vein that was on the point of bursting. If I had any doubts about whether I should have gone into management, they died in that moment.

'No football manager is an island. He needs a good team behind him on and off the field. It would also have been nice to hear the real story of Páidí's relationship with John O'Keeffe. Johno is a lovely guy and a real gentleman. Páidí initially wouldn't have been given the Kerry job because people thought he was a loose cannon. These people underestimated Páidí. At first, he was given Seamus McGearailt to "mind" him. There is no doubt that Seamus kept Páidí under control and made a massive contribution to Kerry's success in 1997. What people don't realise, though, is that if Páidí was unsure about something he was always willing to get advice but he would do indirectly and not from anyone close to the Kerry camp. Then when Seamus moved on, Johno was parachuted in on him because certain people would have thought Páidí was incapable of training the team on his own. The nature of the imposition put a strain on the relationship straight away. A comparable relationship would have been that of Eddie O'Sullivan and Declan Kidney. At the best of times Johno and Páidí would not have been bosom pals.

'A lot of Páidí's most vocal critics were people with agendas. His interview in South Africa was ill-advised. Calling the Kerry fans "f**king animals" was not very clever. It was not good for Kerry football to have its dirty linen washed in public nor to have colleagues and former colleagues on opposite sides. There were no winners in that situation and it left a bitter legacy and a sour taste.'

After bad defeats against Meath in 2001, Armagh in 2002 and Tyrone in 2003 Páidí Ó Sé's reign as Kerry manager ended badly.

When the going got tough for Kerry in Croke Park in successive years against Meath, Armagh and Tyrone respectively Páidí was unable to come up with a Plan B to reverse the situation.

The wounds from those three losses cut deeply, not because Kerry lost but that they lost so tamely on each occasion. That is not the Kerry way. To lose abysmally once was bad; for it to happen twice was shocking, but for it to happen to Kerry three years in a row in Croke Park, the ground they think of as their second home, was the end of the world. In some counties, success is accidental. In Kerry it is compulsory. After failing so spectacularly three years in a row, Páidí's days were numbered. The only problem was that Páidí himself didn't see it that way.

2003 was Páidí's year of the U-turn. In January he gave an interview with *The Sunday Independent* on a team holiday in South Africa and famously said, 'Being the Kerry manager is probably the hardest job in the world because Kerry people, I'd say, are the roughest type of f*****g animals you could deal with. And you can print that.'

Páidí also caused another controversy with his implied criticism of John O'Keeffe's training techniques coupled with a suggestion from Páidí that he himself would be more 'hands on' in 2003. The controversy continued for more than two weeks when Ó Sé returned home to meet with O'Keeffe and the county board to restore harmony.

In response to his 'animal' comment the board issued a statement: 'The Kerry County Board disassociates itself unequivocally from the remarks made by Páidí Ó Sé. We apologise to all the people who were offended and we assure them that we do not in any way condone them.' O'Keeffe issued his own statement, stating that he would not be taking a scheduled session until the 'air was cleared'.

A short time later, Páidí was forced to meekly apologise: 'I regret very much if I have offended all or some of my Kerry supporters who have been very loyal to me.' In relation to O'Keeffe, Páidí apologised for any offence caused. 'I have no question mark of any kind over Johno's physical training techniques. As an individual, he is a man of the highest integrity.'

Then, after his reluctant resignation as Kerry manager in October, he said, 'I wouldn't rule anything in or out, but I couldn't see myself at the present time having the bottle to go in and train another team against the green and gold jersey.'

A week later, after taking over as Westmeath manager he said, 'I now want to transfer all my professional allegiance to Westmeath and will endeavour to coach and improve the team and achieve success in the future.'

# 96

## IT'S NOT ONLY WORDS

*Pat Spillane Lands Himself in Hot Water*

TV pundits can talk themselves into serious trouble. Joe Brolly and Pat Spillane have had plenty of experience in this respect.

Pat Spillane regularly put his foot into his mouth on the *The Sunday Game*.

'I have annoyed counties that people would not expect me to annoy. In the 2004 Carlow versus Longford match in the Leinster Championship, with Luke Dempsey have only been appointed Carlow manager three weeks previously, I confidently predicted in my column that it is a bit like rearranging the deckchairs on the Titanic and they have no chance. What happens? Carlow create the first big shock of the Championship and beat Longford. In one of his typical media-shy performances, when Luke was interviewed afterwards, he said the Carlow players took a few weeks to get used to his "style of football". Carlow fans were not amused at my bemusement.

'Another time I was reviewing a Carlow match with Joe Brolly sitting beside me. He whispered a comment in my ear as I was seriously analysing the Carlow team. I burst out laughing. The

RTÉ switchboard went into meltdown about how much I had disrespected the poor Carlow team. I got the blame, but it was all Brolly's fault! I was afraid to set foot in Carlow for ten years afterwards.'

Sometimes it appears that elements within the GAA think that RTÉ should be an extension of the GAA's PR department, but if you want publicity you have to expect it warts and all. One of the biggest warts is violent play but speaking out about this has brought Spillane no end of trouble.

On *the Sunday Game*, after Armagh played Derry in the Ulster Championship in 1996, Spillane infamously used the word 'thugs' to describe what is euphemistically known in the GAA vernacular as 'robust play'. The following Sunday, RTÉ asked him to withdraw the remark but certainly not to apologise.

'I decided to do it off the cuff. All was going really well until I said that if they behaved that way off the pitch, they would be guilty of "criminal" behaviour.

'To thine own self be true. It was all very well for Shakespeare to write that, but he obviously hadn't a GAA analyst in mind when he got that brainwave. Telling it as it is, in my signature style, has got me into no end of trouble.

'The morning after my aborted attempt to diffuse my "thugs" comment I was hauled in front of the Head of Sport in RTÉ, Tim O'Connor. It was one of the scariest moments of my life.

'There are three times in my life I felt intimidated. The first was when the Dean of St Brendan's caught me out of the dormitory late at night and reprimanded me. The second was when a tax inspector gave me a grilling about my taxes. The third time was when Tim O'Connor carpeted me. I was in fear because I thought it was the end of the line. To be perfectly honest, it looked like it was curtains for me in RTÉ. Obviously, RTÉ Sport were afraid of legal action. They had been taken to the cleaners just before that after what seemed a harmless enough remark. They were panicking a little that they were going to get stung again. In the end they scripted an apology which I read out from an autocue and I got away with it. I checked it out with a barrister friend of mine afterwards and asked him if calling someone a "thug" is libellous. He said yes. It is only okay to call someone a blackguard.'

# 97

# WHAT IT SAYS IN THE PAPERS

*Ger Loughnane's 'Attack' on Wexford*

The Germans have a word, Gedankenkarussell ('thought carousel'), when you return again and again to the same problem despite your best efforts not to think about it.

Ger Loughnane often found himself experiencing that phenomenon. He often found himself embroiled in controversies. Many were of his own creation. This one was not.

His attitude is generally it does not matter what they say in the jealous games people play. But on this one occasion he felt very differently:

'Jim O'Sullivan did a lengthy interview with me in shorthand after we won the semi-final against Kilkenny in Buswell's Hotel in 1997. At one stage he asked me who did I think would win the second semi-final between Tipperary and Wexford. I answered, "I'm certain that Tipperary are going to win it."

He replied, "Surely Wexford will be way too tough for them?"

I responded, "The biggest mistake you could make is think that roughhouse tactics could work against Tipperary." I went on to say that if you look back at the history of Tipperary hurling

362

you will not beat them by roughing them up. We had played them earlier that year in Cusack Park and tried that with them, but they beat us. The only way you could beat them was by outhurling them.

'The following Thursday or Friday I was over in London with my wife, Mary. I rang my two sons at home and they told me that a big headline had appeared in *The Examiner* to the effect that I had said Wexford were hatchet men. I didn't know the exact wording at that stage.

'On the Monday morning I was walking down a street off Oxford street in London and I saw a shop with *The Irish Independent*. I was shocked to discover that Rory Kinsella had been asked in his post-match interview what he was going to do about Ger Loughnane's comment that Wexford were guilty of "roughhouse tactics". What struck me immediately was that if Wexford had qualified for the All-Ireland there would be no denying that I had said it and it would really have polluted the atmosphere coming up to the final.'

## NOTHING BUT THE TRUTH?

Loughnane sought to undo the damage from his perspective. But he was not as successful as he would have wished:

'I was debating in my own mind whether I should let it go because Wexford were out, but I decided it was too serious to leave it. When we got home, I rang *The Examiner* and asked for Jim O'Sullivan. Most people don't realise that the person who writes the article does not write the headline. The problem was not Jim's article but the headline which accompanied it: "Loughnane accuses Wexford of roughhouse tactics". The headline writer obviously wanted it to be as sensational as possible. The then editor, Brian Looney, came on the line. I explained how damaging the headline would have been if Wexford had qualified for the All-Ireland. He said, "I admit we made a high tackle. What are you looking for?" I explained that all I was looking for was an apology. They published it down the page, but who reads an apology at the bottom of the page?

'*The Sunday Independent* had reproduced the article. I then contacted their sports editor, Adhamhnan O'Sullivan. They also printed an apology, but few people saw it. To this day, most people in Wexford think I said something I never did. Ever since, I've always insisted that if somebody was coming to interview me they had to have a recorder.'

# 98

## SHAFTING JIMMY

*Keaveney's Suspension*

He was like a light bulb. When he walked into the room every head turned in his direction.

Jack Lynch told me he saw television as a mixed blessing for the GAA:

'I have seen at first hand how television has changed politics. I think it has created a culture which favours style over substance. Television favours politicians like John F. Kennedy who are very telegenic. I am not sure some of our politicians who have made a remarkable contribution to Irish life would have the same careers they had today because television would not have been kind to them. They didn't have movie-star looks or personalities, but they got things done.

'I have no doubt that television will be good for the GAA and will bring hurling, in particular, to a new audience and bring the great players like Jimmy Barry-Murphy to a mass audience and give him the type of platform that Christy Ring never had.

'I do worry, though, that it will create a new style of reporting and commentary that is more sensational and personality-based.

Gaelic games has a great history of print journalism with people like Paddy Downey always producing thoughtful articles and comment. I fear a little, though, that television with its need for drama and immediate comment will create a need to amplify controversy and demonise people. I fear that this trend will be replicated in sections of the print media who have to keep up. Entertainment is important but not at the expense of damaging players' reputations.'

Seán Óg O'Ceallacháin was the first presenter of *The Sunday Game* in 1979, a rare programme then devoted exclusively to Gaelic games. Seán Óg's contribution to Gaelic games is well known because of his varied career as a Dublin county footballer and hurler, referee and sports commentator and reporter.

Seán Óg had a good team behind him in RTÉ, with Maurice Reidy as the editor and John D. O'Brien as director. They made the brave decision to have Liz Howard as one of their main analysts. Liz was an All-Ireland camogie player brought up in a hurling household; her father was the great Limerick All-Ireland star Garrett Howard. For years she was PRO for the Tipperary County Board.

In 1979 Liz hit the headlines following her comments about the Leinster football final on *The Sunday Game*. Legendary Dublin full-forward Jimmy Keaveney was sent off for an elbow offence on Offaly defender Ollie Minnock. Liz was in no doubt that the sending off was very harsh. The next day *The Irish Press* carried the headline 'TV personality supports Jimmy Keaveney' over a front-page story. Keaveney was asked to attend a meeting of the Leinster Council Disciplinary Committee, to explain his actions.

The Dublin County Board invited Liz to attend the meeting and give evidence in support of Jimmy. She did and so did Ollie

Minnock, who pleaded for leniency on Keaveney's behalf. Their pleas for mercy fell on deaf ears and Keaveney was suspended for a month, ruling him out of the All-Ireland semi-final against Roscommon. On the day of the match Liz was going into Croke Park when she was accosted by a big Dublin fan who shouted at the top of his voice: 'Look at her. She's the wan who shafted Jimmy Keaveney.'

# 99

## CON'S COMPETITION

*Roscommon v Armagh*

A dramatic one-point Connacht final victory in 1977 was secured for Roscommon with a late goal in the Hyde despite a stellar performance from Galway's Brian Talty and Dermot Earley having the middle finger of his right hand severed in an accidental clash with Johnny Hughes. He was left with an enduring legacy from the game with a line across his middle finger with five little strokes which marked the points of his five stiches.

Earley found himself embroiled in controversy in the All-Ireland semi-final against Armagh. With the score tied at Armagh 3–9 Roscommon 2–12 as he faced up to a long distance free, the last kick of the game, Gerry O'Neill (brother of former Irish manager, Martin), the Armagh trainer, ran across the field in front of him and shouted something at him. The kick sailed high and wide. There was much press comment on the 'O'Neill-Earley' incident in the following days. In his column in *The Evening Press* Con Houlihan offered two All-Ireland tickets to the person who could tell him what O'Neill said to Earley.

The Roscommon star was not unduly distracted: 'I had no idea what he said to me that time. I wasn't even aware that he was talking to me. All I wanted to do was drill the ball over the bar.'

What did bother him was the outcome of the game:

'We were seven points up with ten minutes to go in the All-Ireland semi-final against Armagh but we lost concentration and let them back to draw the game. You could feel the giddiness running through the team. We thought we had one foot in the All-Ireland final. We were shell-shocked in the dressing room afterwards. We had been much better than them but in the replay they beat us by a point.

'It was pretty much the same story two years later when we snatched defeat from the jaws of victory against Dublin in the semi-final to again lose by a point. If we had won either of those two semi-finals, the experience of having played an All-Ireland final would have been invaluable when we took on Kerry in the 1980 final.'

It is not the loss in the replay in 1977 that most irks Roscommon's three-time All-Star Harry Keegan today:

'Everybody keeps talking about the Kerry-Dublin semi-final that year and it's regularly shown on TV but people forget that we produced two great entertaining games, which almost 100,000 people came to watch. Yet neither of the games is ever shown on television. The other so-called "classic" was really a game of rugby league, there was so much hand-passing. We played Armagh again in the 1980 semi-final and that was a very entertaining, high-scoring game but it is never shown on TV whereas our final in 1980 is shown, even though it is a much poorer game.'

### PRIDE AND PREJUDICE

In 1980, Roscommon and Armagh would again face each other in an All-Ireland semi-final. Dermot Earley took confidence from the blend of youth and experience:

'The spine of the team were very experienced but the new lads brought another dimension. Tom Heneghan did a great job as our manager. He was ahead of his time as a coach. With Tony McManus, Mick Finneran and John O'Connor in our forward line we had three guys who could get you scores. Their worth was really shown in the All-Ireland semi-final in 1980 against Armagh, when, after failing in four previous semi-finals, we finally qualified for the All-Ireland. Tony's goal that day typified what our forward line was capable of. Tom once said to us: "Our tactics are very simple; get the ball fast into the forwards." There was none of the passing to the side or even backwards that you see today.'

One of Dermot's children would unwittingly embroil him in controversy:

'In 1980, as we left our Dublin hotel before the All-Ireland semi-final against Armagh, David, who was four and a half at the time, was togged out in his Roscommon's outfit and by my side. David was part of all our build-up and saw himself as an unofficial sub on the team. It had been patiently explained to him that he would accompany the team to the hotel but would then travel separately with his mother to the match. When the point of separation came David went into hysterics. After all efforts at placating him had failed I reluctantly allowed him to travel with the team.

'David was watching the teams getting ready for the parade from the dugout when Danny Burke (team selector) urged him to join me on the pitch. This caught me by surprise, but I had no option other than to take him by the hand and parade with him.

'As Roscommon already had a mascot there was controversy after the match about the incident. A press report referred to the "immaturity" of Roscommon for allowing the situation to arise.

GAA headquarters issued a directive before the All-Ireland final saying that no mascots would be allowed for the big game.

'After the Armagh match, the Roscommon fans were so ecstatic that David became frightened as he was engulfed by a sea of blue and yellow when Roscommon fans invaded the pitch. Having successfully retrieved and consoled him, I was then able to savour the joy of winning.'

### FEELING UNWELCOME

Harry Keegan has one particularly strong memory of playing Armagh:

'We played them in a fierce match in the League at the height of the Troubles. There was a skirmish and a lot of "scelping" in that match. They beat us by a point. We were delighted they beat us because there were rocks and stones reigning down on us after the game in the dressing room. What would they have done if we won! It was not one of my favourite places to go as they were one of the few crowds I found abusive. I'm sure the Troubles did have an impact on them, but I couldn't understand why they took it out on Roscommon above any team.'

# 100

# RING WRONGED

*Christy Ring Gets an Apology*

Nobody did more to transform our national game into our national soap opera than Christy Ring. Such was his legend that it was said he could shoot the eye out of your head from two fields away.

One of Ireland's national treasures Bill O'Herlihy told me he often saw Ring at close quarters growing up in Cork in the 1940s and '50s.

'My generation was very lucky because we grew up at a time when sport in Cork was terrific. Cork hurling was the best hurling in the country at the time by a distance. In Cork City, you had Glen Rovers, Sarsfields, Blackrock and St Finbarrs, which was in my parish. They had unbelievable teams and there was unbelievable tribalism involved. Ring was the greatest hurler I've ever seen, and I saw a lot of him, because my father, God rest his soul, loved hurling and brought me to a lot of games. But you would have an extraordinary attitude to Ring. When he was playing for Glen Rovers you hated him because you were from the Barrs, but if he was playing for Cork you thought he was a god. He was a very nice man but he had this aura about him and he wasn't the easiest man I've ever talked to. He was difficult because he was shy, not because he was rude.'

Ring took no prisoners on the pitch. To take one example he had some tasty encounters with Tipperary. In the 1961 Munster final, Ring and John Doyle became embroiled in a punch-up while Tom Moloughney was knocked to the ground, allegedly after being struck by Ring. In the aftermath, Ring was wrongly named in some national newspapers as having hit both Doyle and Moloughney. The National Union of Journalists subsequently issued an apology to him.

# AFTERWORD

*A Love Letter*

Wandering the world of dream and memory, life was simpler back then.

In my final year in Roscommon CBS we got a new principal. Brother Donnelly was a very kind man. He could also have talked for Ireland. We discovered that when he became our religion teacher. Three times a week he would come into us. He stood at the top of the classroom, looked out the window and talked about whatever came into his head from the first minute of the class to the last without ever catching his breath. Years later, I discovered that this technique is known as 'a stream of consciousness'. We were polite and respectful but we collectively shut off apart from the enterprising few who quickly saw these classes as the ideal time to copy their homework.

Yet Br Donnelly's religion class provided me with the most magical moment of my schooldays. Six months earlier, Pope John Paul II had visited Ireland and brought the nation to a standstill, but that event was as nothing when compared to this.

The class began as normal but about twenty minutes into Br Donnelly's monologue there was a knock on the door. A man walked in and as I was at the back of the class and close to the door I couldn't see his face. I thought to myself: *he looks like . . . but he couldn't possibly be . . .* Then he handed over a big set of keys to Br Donnelly. They nodded to each other, but being a true professional our teacher continued to talk away.

Then our guest turned around. It was like a giant surge of electricity miraculously crackled through the room. I struggled to get my breathing back to its normal rhythm. As we digested that it was really *him* he started to walk out. As I looked up at him with a weird amalgam of shock and elation, he winked at me and said four immortal words which are preserved pure in my memory. I have studied all the great speeches from the Sermon on the Mount to Martin Luther King's 'I have a dream'. I have read all the great documents from the 1916 Proclamation to the Declaration of Independence but no words have ever impacted on me the way these did:

'How're ye lads?'

They were so spellbinding because they came from one of my heroes John 'Jigger' (because of his dancing feet) O'Connor. The nickname captured John's balletic quality. Six months later, Strokestown's Superstar produced the most magical moment I have ever witnessed when he scored a goal in the first minute of the 1980 All-Ireland. After twelve minutes Roscommon led the greatest team the GAA world had ever seen, Kerry, by 1–2 to no score. Those were the most thrilling twelve minutes of my existence when it seemed that all the secret, barren parts of my life would turn green and bud with new energy. Foreigners to the world of intense emotion will not understand this but all fans of Gaelic games will. If this is what heaven feels like, then we have no need to fear dying. The scar tissue from that narrow defeat still has not healed, something greater than we Rossies could be expected to bear.

Thirty years later I achieved one of my life's ambitions and spent a day with Jigger. The first question I asked him was: what was he doing in our classroom all those years earlier? He had absolutely no memory of it! He was humble and generously deflected all the credit for his performances in the county jersey to his teammates.

Jigger is not Roscommon's greatest player, but he was the most thrilling. The best soccer player I ever saw in the flesh was the Dutch master Ruud Gullit. He was a proponent of 'sexy football'. He would have loved John O'Connor. Jigger played samba football. With his long, flowing hair in a headband he looked more like a Brazilian international than a Roscommon footballer.

He was a phenomenon capable of reducing the best and swiftest defenders to impotent pursuit, of leaving them as miserable stragglers baffled by astonishing surges of acceleration and devastatingly sudden changes of direction.

Jigger could do things others would not even dream of, drawing from a deep well which never seemed to run dry. He would do flicks and weaves that would electrify the fans and could chip in some great scores in repeated incantations of hope. When he was on fire like the All-Ireland semi-final against Kerry in 1978, he was virtually unmarkable – though I think Jimmy Deenihan left quite a few marks on his jersey that day! Roscommon had played well in midfield and in attack in the Connacht final against Galway, and won well, but were unable to reproduce that form against Kerry – except Jigger. In many ways, he seemed to carry the fight to them on his own at times but his Herculean efforts plummeted like echoless stones into a void against the might of the Kingdom.

Jigger was a special talent and a one-off. He had an X factor that few players possess. Matt Connor had *it*. Maurice Fitzgerald had *it*. Joe Canning had *it*. David Clifford has *it*. That *it* is hard to explain but it involves a unique capacity to make the heart skip a beat.

Jigger had the talent to be one of the greats of the game outside Roscommon, where he rightly remains a much-revered figure, but he had a temperament that needed to be carefully nurtured. What would work with most of the rest of the team would not work with Jigger and he needed to be managed in a unique way. Sadly, once Tom Heneghan stepped down as county manager that did not happen and Jigger was lost to the game. The Primrose and Blue has never seen such a free and beautiful spirit since. One of my favourite films is *The Shawshank Redemption*. Whenever I hear Morgan Freeman musing to the effect that some birds are not meant to be caged, I immediately think of John.

Nothing showcases the magnificence of the GAA better than 'the GAA funeral'. Think of the passing of such figures as Christy Ring; Ger Michael Grogan, Michaela Harte, Páidí Ó Sé and Niall Donohue to name but a few. In 2022 we poignantly saw these in the passing of those gone too soon like Damian Casey, Ashling Murphy, Red Óg Murphy, Paul Shefflin, Dillon Quirke and Kate Moran. We are great at saying how wonderful people are after they die. Maybe it is time that we raised our game and told people how special they are to us while they are still here. We should appreciate what we have before time teaches us to appreciate what we had.

Jigger we loved you then.

We love you now.

We will always love you.

In those fleeting moments you ignited our souls.

We flew higher because of you.

Others carried the piano but you were the true artist when you played.

# ACKNOWLEDGEMENTS

I am deeply honoured that Dublin legend Charlie Redmond wrote the foreword for the book.

I am profoundly grateful for the support of two of my sporting heroes Seán Boylan and Joe Connolly for their practical support.

Special thanks to Lee Keegan, Ger Loughnane, John O'Mahony, Pat Spillane, Paul Earley, Hannah Tyrrell and Jackie Tyrrell for their assistance.

Clare Colossus Anthony Daly has always been very generous with his time and stories which I really appreciate.

Thanks too to the many players and managers of the past and present, too numerous to mention, who kindly shared their memories with me.

My deepest gratitude to Brian Darcy for his ongoing support of my books.

Ace goalkeeper Emma Dennis is to Round Towers Lusk what Stephen Cluxton was to Jim Gavin's Dubs. She is an ongoing inspiration for her unique ability 'to see the sun when it would rain'.

Thanks to Simon Hess, Campbell Brown, and all at Black & White for their help.

As work on this book commenced, a great oak fell in the forest with the passing of Athleague's Albert (Bert) Fallon. He achieved life's ultimate distinction. He left the world a better place than he found it.

We lost Conor Heaphey, a noted GAA stalwart too. He was one of the great Ballylongford and Shannon Rangers players and was later involved in management roles with both teams. Kerry will be poorer for his passing.

Another sad loss to the GAA family was Dundalk's Brian Sloan. He was a gentleman for all seasons. His remarkable courage was an inspiration to all. May his great love continue to be an invisible cloak to shield his family.

Last December we said a final goodbye to a keen GAA fan in Margaret Proudfoot.

Her devoted family have not learned to live without her but have learned to live with the great love she left behind.

Likewise Fr Mick Reynolds went to meet his God. A hero of the Biafran war, his real heroism was in his many everyday acts of goodness and kindness.

In the circle of life, in March Ferdia Niall Mulvin was born to his proud parents Róisín (star of the famous Roscommon team that beat Kildare 1–18 to 0–8 in the 2001 All-Ireland final) and Garret. On a day when everything was as fresh as the bright blue sky, no joy on earth brought greater pleasure than this baby boy to love and treasure.

# ABOUT JOHN SCALLY

A native of Roscommon, John Scally is the author of over 40 books, including the bestselling sports books *101 Great GAA Teams*, *The People's Games*, *Great GAA Rivalries* and *100 Great GAA Moments*.

He won a McNamee award for best GAA programme for his radio documentary on Roscommon football, *Come on the Rossies*.

# ALSO BY JOHN SCALLY

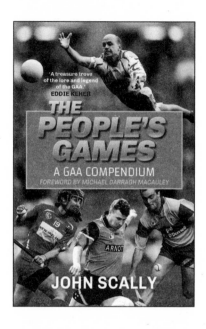

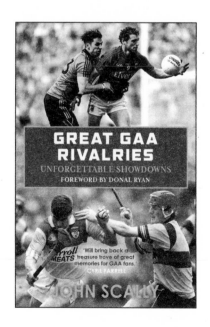

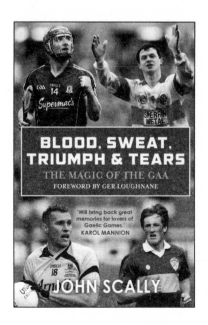